THE STORY OF FOOD

OTHER AVI BOOKS

NUTRITION AND BIOCHEMISTRY

MILESTONES IN NUTRITION   *Goldblith and Joslyn*
PROGRESS IN HUMAN NUTRITION, VOL. 1   *Margen*

FOOD SERVICE

CONVENIENCE AND FAST FOOD HANDBOOK   *Thorner*
FOOD SANITATION   *Guthrie*
MEAT HANDBOOK, 3RD EDITION   *Levie*

FOOD SCIENCE AND TECHNOLOGY

ATTACK ON STARVATION   *Desrosier*
BREAD SCIENCE AND TECHNOLOGY   *Pomeranz and Shellenberger*
BREADMAKING AND FLOUR CONFECTIONERY, 3RD EDITION   *Fance*
CHOCOLATE, COCOA AND CONFECTIONERY   *Minifie*
COOKIE AND CRACKER TECHNOLOGY   *Matz*
ECONOMICS OF FOOD PROCESSING   *Greig*
ECONOMICS OF NEW FOOD PRODUCT DEVELOPMENT   *Desrosier and Desrosier*
EGG SCIENCE AND TECHNOLOGY   *Stadelman and Cotterill*
FOOD OILS AND THEIR USES   *Weiss*
FOOD PROCESSING OPERATIONS, VOLS. 1, 2, AND 3   *Joslyn and Heid*
FOOD SCIENCE, 2ND EDITION   *Potter*
FOOD TECHNOLOGY THE WORLD OVER, VOLS. 1 AND 2   *Peterson and Tressler*
FREEZING PRESERVATION OF FOODS, 4TH EDITION, VOLS. 1, 2, 3, AND 4
     Tressler, Van Arsdel, and Copley
FROZEN FOOD COOKBOOK, 2ND EDITION   *Simpson*
FRUIT AND VEGETABLE JUICE PROCESSING TECHNOLOGY, 2ND EDITION
     Charm
FUNDAMENTALS OF FOOD PROCESSING OPERATIONS   *Heid and Joslyn*
HANDBOOK OF SUGARS   *Junk and Pancoast*
LABORATORY MANUAL FOR FOOD CANNERS AND PROCESSORS, 3RD EDITION,
     VOLS. 1 AND 2   *National Canners Association*
MICROBIOLOGY OF FOOD FERMENTATIONS   *Pederson*
MICROWAVE HEATING   *Copson*
PRACTICAL BAKING, 2ND EDITION   *Sultan*
PRACTICAL BAKING WORKBOOK   *Sultan*
PRACTICAL FOOD MICROBIOLOGY, 2ND EDITION   *Weiser, Mountney, and Gould*
PRINCIPLES OF PACKAGE DEVELOPMENT   *Griffin and Sacharow*
SAFETY OF FOODS   *Graham*
TECHNOLOGY OF FOOD PRESERVATION, 3RD EDITION   *Desrosier*
TECHNOLOGY OF WINE MAKING, 3RD EDITION   *Amerine, Berg, and Cruess*

DAIRY SCIENCE AND TECHNOLOGY

ICE CREAM, 2ND EDITION   *Arbuckle*
JUDGING DAIRY PRODUCTS   *Nelson and Trout*

THE STORY OF FOOD

by IRA D. GARARD, Ph.D.

Professor of Chemistry, Emeritus
Rutgers—The State University
New Brunswick, New Jersey

WESTPORT, CONNECTICUT
THE AVI PUBLISHING COMPANY, INC.
1974

641.1
G16

2891

ISBN-0-87055-155-8

Printed in the United States of America
BY MACK PRINTING COMPANY, EASTON, PENNSYLVANIA

Preface

This book was written as an introduction to the subject of Food and Nutrition. Technicalities have been avoided as far as possible; many who wish to study the subject may have a meager scientific background. In addition, I have attempted to explain the physical, chemical and biological principles necessary to the understanding of the various topics. Although the treatment of the vast field of nutrition is necessarily brief, the book contains the known facts about the nutrients in sufficient detail for personal application.

The information in the book includes the changes in the sources of the food supply from its wild state to the present; the processing of some of the more important foods; the legal regulation of food and its difficulties; the chemical nature of food and digestion; the essentials of nutrition and how to meet them. The Bibliography and the General References, at the end of the book will enable the student to study any topic in greater detail.

Some of the information comes from my own experience and all of it from authentic sources. I have avoided the fads in diets that so often appear in the news or in advertisements.

The information and explanations in the book will be found useful by students and teachers of nutrition and dietetics, food technologists, nurses, restaurant managers, doctors, and others concerned with human feeding problems.

The last chapter contains some practical suggestions for buying, storing, and cooking food and an estimate of the future of the food supply.

I wish to express my indebtedness to Dr. Mabel E. Baldwin for her suggestions and criticisms.

IRA D. GARARD

Lakeland, Florida
November 1973

Contents

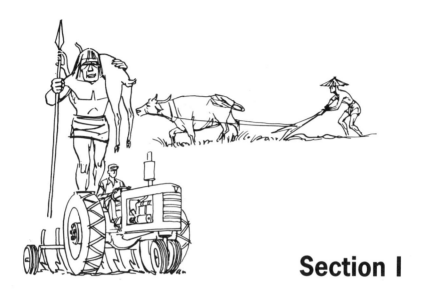

Section I

Our Food Supply—A History

CHAPTER 1

Man Finds His Food

Food and drink have been the most pressing problems man has ever had to face, and the gnawing pangs of hunger have been his greatest incentive to work. For some men, working may have become a habit, but the fear of destitution has always been the greatest spur to human diligence.

There are no records of the food of primitive man, and so we can only guess at what he ate. The selection presented different problems in different places. Near the ocean marine life offered possibilities, but it must have taken the courage of desperation to sample mussels, oysters, clams, or octopus. To catch fish required the invention of an effective method of getting off shore. The inland people had snails, crayfish, and fresh-water fish as possibilities. Land animals of some kind were everywhere, but the problem was to catch them, and so thousands of years ago man was driven to the necessity of hunting and fishing. We humans are largely carnivorous, as both the earliest records and the menu of any first class restaurant testify; therefore we must suppose that everything from the mammoth to the mouse has served as food for someone, sometime.

The hunting of birds and fleet-footed animals required the invention of traps and weapons more effective than the wooden club or a small stone. This need for weapons produced the spear, the bow and arrow, and eventually the rifle and shotgun. Centuries later the nylon fishing line was invented, for some of us still like to acquire a bit of our food in the primitive manner.

Potential foods of plant origin were less obvious to early man than animal foods and less palatable, but curiosity, hunger, or the eating habits of other animals led to the sampling of leaves, fruits, nuts, and roots. Eventually the most appealing botanical items were included in the food supply.

Archaeologists have dug into the earth here and there to learn what they could about the nature of early man and his habits. They have given names to the various types of man that they found, and the name *homo sapiens* is the one they gave to what we now call the human race; it means "wise man" although there are times when it seems that the name may not have been well chosen.

Homo sapiens may have been around for the past 100,000 years or more, and so he had a long time to hunt, fish, and migrate with the seasons, for agriculture and the domestication of animals and plants is comparatively recent.

DOMESTICATION

In spite of the superiority of intelligence of homo over the other animals, it took several thousand years for him to think of settling down and producing his food with less effort than he had been spending, for man was and is naturally a migrating animal.

When he finally got around to it, homo built himself a house of some sort where there was no cave available, and gradually domesticated horses, cattle, dogs, sheep, and goats. In the Near East this process began before 7000 B.C. From the day the first man, or probably woman, decided to settle down, build a shelter, and raise plants and animals to provide food and clothing for the family, agriculture has developed slowly and at different rates throughout the world. Fields were cultivated in Sumer in 3000 B.C., in China and Sweden by 1300 B.C., in England not until 800 B.C., and in the Americas agriculture was still very primitive in A.D. 1500. The foods the primitive farmer raised were very important, because those he liked best, meat and fish, did not keep well in hot weather, and it was a nuisance to catch fish or butcher every day.

Fish were domesticated in ponds by a few wealthy men as early as 3000 B.C., and by 400 B.C. raising fish was a going industry in both Persia and China. The industry did not flourish as one might expect, and even though some fish are now raised commercially, we still prefer to catch our fish wild. The world-wide catch is estimated at 50 million tons annually, but only 30 million tons are used directly as human food; the remainder becomes feed for cattle, pigs, chickens, and cats. Fish constitutes only 1% of the human diet throughout the world.

Although man has been domesticating plants and animals for several thousand years, he has not tamed so very many. A French scientist estimates that he has only domesticated some 50 species of animals out of a possible 2 million and some 600 plants of a possible 250,000.

The items in our present food supply are not as recent as we might imagine. In the Near East and India some 3000 years before the Christian era, the natives were eating apricots, apples, cherries, dates, peaches, pears, grapes, melons, olives, beans, garlic, onions, lettuce, eggplant, peas, cucumbers, turnips, radishes, and several kinds of nuts. They also went in for spices and were familiar with mint, coriander, saffron, thyme, and possibly several others—for spices are mostly of Asiatic origin and that continent still supplies us with many of them.

Although only a few of our fruits and vegetables have been added to the human food supply within the past 5000 years, many of them have been taken to other than their native regions and many of them have been improved by the plant breeders who still continue that activity. New varieties of tomatoes, citrus and other fruits, grains, and vegetables have been developed through the years, some of them recently. In the fall of 1968 a new variety of corn was announced that contained twice as much protein as the usual varieties.

The plant and animal breeders may try to produce varieties that are more disease resistant or have other desirable characteristics. The wheat breeders, for example, try for disease resistance, better yields per acre, stronger straw (so that the wheat does not fall over before it can be harvested), resistance to shattering, or wheat that makes better flour. The animal breeders have produced turkeys with more white meat and cows that produce more or richer milk.

Besides the plant and animal breeders there are other agricultural scientists who are interested in the destruction of rats, mice, and other animals that destroy great quantities of farm crops. Then there are the insects and plant parasites for consideration; they have increased in number and variety along with the increase in agricultural production. If anyone doubts the importance of the efforts to destroy these pests, let him set out an apple tree in his back yard and wait for the crop. A commercial apple grower in Pennsylvania tells me his apple trees must be sprayed 12 times a year to get saleable apples. Most fruit trees need one or more sprayings a year to defeat the destruction of the fruit by some insect or plant disease. The United States Department of Agriculture, the State experiment stations, and the agricultural colleges have men and women employed full time to search for more effective pesticides. The big problem is to find something that will kill the pest and not the rest of us. Some of those now in use are very poisonous to us and other domestic animals. Consequently, every nation tries to have all pesticide removed from the food before it gets to market. If the food plants and animals cannot be protected from their pests, all of man's labors to improve the food supply will go for nothing and homo sapiens will starve.

TABOOS

The noble efforts of nature and man to provide the human race with food have been frustrated in many instances by the taboos of certain tribes and religions.

The Koran forbids the Moslems to eat pork, which is also forbidden the Jews. According to Deuteronomy, Chap. 14:

These are the beasts which ye shall eat: the ox, the sheep and the goat. The hart and the roebuck and the fallow deer and the wild goat and the pygarg and the wild ox and the chamois. And every beast that parteth the hoof, and cleaveth the cleft into the claws and cheweth the cud among the beasts that ye shall eat.

Nevertheless, these ye shall not eat of that cheweth the cud or of them that divide the cloven hoof: as the camel and the hare, and the coney; for they chew the cud, but divide not the hoof; therefore they are unclean to you.

And the swine because it divided the hoof, yet cheweth not the cud, it is unclean to you; ye shall not eat of their flesh, nor touch their dead carcass.

These ye shall eat of all that are in the waters: all that have fins and scales shall ye eat; and whatever hath not fins and scales ye may not eat, it is unclean to you.

Ye shall not eat anything that dieth of itself, thou shall give it unto the stranger that is within thy gates, that he may eat it; or thou mayest sell it unto an alien . . ..

The first clause of this last statement is approved by our present food law, but the law does not permit either giving or selling it to a stranger or a foreigner.

Hindus eat neither meat, fish, nor eggs; but they do use milk, butter, and cheese although one Indian sect is strictly vegetarian. In many parts of Africa fish and milk are taboo, and Europeans and Americans simply do not care for dogs, cats, rats, snakes, or insects as food.

PROGRESS IN AGRICULTURE

Fulfilling the ever-increasing demands for food has required ingenuity and invention since the beginning of domestication. The primitive farmer dug up the ground with a sharp stick and planted his seeds. Grain was harvested by pulling off the heads and threshed by rubbing them between the hands. As the need for bigger crops increased, the sharp stick gave way to the invention of the hoe, which in turn was succeeded by the plow to be pulled by a man or woman while another guided it. Pulling the plow required the invention of a rope, but plowing increased the size of the field that could be planted. It must also have resulted in some reflection on the possibility of an easier way to do the job. Once a machine has been invented it is usually easy to improve it. So the plow has been improved through the centuries, but the primitive method of drawing it has not entirely disappeared. During World War II, and within 40 miles of New York City, I saw a man and a woman plowing a field to plant a vegetable crop; the woman was pulling the plow and the man was guiding it.

Imagine the admiration of the first man, about 3000 B.C., who made a rope harness and hitched the family cow to the plow. This idea hastened the use of the ox and other animals with little work to do; the dog, goat, camel, water buffalo, donkey, and horse have all taken turns at the task and somewhere in the world each of them still pulls the plow. Animals were domesticated for labor as well as for food: the dog was hunter, shepherd, and companion; the ox was a laborer; the horse and the camel were for rapid transit; and the cat was supposed to work on the rodent problem.

Increase in the amount of grain that could be raised acted as a spur to the improvement of harvesting methods. Archaeologists have found sickles with flint blades and wooden handles in Mesopotamia, which are thought to be 6,000 years old. After the beginning of the bronze age, sickles with blades made of that metal became common. It is impossible to say just when this was, because the use of bronze began at different times in different parts of the world. In his *Outline of History*, H. G. Wells places the beginning of the bronze age in Egypt between 6000 and 1000 B.C. In Mesopotamia bronze was probably used as early as it was in Egypt, but in North America it was unknown in 1492. The sickle was the only tool for cutting grain for centuries. It was succeeded by the cradle, the reaper, and the binder—all comparatively modern.

Threshing soon advanced from a hand operation to the threshing floor, where the harvested grain was spread out and the seeds beaten out of the husks with long poles, or tramped out under the feet of oxen.

Early in the history of the race, agriculture took a new turn as people began to gather in villages. The earliest village on record is Jarma in what is now Iraq. It dates from 4750 B.C., and by the year 3000 B.C. there were market towns throughout Mesopotamia. Some villages grew into cities and this congregation of people brought about division of labor. As early as 4000 B.C. farmers began to produce not only their own food, but also food for the villagers.

The inventors continued to improve farm implements. The present century has seen the appearance of the combine, which cuts and threshes the grain in one operation; and the plow, the cultivator, and the combine are now pulled by the tractor. The horse and wagon have also been replaced by the truck, so that farming today bears little resemblance to the same operation even a century ago.

In fact, about a century ago the farmers began to specialize and we now have the wheat farmer, the corn farmer, the apple grower, the cattle raiser and many other agricultural specialists. This latest stage in agriculture is more recent than we think. I have cut wheat with a cradle and bound it into sheaves to be stacked and threshed by a steam-powered thresher; it was the regular method in hilly country far into this century. Cyrus McCormick invented the reaper in 1834 and its use soon spread over the level areas of the Middle West, but did not reach the small, hilly, general farms of the eastern states until after 1900. In 1850, one farm worker raised food for 4 people, in 1950 for 25.

CEREALS

Specialization took place gradually, but as early as 1888, 45 steamboats and 57 sailing vessels left Chicago for Buffalo with 5 million tons of grain to be shipped by rail or the Erie canal to the cities of the east for consumption or export. The Midwest had already become the nation's granary.

Cereals became the common food of the human species very early in its history because they are easily stored, retain their quality, and keep the whole year long. Rice, barley, and wheat are all of ancient origin; wheat was cultivated in Mesopotamia before 5000 B.C.

While the people in Europe, western Asia, and the Americas were raising wheat, rye, and barley, the Orientals were planting rice, which has always been their cereal. Maize, or corn as we call it, was the cereal of the American Indians. The plant was native to the Americas and had some advantages for primitive farmers over all the other grains. It grows on tall, strong stalks and each stalk produces one or more ears, each full of grain, whereas all the other grains produce a head at the top of a slender, weak straw and each head contains only a spoonful of grain. Moreover, the corn could be planted between trees or rocks with a few stalks here and there and the hoe could destroy the weeds around them. The ears could be pulled from the stalks, husked, and the corn shelled from the cob by hand. The fodder (the cornstalks and their leaves) was much better feed for the cattle than the straw from the small grains. Because of all these advantages the American settlers planted corn and it has since become our biggest cereal crop.

TRANSPORTATION AND STORAGE

Besides the production of the cereals, a fixed residence permitted the planting of fruits and vegetables and the raising of animals for food. At the same time, it created problems of preservation, transportation, and storage. All these food products are seasonal; consequently if they are to be available throughout the year, they must be stored or transported long distances. Only the cereals, dried beans, peas, and lentils were easy to store because only foods of low water content keep well.

Although the transportation and storage of dry food does not seem to have been a serious tax on human ingenuity, prevention of the spoilage of fresh foods was another matter. The two oldest methods of preservation are drying and salting. Drying was in use in 7000 B.C.—fruits and vegetables were dried in the sun. Salting was used mainly for the preservation of meat. The Sumerians left no evidence that they smoked meat, but the practice was common in Egypt.

FOOD PROBLEMS IN AMERICA

It has been claimed that the American Indians of the two continents used some 1700 plants for food, but only a small fraction of these 1700 foods have ever been cultivated or eaten by Europeans on either side of the Atlantic. However, the immigrant Europeans found many native foods to add to the wheat, fruits, vegetables, and animals they brought with them. As they spread out over the two continents they discovered potatoes, tomatoes, squash, peanuts, pecans, lima beans, maple sugar, chocolate, vanilla, green peppers, and avocados. These native foods were localized; nobody had all of them. The sugar maple, for example, does not thrive south of the latitude of the city of Washington and so only those who lived in the northeastern colonies had maple sugar. Corn does not grow well very far north. Sweet potatoes and peanuts grow best in sandy soil, cranberries prefer bogs, and banana plants and citrus trees do not withstand freezing.

CHANGING AGRICULTURE

At first the American settlers produced their own food on family farms. Even the villagers had vegetable gardens and many of them had fruit trees, kept a cow, and raised poultry and pigs. Cities grew slowly; at the time of the American Revolution, 170 years after the settlement at Jamestown, the largest city was Philadelphia with its 40,000. New York had 25,000 and Boston 16,000. When the first census was taken in 1790, the population of the entire country was only 3,929,214 of whom only 3% lived in cities of 10,000 or more; in 1960 nearly 70% of our population was urban. This change in population has continued, and the nature of the food supply has had to change with it.

The principal factor in the changing food supply was the improvement in transportation. As the town grew, the kitchen gardens could not keep up with the increase in population. The larger the town the more land was needed to supply it with food; but with the primitive roads and oxen or horses for transportation, 20 miles was about the farthest food could be hauled in a day, even in good weather. The invention of a practical steamboat in 1807 relieved the situation for those cities along the rivers. Then came the Erie Canal in 1825 and the first railroad in 1830. The extension of canals and railroads was the main improvement in transportation before 1900 when the introduction of the automobile and the truck brought about the construction of hard-surface roads. As late as the 1850s, cattle were driven on foot across the Alleghenies to the cities of the Atlantic coast, but as early as the 1920s the airplane was carrying mail and small packages. Air transportation of freight has gradually increased so that now, such perishable foods as fish and oysters can be delivered hundreds of miles from the sea in a few hours.

The diet of rural America was largely seasonal and varied with the locality. As the people moved westward, first from Europe, then across the Alleghenies, and finally across the plains and the rockies, they took their seeds and their animals with them. Some crops grew well in the new environment and some did not; and so the diet of the North Americans was only as uniform as soil and local foods permitted. In western Pennsylvania, for example, the food was much the same as that of the settlers to the north and east of them and west to the Mississippi river. In fact, there was little change in the food of this region until after the beginning of the present century.

The western Pennsylvania farmer raised cattle, sheep, hogs, chickens, and turkeys. Land was cheap and there was ample room for cattle and sheep to graze and for the growth of Indian corn, oats, and hay to feed them.

Corn and wheat were the staple grains with buckwheat in a few localities. Pumpkins and beans were planted in the corn fields where the bean vines could climb the cornstalks. Near the house there was a vegetable garden with potatoes, peas, bush beans, lima beans, cabbage, lettuce, tomatoes, beets, parsnips, turnips, onions, and radishes. Close to the house there was also an orchard of apple trees and often some peach, pear, and cherry trees. Every villager raised some fruits and vegetables.

As the forests were cleared, several maple trees were left standing and, if the farmer had plenty of land, he might set out a grove of these trees to increase his supply of maple sugar. Sugar cane would not thrive north of Virginia, but some of the northern farmers raised sorghum. Here and there some thrifty farmer had a cane mill with which he converted his sorghum, and that of his neighbors, into a heavy, sweet syrup.

The general store in the village or at the cross-roads supplied coffee, tea, salt, soda, spices, and, after there were wagon roads over the mountains, these stores carried cheese, canned goods, and a few other food items. The village mill ground the farmers grain and an adequate number of distilleries converted part of the grain into whiskey. Once a year, in midwinter, the general store might have a few small tubs of saltfish from the Great Lakes or a small barrel of fresh oysters from the Atlantic.

Such was the supply of food of many a locality in the United States until about the year 1900. It made a far better diet than many a prosperous American eats today; but most of these foods are seasonal, which meant better quality but less variety, especially in winter. There were always milk and eggs the year round, and poultry could be butchered at any time; but cattle, sheep, and hogs could be butchered only in cold weather so the meat could be used, smoked, salted, or fried down before it spoiled. The principal meat was pork; cattle were a cash crop for they could be driven over the mountains, sold, and butchered in near-by cities of the region.

In November the farmer would butcher a number of hogs according to the size of his family. Hams, shoulders, and side meat were packed in salt for six weeks or so and then removed and cured with smoke from hickory or some other hardwood; every farm had its smokehouse. Sausage was made from the trimmings of the shoulders and hams, hearts, livers, and other bits of meat. The farmer's wife "fried down" the sausage, backbones, and the spareribs; that is, she fried the meat, packed it in earthenware crocks, and covered it with melted lard rendered from the fatter parts of the hog. This process preserved the meat for at least a year.

The older houses had no cellars and so there was a milkhouse, cooled by water from a spring or well. It served to keep milk, butter, and eggs fresh until they were used or sold to the village store or to an itinerant huckster who collected such produce for the larger towns.

Grains and beans kept well if they were dry; fruits and vegetables were the real problem.

Many a farmer constructed what he called a cave, or a root cellar. If his house was on a hillside, he simply dug into the side of the hill, bolstered up the roof with slabs or heavy boards, walled up the sides with boards or field stone, built a door frame, hung a door, and built bins along the sides and across the rear. If he lived on level ground, the cave was more of a problem, but the early American farmer was used to problems, and so he dug a rectangular hole 4 or 5 ft deep with a ramp or steps at one end for access. He walled up the sides to the proper height, put on a peaked roof of boards or slabs, and then covered it with the dirt he had dug from the hole. Grass or weeds kept the dirt from washing off the mound when it rained.

These caves withstood temperatures far below freezing. On a very cold night, the farmer put a tub of water in the cave and hung a heavy blanket over the door, which protected the food at outside temperatures down to zero Fahrenheit or below. Water freezes at a higher temperature than either fruits or vegetables and emits 80 calories of heat for each gram that freezes. This was enough heat to keep the temperature in the cave above the freezing points of the food as long as there was any water left in the tub.

The caves were used to store apples, root vegetables, cabbage, onions, and perhaps a few other items. If a farmer raised more of these crops than his cave would hold, he buried the rest in the garden in a hole lined with straw, and covered them with a foot or more of dirt according to the local climate. Then when the supply in the cave became low, he dug up his cache and replenished the stock in the cave. The food would keep until late in the spring and some of it until the new crop came in.

Apples, pears, peaches, and blackberries were dried in the sun, but sweetcorn was the only vegetable dried. Drying was the cheapest way to preserve these foods, but the products were not very good. They all changed flavor—apples, for example, turned brown and developed an indescribable flavor that no fresh apple ever had.

Canning gave a better product than drying, but the equipment was poor and expensive. In many communities there were potteries, or "pot shops" as they were generally called locally, that made thick-walled jars of various sizes from clay. Where there was no such shop nearby, the local store would supply the jars. These jars were taller than wide, and the inside of the mouth was a flat surface that accommodated an almost flat tin lid. The housewife cooked the food, scalded the jar, poured or dipped the food into it, put the lid in place, and poured melted sealing wax around the edge of it.

The jar was of any size from a pint to 2 gal., but the quart and the half gallon were the most popular sizes.

Later, glass jars arrived at the country stores. They were closed with a rubber gasket around the mouth and a cap that screwed or clamped on top of the jar and held the gasket in place. These were an improvement over the earthenware jar in convenience, but canning remained an art the housewife learned from her mother. A successful method was followed as closely as any recipe for baking a cake. If the canner grew careless and let a filled jar cool before she sealed it, the food might mold, or ferment and burst the jar. The women took great pride in their art, and the ability to get through a season without any spoilage was a victory. The canned foods were usually fruits, tomatoes, beets, snap beans, sweetcorn, or peas.

After sugar became plentiful, the housewives preserved a lot of fruit as jam or jelly, with sugar serving as the preservative. Although some of the jam was put into jars, the jelly was poured into glasses where it set to a solid, but there was no good way to close the glass. The usual makeshift was to place a piece of paper on top, fold it down around the sides and tie a string around it. This protected the jelly from dust and insects, but molds often grew on the surface. One ingenious woman of my acquaintance cut circles of white paper the exact size of the jelly surface, soaked them in brandy and laid them on the surface before she tied the paper over the top. Fifty percent alcohol is a good preservative, but how general this procedure was is not a matter of record. After paraffin became available many women melted that and poured a thin layer over the surface of the jelly.

The worst time of the year for those living under such an economy was the spring and early summer. If the family had calculated badly or if there had been a short crop, food began to run out in March or April and the family ate flour and cornmeal products, poultry, eggs, milk, butter, and cottage cheese, for there was little fresh food from field or garden before July.

With the advances in food processing and transportation of the past 50 years, our present food supply bears little resemblance to that of any earlier period in the history of the world. In fact, much of it is now overprocessed in order to transfer the labor of the housewife to the factory. The processors have devised new or better methods for preserving food, and modern transportation has brought food from far places. Specialization in production has also increased and in some areas of the country one may see thousands of acres of watermelons, snap beans, tomatoes, or some other food crop.

Our food habits and requirements have been established by thousands of years of food history. What a major change in available foods would do to the growth and health of man is an interesting subject for speculation.

CHAPTER 2

Processing the Cereal Grains

Agriculture and fishing are the means of food production today. Anything that happens to food between its harvest and its arrival in the kitchen is transportation, storage, or processing.

Food processing is a multiplicity of industries, and many a task formerly part of kitchen routine is now a commercial process. Washing apples, dyeing oranges, peeling potatoes, grinding grain, baking bread and cakes are all commercial food processes. In this chapter, I shall describe some of the methods for processing the cereal grains.

MILLING

One of the oldest and most important of the food processes is the grinding of grain. Whole grain is tasteless and indigestible, and some ancient genius decided to aid his teeth by crushing the grain between stones. If a little crushing is good, more is better, and so improvements in the process were the stone mortar and pestle and then the stone mill which was used to grind grain from the beginning of history to the middle of the 19th century.

From the earliest settlements in America to about the year 1900, no farmer who raised grain was far from a mill. As the population moved westward and means of transportation improved, the local mill began to give way to the large commercial mill. The first milling center was in Richmond, Virginia. As the population and the wheat fields moved westward, it moved from Richmond to Rochester, N.Y., from Rochester to St. Louis, and, as the North Central States began to concentrate on raising wheat, to Minneapolis, which is still the milling center of the whole country.

The amount of the common grains available to us is indicated by their production, which in 1970 was: corn 4109 million bushels, wheat 1378, oats 909, barley 410, and rye 38 million. We do not eat all this grain; some is used to feed cattle, hogs, and poultry, some is made into beer and whiskey, and some is exported.

The human consumption of grain in the United States in 1970 was 110 lb of wheat per person as flour and 2.9 lb as breakfast cereals; 7.4 lb of corn as cornmeal and 20.7 lb as other products made from corn, such as cornstarch, corn sirup, corn sugar, hominy, and

14

breakfast cereals; 1.2 lb of rye flour; 3.7 lb of barley in several ways; and 7.4 lb of rice.

Wheat

Different kinds of wheat differ in composition; the protein content, for example, varies from 7.5 to 17%. The higher protein wheats are used to make bread flour and the low protein wheats are used for cake and pastry flour.

The first step in the modern manufacture of flour is to clean the wheat. This is done by passing it over shaking screens in a current of air. Most of the weed seeds that may be present are smaller than the grains of wheat and drop through the screens, while the air current carries off the dust and chaff.

Very dry wheat is hard to grind, and with more than 14% water neither wheat nor flour keeps well; consequently, a modern mill conditions wheat to 14% moisture. This makes it easier to separate the bran from the flour and increases the yield of flour the miller gets from a bushel of wheat.

The grain of wheat consists of four parts: the bran, the aleurone layer, the germ, and the endosperm (Fig. 2.1). The bran is the brown outer coat of the seed and is made up of flat cells which are brittle when they are dry, and tough and paper-like when they are slightly moist. The germ is a short thread-like structure at one end of the seed. It contains most of the fat in the seed and is tough and rubbery. The aleurone layer is a series of coarse cells just under the bran, and the endosperm is the central part of the seed composed of fine particles of starch and protein.

The task of the mill is to separate these four parts of the wheat seed and grind them. The old stone mills did not grind the bran and the germ very much and they were screened out together as the bran fraction. The remainder was passed over a much finer screen; the flour went through and the coarser aleurone particles along with a little of the bran was therefore called middlings.

The operation of a modern roller mill is much more complicated. The wheat takes a long journey through scales, cleaners, rollers, and sifters. Each is a separate machine and each is connected to the next by a conveyor, so that the process is one continuous stream from the wheat storage bin to the silo or the bags that receive the flour. The bran and the germ are ejected at some point along the way and reach their own packaging or storage facilities.

The first few sets of rolls that the wheat meets are called break rolls. They are made of steel and corrugated. Of different sizes, sometimes as large as 10 in. in diameter, they are set just close enough

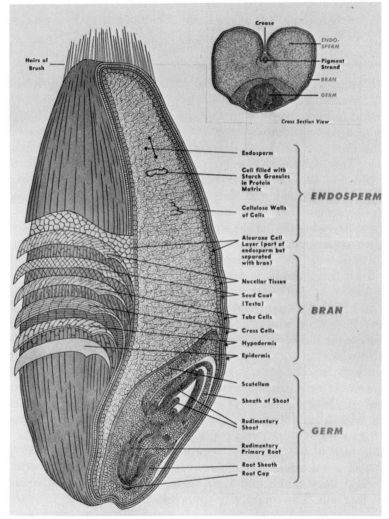

Crease

ENDO-
SPERM

Pigment
Strand

BRAN

GERM

Cross Section View

Hairs of
Brush

Endosperm

Cell filled with
Starch Granules
in Protein
Matrix

Cellulose Walls
of Cells

Aleurone Cell
Layer (part of
endosperm but
separated
with bran)

Nucellar Tissue

Seed Coat
(Testa)

Tube Cells

Cross Cells

Hypodermis

Epidermis

Scutellum

Sheath of Shoot

Rudimentary
Shoot

Rudimentary
Primary Root

Root Sheath
Root Cap

ENDOSPERM

BRAN

GERM

Courtesy of Wheat Flour Institute

FIG. 2.1.   WHEAT KERNEL

together to crack the wheat. There are several sets of these break
rolls, and since some flour is produced by each set the product is
sifted after each cracking. The coarser material goes on to the next
set, which are usually smaller than the previous ones and are closer
together. In each set of rolls, one turns faster than the other so there
is a grinding action as well as the crushing.

After the break rolls have done their duty and the product has been
sifted, it goes to the reduction rolls, which are smaller than the

break rolls, smooth and set closer together. Here again the rollers alternate with sifters. The total number of rolls differs with the mill, but there are usually at least a dozen sets. One miller told me that his mill had 18 and another claimed 36. There are also some machines not mentioned that perform mysterious functions such as throwing out the bran or the germ.

The screens in a flour mill are usually made of wire cloth like a window screen and differ in mesh according to the job they have to do. The finest one, however, is a closely-woven silk or nylon cloth and is called a bolting cloth. Several years ago I knew of a small mill that was owned by three brothers. The mill had an unusual demand for bolting cloth, not only from the wear in the mill, but also from the wives' demand for dress material.

The several flour streams can be combined in different proportions to produce different kinds of finished flour. A bread flour may contain as much as 14% protein and a cake or pastry flour as little as 7.5%. The general purpose flour of the grocery contains about 12% moisture, 10.5% protein, and 0.3% fat.

A whole wheat flour is made by grinding the entire grain into one stream; it contains about 13% protein and 2% fat. Because of the difference in composition, whole wheat flour doesn't keep as well as white flour. The fat becomes rancid and the insect eggs (from the crease in the grain of wheat that escaped the cleaning process) hatch and a large insect population soon appears. There are machines for destroying these insect eggs, but even when they are used, some eggs escape destruction. White flour is less subject to insect infestation but by no means free from it, especially in warm climates.

Flour has a pale cream color, but today nearly all the flour sold either to the bakers or the grocers is bleached. The bleaching is done with chlorine, compounds of nitrogen and chlorine, or benzoyl peroxide. The treatment oxidizes the pigment in the flour and usually the fat, and destroys the natural flavor of the flour. The bleaching is incidental; the real purpose of the treatment is to age the flour. Freshly ground flour does not make very light bread. If the flour is stored for several months the action of the air ages it and it makes lighter bread. The bleaching causes much the same improvement in a short time at the expense of the flavor of the flour, but it saves the cost of long storage.

The protein of wheat is called *gluten* from its glue-like tendency to hold the starch particles together to make a firm bread, but too firm for a cake, hence the lower protein content of a cake flour.

The plant breeders have produced better varieties of wheat and the millers have improved the flour, but the use of wheat products has declined as the country has become more prosperous. We seem to prefer other foods although they are more expensive than bread. This preference is indicated by the amount of flour we each consume annually, which was 212 lb in 1910, 177 in 1920, 160 in 1930, 157 in 1940, 135 in 1950, 118 in 1960, and 110 in 1970.

Corn

The protein of corn does not have the adhesive quality of wheat gluten, and so the ways in which corn is used for human food are different from those of wheat. The old stone mills simply ground the corn and passed it through a screen to remove the hulls. This left some of the germ in the meal, and since the germ has a high fat content the meal did not keep well, but this old style meal is still available in some localities. The modern roller mills clean the corn, remove the hull and the germ, and then grind the endosperm to a meal, which is much coarser than a flour (Fig. 2.2). The old style corn meal contained as much as 9% protein and 3 to 4% fat. The newer product contains less than 8% protein and about 1% fat. Recently the plant breeders have produced a variety of corn of much higher protein content.

For many years corn meal was used to make mush by boiling it with water and a little salt. The mush was of the consistency of morning oatmeal and was often eaten with milk as the main supper dish. Any excess was put into a pan or a crock where it solidified, was cut into slices, and fried for breakfast. This wide use of corn meal has now become practically extinct in the United States.

Some corn meal now appears on the table as corn muffins, which generally contain as much wheat flour as corn meal; the corn meal supplies the color and the flavor, and the gluten of the flour holds the product together. Corn meal alone does not make good bread because the corn protein does not hold it together, and it crumbles when an attempt is made to spread it with butter or jelly. Nevertheless, a corn bread called by the Indian name "pone" was a regular item of food in many a home in earlier and less prosperous years and was eaten with molasses on it or fat meat with it.

When food was scarce during World War I, we shipped some corn meal to our French and British allies. It was unfamiliar and they wouldn't eat it, whereupon, our government made a drive to induce us to eat more corn so we could ship more wheat to our friends overseas.

Even we Americans are about to give up corn meal as we become more wealthy and more urban; we averaged 117 lb each in 1899, 21

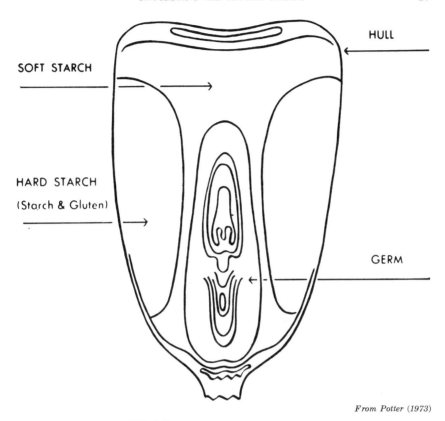

HULL

SOFT STARCH

HARD STARCH

(Starch & Gluten)

GERM

From Potter (1973)

FIG. 2.2. CORN KERNEL

lb in 1931, and 4 lb in 1970. However, the total consumption of corn in 1970 was 28 lb per capita and so there are obviously other ways of eating corn besides the corn meal products. There is hominy (grits, mostly) and even though its use has also declined, we still ate 3 lb each in 1962, as well as 1.8 lb of breakfast cereal made from corn.

Wet Corn Milling.—The greater part of the corn eaten today is in the form of some product of the wet milling industry.   These products are corn syrup 11.3 lb, corn sugar 3 lb, cornstarch 1.8 lb, and a small amount of corn oil.

The wet milling of corn justifies its name by using water from the beginning to the end of the process. After the corn is cleaned it goes into a large tank of water where it remains for about two days. The average corn kernel contains 11% moisture, 72% starch, 10%

protein, 4% oil, and 2% hull. During the steeping period some
protein soaks out of the grain, which makes the water a good home
for bacteria and other microorganisms. Consequently, sulfur dioxide
is added to the water, not only to prevent the growth of these
organisms, but also to bleach the yellow pigment of the corn and to
help loosen the hull and the germ. During the soaking, the kernel
swells and the hulls and the germ can then be separated from the
endosperm more easily.

When the soaking is finished, the swollen grains are passed through
a machine that loosens the hulls and the germ, breaks the endosperm
into small pieces and discharges the product into a trough of water.
The germs, which are rich in oil, float on the surface of the water
and go over a dam at the end of the trough. They are collected,
dried, and pressed for oil, which is refined and eventually goes into
soups, salad dressings, margarine, paint, or bottles for the grocers'
shelves.

The hulls and endosperm, still in water, are passed along to a
stone mill that grinds and separates them. The starch is washed
several times to remove the last traces of protein, then dried
and ground. It may or may not receive further treatment to adapt
it for use in puddings, in the laundry, for paper sizing, or for some
other use.

Some starch goes to a part of the factory where it is converted into
corn syrup or corn sugar. There the starch is suspended in water
again, and a small amount of hydrochloric acid is added. The suspension is heated, and several successive changes occur as the starch
reacts with the water (hydrolysis). The first product is *dextrin*
followed by several complex sugars, then *maltose*, and finally the
simple sugar, *glucose*, also called *dextrose*—a chemist uses whichever
name comes to mind first. It is impossible to stop this process at
any single stage until the last, because each product begins to change
to the next as soon as there is any of it formed; for example some of
the maltose changes to dextrose before all the complex sugars have
become maltose. To stop the hydrolysis the mixture is discharged
into a tank where it is cooled and the acid neutralized.

The first commercial product is mostly dextrin—a stiff, gummy
mass called "glucose" in the industry. It is used to make soft candy
because it keeps the sucrose from crystallizing into a hard chunk
like a piece of rock candy or lump of sugar. If the hydrolysis is
allowed to go further, the product contains less dextrin and more
sugars, and is the corn syrup of the market. The hydrochloric acid
is neutralized with sodium carbonate and so the "glucose" and the

corn syrup contain the sodium chloride that is formed. But sodium chloride is common salt and there is only about 0.2% of it.

The corn sugars are not as sweet as the common sucrose, and so some manufacturers often add cane or beet sugar to make a sweeter table syrup. The label always mentions the sucrose if it has been added. Corn syrups differ in composition depending on the exact point where the action was stopped and whether or not sucrose was added. Two syrups on the market were found to contain:

	Water	Dextrin	Maltose	Dextrose	Sucrose
(1)	25.3%	35.4%	22.2%	7.5%	7.1%
(2)	25.2	9.1	25.5	28.0	—

If the process is allowed to go to completion, the acid is neutralized, the water is evaporated, and the dextrose crystallizes as a fine white product.

During World War II, when cane and beet sugars became scarce, some manufacturers of corn sugar offered packages to the housewives through the grocer, but it was a new product and they looked on it as a substitute and did not buy it. Consequently, it was withdrawn from the trade when the more familiar sucrose again became plentiful.

Corn syrup, corn syrup solids (that is, dried corn syrup), and dextrose are used for many purposes. The candy industry uses more than any other, but they also go into soft drinks, cakes and cookies, pie fillings, jams, jellies, canned foods, and other composite food products. The wet-milling of corn has grown through the years and now produces well over 2 billion lb of these products annually.

Rice

Rice is the cereal food for most of the world's population. It is to the East what wheat is to the West. In fact it has been reliably estimated that rice is the principal food of over half the people in the world. About 95% of the rice is grown in the Orient, but several European and South American countries grow and eat considerable rice, and we grow some in Louisiana, Texas, Arkansas, and California.

A little rice is ground to flour, but the vast majority of it is consumed in the whole grain simply boiled.

Barley

Barley produces more grain to the acre than wheat and also grows under less favorable conditions, such as less rainfall or a shorter growing season. Unfortunately, the flour is less satisfactory than wheat flour for making bread. Therefore, our chief use for barley is the manufacture of malt, which in turn is used to make beer, ale, whiskey, and malted milk. Other countries use more of their barley for human food. Russia, India, Germany, and Spain all grow large quantities of it, and in Japan it is next to rice in importance, for it will grow on mountain sides where rice does not flourish.

Rye

Most of the rye we produce in this country is used for cattle feed or to make beer or whiskey. It is more easily grown than wheat, particularly in cold countries, which makes it a popular cereal in northern Europe. Russia is the leading grower of rye followed by Germany, Poland, Czechoslovakia, France, and Spain. The Europeans eat far more rye bread than we do and so most of their rye is ground into flour and used in the bakeries.

BAKING

Over half the people in the world eat their cereal as porridge, such as boiled rice, hominy, and oatmeal; but someone invented bread a long time ago and it rapidly gained in favor. Unleavened bread and ovens to bake it have been found in several places scattered over Europe and Asia. These discoveries date from about 5000 B.C. Bread has two advantages over porridge: the higher temperature used in baking gives it more flavor, and it keeps much better than porridge because it is drier. In fact, baking was one of the inventions that sped the human race on its way to our present way of life, for the unleavened bread was soon followed by the leavened product.

History does not record when or how leavened bread was invented, but salt rising bread, which is now almost forgotten, gives us a clue. The nature of this product is indicated by my own experience with it.

Long years ago, I taught a country school in the hills of southern Pennsylvania and lived at the home of a farmer who would not eat bread made with yeast, and so his wife made salt rising bread. The bread was made by mixing a dough and allowing it to stand over night in a warm place. Gas formed and the bread became lighter but not very light by present day standards. Nobody knew what made the dough rise, but some thought it was the salt, and that opinion gave the bread its name. The dough not only became lighter but also sour. During the baking a sour odor pervaded the house and a sour taste remained in the bread. In late November cold weather arrived, and in that primitive farmhouse the dough could not be kept warm enough overnight so we ate baking powder biscuits at every meal through the winter and well into the spring.

Several years after my experience, a food scientist became curious about this salt rising bread and investigated it. He found that the gas is produced by certain kinds of bacteria that fall into the dough from the air or are added with one of the ingredients; the dough contained a little corn meal, which was suspected as a possible source. Whatever their source these bacteria not only produced carbon dioxide to raise the dough, but they also changed the sugar to lactic acid—the acid of buttermilk—hence the sour odor and taste. Few people liked this bread and it has now almost disappeared from the American scene.

Commercial bakeries were common in ancient Egypt and made many kinds of bread and rolls long before the Christian era.

In many countries the wives of the farmers and of many villagers baked the family bread. In this country they used a "starter" method in most cases. They boiled potatoes, mashed them and added sugar, water and yeast. The yeast came from a brewery, a distillery, or a neighbor. When baking time came, which was at least once a week, part of the fermenting mixture was added to the dough, but some of it was always kept to add to another potato broth for future use and was called a "starter." By this method the yeast could be kept alive indefinitely unless it got too cold or was kept too long and "ran out." Yeast is a plant that lives on the sugar, protein, and other nutrients from the potato, and if it used up all these materials it would starve to death. If the starter ran out, a young son was given a cup and sent to a neighbor to "borrow" some.

In 1868 a brewer by name of Fleischmann began to grow yeast, mix it with corn meal or flour, press it into cakes, and dry it. Then the baker and soon the housewife could buy these cakes of yeast at the grocery. This development gradually ended the use of the starter, and the yeast jug no longer startled the family by popping its cork.

When the housewife made bread, she first sifted the flour into a large pan. This removed or broke up lumps of flour and also removed splinters, cloth fibers, or any other foreign matter that may have gotten into the flour. It also mixed the flour with air, for yeasts, like any other living organism, require air to breathe.

She added salt, yeast, and water and mixed the batch thoroughly to a rather stiff dough. She then set the pan aside in a warm place for a time, often overnight. During this period the yeast produced bubbles of carbon dioxide, which caused the dough to expand and

FIG. 2.3.   DOUGH MIXER

sometimes run over the sides of the pan. Besides the rising, other
changes occurred; substances were formed that improved the flavor
of the bread, and the gluten "developed." A good bread flour should
have over 10% gluten, and the gluten from some kinds of wheat is
better than that from others. The housewife, of course, used whatever
flour came to hand, generally that made from the wheat grown on
the family farm; but she learned by experience that some flour made
better bread than others, and if she bought the flour at a store, she
soon developed a preference for some brands over others. Why
glutens differ and what happens to them as they develop, she did not
know, and I hasten to add that the cereal chemist of the 1970s does
not know much more about it than she did. He knows the gluten
"develops," that is, it becomes more adhesive and rubber-like so

it holds the gas bubbles better; just how it does this is the gluten's own secret.

When the dough had raised enough to suit the housewife, she "worked it down" to remove the big gas pockets and thus produce a more uniform "grain" in the loaf. She next divided the dough into portions and rounded them into loaves to close up the surface where she had torn the dough apart, so the gas would not escape. She put these loaves into pans and set them aside to rise to about twice their volume, and then baked them.

From the above description it is evident that baking bread at home is an art. The housewife learned by experience how much flour she needed for the amount of bread she planned to bake—also how much salt and how much yeast, how long to let it rise, and how much dough to use for a loaf. Then she baked it in the oven of a wood, or coal stove, and guessed at the time and temperature. If the bread did not turn out well she guessed at the reason and tried to correct it next time.

The bakers have simply standardized and mechanized the baking process used by housewives for centuries. They sift the flour and weigh it and then weigh the water, salt, and dried yeast. They have mechanical mixers that may mix a batch of 1000 lb (Fig. 2.3). They time the mixing accurately because overmixing makes the gluten soft and sticky, ruining it.

The dough from the mixer is discharged into a trough, which for some strange reason is pronounced to rhyme with dough. It is commonly about 10 ft long, 2 ft wide, 2 ft deep, and mounted on small wheels so it can be easily pushed across the floor into the fermentation room. The trough is filled about half full to allow space for the rising of the dough.

At this point the baker calls his mixture a "sponge." The fermentation room is air conditioned to 80°F and 75% humidity. Yeast grows well at this temperature, and the air is kept moist so the sponge will not dry on the surface and form a bothersome crust. The sponge remains in the fermentation room 4 or 5 hr after which it goes back to the mixers, flour and some other materials are added and then back to the fermentation room for further rising.

After the second fermentation the sponge goes to a machine that cuts it into uniform pieces of a definite weight because the laws are fussy about food that weighs less than it claims to; if the wrapper says 16 oz, 16 oz it must be. The housewife did not sell her bread and so she did not have to be so particular on this point.

From the divider the loaves go to the rounder, which is a machine that seals the cut edges just as the housewife did by hand. The rounded loaves go to a proof room, which is a bit warmer than the fermentation room, to rise some more and thus recover from the cutting and rounding. After a half hour or so of proofing the loaves go to a machine that shapes them and puts them into pans, which then go to the oven. In one common type of oven the pans pass through a long heated tunnel on a moving metal melt. The oven is heated to 400°F or thereabout. There is so much water in bread that the inside of the loaf is cooked at the boiling temperature of 212°F, but the higher temperature of the oven dries out the surface and toasts it slightly to form the crust. The bread travels slowly through the oven; the exact time depends on the temperature, but it is usually about an hour.

The modern baker's bread is of more complicated composition than the home product. To begin with, the flour is bleached at the mill to improve the protein. In the past 25 years bread flour has been enriched (see Chap. 20) in order to add some minerals and vitamins needed in white flour for better nutrition. In addition to these substances added to the flour at the mill, the baker has some of his own that he adds at the second mixing. Yeasts are plants and require food and fertilizer. For food, the baker adds malt syrup, which changes some of the starch to dextrose for yeast food. He may also add some sucrose to improve the flavor of the bread and also as food for the yeast. The yeast fertilizer consists of ammonium salts and phosphates. These are in very small amounts and they are edible; in fact, the phosphates are among the requirements of the human diet. The baker may also add shortening and other substances to make the bread soft or to keep it from molding. There are legal standards for bread that specify what substances may be added and how much of some of them. The label on the wrapper is very informative as to these additives.

Other cereal food processes besides milling and baking have appeared through the years. Among the most important is the manufacture of everything from oatmeal and farina to the crisp luxuries of the breakfast table. Less important but just as enjoyable are cakes and pies, popcorn to help us through a movie, and snacks for the cocktail hour.

CHAPTER 3

Food Preservation

Most foods of botanical origin are seasonal; in the temperate zone all of them are. Consequently, if we are to have these fruits and vegetables out of season or at a distance from where they are produced, they must be preserved. Cold storage and rapid transportation have gone a long way toward solving the fresh produce problem, but they are still far from able to maintain an adequate food supply through the long winters of the north.

Meats also must be preserved. Salting is one of the oldest methods of food preservation, and has been used mainly to preserve meat. Generally some drying goes along with it.

DRYING

The oldest method of drying food is to expose it to the sun, a method still used. Fish are cleaned, salted, and placed on wooden racks in the sun (Fig. 3.1).

Sun-drying is cheaper than using fuel for heat. The drying of prunes, raisins, apricots, and peaches has a long history in California where the climate is warm and there is little rain during the harvest season. Grapes are harvested and dried on wire trays on the ground between the rows of vines or in a drying yard until they have been reduced to 9 to 12% moisture (Fig. 3.2).

Prunes are shaken from the trees and taken to a drying plant where they are cleaned, placed on trays, and exposed to the sun in a drying yard. They are dried to 16 to 19% moisture and stored in bins to allow the moisture to distribute evenly, for they are drier on the outside than they are in the interior. When marketed they are rehydrated with steam or boiling water to 28% moisture and packaged. The rehydrated product does not keep as well as the drier prunes, but one advantage is that the housewife can cook them without a long preliminary soaking.

Apricots and peaches, like prunes, are brought to a drying plant, cleaned, cut, seeded, and placed on trays with the cut side up because the water evaporates faster from the cut surface than from the skin. One of the difficulties of drying a cut fruit is an enzyme in the fruit that turns the surface brown as soon as it is exposed to the air. To avoid this, peaches and apricots are put into a room filled with the fumes of burning sulfur. The sulfur dioxide inactivates the

27

FIG. 3.1. DRYING FISH

enzyme, bleaches the fruit, and helps to preserve it. After the fruit
has been sulfured the trays are transferred to the drying yard,
and the fruit is dried to 18% moisture or less.

Although the California climate is favorable for drying fruit,
the fruit is exposed to dust and insects and the drying conditions are
hard to control; consequently, more sophisticated methods have
been coming into use for several years. One of the big advantages of
dried foods is ease of transportation—because they are lighter and
take up much less space than the same foods in the fresh condition.
For this reason war has been a big factor in the invention of artificial processes for drying food. With over four million Americans
under arms in World War I, and most of them at sea or in Europe,
it became necessary to have more dried food to feed them. Unfortunately, there was no food-drying industry except the production of dried fruit in California and dried fish in New England.
The troops were supplied with fresh and canned foods. Beef, frozen
in Chicago, was delivered to the front lines in Eastern France, still
frozen. Raw potatoes were shipped in quantity, and tomatoes
and other fresh foods, when available, were bought locally in France;
but fresh foods began to overtax the supply lines as more and more
soldiers went to Europe.

Some food processors tried to dry vegetables, but, unfortunately,
they didn't know how to go about it, and the war was over before
they learned. One product that did get to France was dried potatoes.
The potatoes were cut into strips and dried with artificial heat.
They turned brown and had an unimaginable flavor. The cooks
made mashed potatoes out of them, and some of the hardier and
hungrier soldiers ate them.

Courtesy of USDA

FIG. 3.2. GRAPES DRYING

The state of the food-drying industry from 1918 to 1941 may be illustrated by the experience of a chemical engineer. His family was in the pineapple industry in Hawaii, and he noticed that when the pineapples were cut into familiar rings for canning, a lot of juice was lost. He devised a successful method for drying this juice, but nobody wanted dried pineapple juice and so the venture was not a financial success. He then returned to the mainland and set up an experimental plant for drying vegetables. He turned out satisfactory potatoes, carrots, onions, and a few other vegetables. He then went to Idaho and set up a commercial plant to dry the famous Idaho potatoes. Here again, he found there was no demand for his product. At that point he gave up. Today, over 1 billion lb of potatoes are dried each year to produce 160 million lb of dried potato powder.

When we became involved in World War II and had 12 million men in uniform scattered over the world, many of them in the tropics, supplying them with fresh foods or even canned foods was out of the question because of the long distances and the climate. Dried foods were a must, both because of their advantage in transportation and their keeping qualities. We had been supplying some food for the British, but it is impossible to describe the furor in the food processing industries when we were plunged into the war in December 1941.

THE FOOD TECHNOLOGISTS

A food technologist is anyone who concerns himself with the scientific aspects of food processing. Most of them have been educated as chemists, bacteriologists, or engineers. The Americans of that profession were unorganized until July 1939 when several of them assembled at Cambridge, Mass., under the leadership of Professor Samuel C. Prescott of the Massachusetts Institute of Technology. A society was organized for the exchange of ideas and the advancement and improvement of the food processing industry; it was named the *Institute of Food Technologists*, the IFT for short. These technologists soon faced an emergency in their industry.

The third annual conference of the IFT met in Minneapolis June 14–17, 1942. They held nine sessions in each of which some aspect of war-time food problems was discussed. Even at a smoker held one evening, food problems were the main topic of conversation. The opening speech of the first session was on the role of food technology in war. It was made by Colonel Paul P. Logan of the Quartermaster Corps of the U.S. Army. At lunch that same day a member of the FBI spoke on sabotage and what to do about it. Incidentally, the food industry got through the war without any sabotage.

Machinery and building materials were scarce and rationed, and so a half day of the convention was spent discussing priorities and substitutes. One session was spent on the conversion of factories from what they were doing to food processing. One session was devoted to food dehydration and one to packages and the packaging of dried foods so they would keep, which was an unsolved problem. Tin was so scarce that even the tin can came in for attention.

Late Wednesday afternoon the meeting adjourned and of the 1200 members of IFT, the 300 who attended the convention left for home determined to do what they could to solve the pressing food problems. Some members were teachers in universities, some were government employees, and some were consultants to industry, but most of them were employed by industries that processed food. All could work on the solution of technical problems and the industrial members could and did inform their management of the problems, difficulties, and solutions they had learned about at the convention.

Fresh and frozen foods average about 75% water and canned fruits and vegetables much the same. There were simply not enough ships to carry so much water to the armed forces so far from their bases of supplies. The problems, then, were mainly three: dehydration, packaging dehydrated foods, and devising new food for army rations.

The food technologist distinguishes between drying and dehydration although the words have the same meaning in general usage. He uses drying for the sun drying operation—dried prunes, dried apricots, dried fish—and dehydration for the artificial-heat process used for eggs, milk products, potatoes, and fruits and vegetables in general. Aside from the difference in the method of processing, the dehydrated products are much the drier of the two—dried fruit may contain 18% water and dried fish 50%. At the time of the 1942 meeting of the IFT it was known that milk, eggs, and vegetables had to be dried to less than 10% water or they would spoil. A closer examination of dehydrated foods later disclosed the fact that most foods had to be reduced below 5% water, and before the end of the war the military food was reduced to less than 2% water to prevent spoilage in the tropics.

While the chemist and the bacteriologist were working on the problem of spoilage, the engineers were building plants to dehydrate the food, and most everybody was testing packaging material. Tin was too scarce to permit the use of tin cans. There was already a shortage of cans for meat, fish, ether, oil, and other essential civilian and military supplies. Glass was too heavy and too fragile for transportation, and so suitable paper and plastic packaging materials had to be found or developed for as many items as possible.

Dehydrators are of several types: tray driers (Fig. 3.3), tunnel driers, continuous belt driers, drum driers, spray driers, and freeze driers. All these except the last had been used before 1942 for one purpose or another, but there were very few in operation. Probably the most common was the spray drier used to make soluble coffee and dried milk. The engineers had to build driers in a hurry, even though metal and everything else needed for the

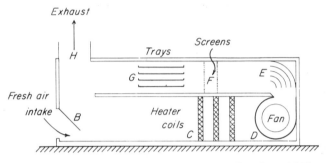

From Potter (1973)

FIG. 3.3.　TRAY DRIER

purpose seemed to be under government restrictions for other war uses. The tunnel drier, which had been developed in the 1930s for drying fruits was the simplest and cheapest. It was composed of a tunnel about 6 ft wide, 6 ft high, and several feet long; it was made of boards, sheet metal, concrete or whatever was available in the neighborhood. These driers were scattered all over the country in places where fruits or vegetables were grown, for the transportation of fresh food overland was as much of a problem for the railroads and trucks as the overseas shipment was for the ships.

Technologists had learned the cause of the trouble with the dried potatoes of World War I; enzymes turned them brown and caused the bad flavor. These enzymes are in the fresh potatoes and as soon as the potato is cut, the air and enzymes begin to operate and work more rapidly as the temperature rises until it gets to 115°F where the enzyme is inactivated. The obvious solution to the problem was blanching, that is, exposing the freshly cut slices to boiling water or steam for a few minutes. This process put the enzyme out of action and then the potatoes could be dried with no change in color or flavor unless the temperature became high enough to scorch them. Many technologists worked on these drying problems, and what they learned was promptly published or disclosed to a scientific meeting—soon all of us knew that practically all cut fruits and vegetables must be blanched before dehydration.

In the tunnel process of dehydration the cut and blanched vegetables were spread on wooden trays that were slid into racks mounted in a frame on wheels something like the pie racks used in a bakery or the hospital carts for food trays. The trucks were just about wide enough and high enough to pass along the tunnel. At one end of the tunnel was a gas or an oil heater and a fan to blow the hot air through the tunnel. In most of the tunnels the trucks were pushed into the end farthest from the heater. As soon as a second truck was filled it was pushed into the tunnel and shoved the first one along toward the hotter end; thus the process was continuous. The fresh food met with air that had already taken up considerable moisture from the food ahead of it, and the one about to emerge was dried by the hottest and driest air.

These crude tunnels dried a lot of food for the army and navy, but the engineers improved them as rapidly as they could. By the end of the war the tunnels had reached a high degree of refinement, and there were companies prepared to build a good drier for anyone who wanted one. One of the improvements was the change from wooden to metal or plastic trays, because splinters in the food had been a problem for the war-time operators.

Liquids, such as milk, eggs, and fruit juices, were spray dried. The spray drier is a funnel-shaped chamber several feet in diameter at the top and several feet high. The liquid enters from a spray head at the top. This device is much like the head on a shower bath and the liquid, which comes in under pressure enters as a fine spray. Hot air comes in at the side and goes out at the top taking the water vapor with it. The dehydrated food settles to the bottom of the drier.

ARMY FOOD

It would be rash to say that the American soldiers of World War II found their food entirely satisfactory. An officer of the Quartermaster Corps visited outlying posts in the Pacific area during the war to study the supply problems and to find out how the men liked the foods served them. When asked how he liked the food, a sailor replied, 'Oh, it's all right what there is of it." "Don't you get enough to eat?" the officer asked and the reply was, "Oh, yes there is enough of it such as it is." And a soldier expressed this opinion of what the army called the K ration: "A man could probably live on it longer than he would care to."

Institutional feeding always brings complaints whether in an army, a navy, a boarding school, or a jail. Mass feeding cannot be done on home cooking, and even if it could, the cooking of one home would be different from that of another. Brides have the same trouble: "This cake is not like the one that mother used to bake."

The food technologists tried to correct the faults in the army food supply with considerable success. Nobody in the armed forces starved or suffered from any dietary deficiency disease, a problem that has always troubled quartermasters. Many an army has lost more men to scurvy than in battle.

DEHYDRATED CIVILIAN FOOD

When the war was over, dozens of plants in this country could produce dehydrated food in large quantity, but the returning soldiers had had enough dried food and civilians had never cared for it. Consequently, many owners closed their plants, but some decided to stay in business.

Some dried food products had been used in the food industries long before the war. Dried eggs had been imported from China for decades, but not until 1927 were eggs dried commercially in this country. Bakers were the main customers for dried eggs and still are. During the war the quality of dried eggs was considerably improved, and so the industry prospered. The baker finds it much easier to weigh a dry product than to break several dozen shell eggs, for eggs must be broken into a cup, one at a time because one bad egg would ruin a batch of several gallons. If a bad egg is broken in a dehydrating or freezing plant, it is discarded, and the cup is sterilized before it is used again.

Several companies continued to improve their dehydrating processes after the war and undertook to introduce the product into the grocery trade. Dried mashed potatoes and dried nonfat milk solids have been the most successful, but the shelves of any supermarket testify to the partial success of several other products.

Dehydrated foods are now commonly called dried foods by the general public and by the technologists too unless they need to make a distinction in a technical conversation. Their chief advantage, both in industry and in the home, is their convenience. A large part of these dried products is used by bakers or other manufacturers of composite foods such as cake mixes, dried desserts, dried soups, salad dressings, and many others. Nonfat dried milk leads the list with 2 billion lb annually and there are 50 million lb of dried eggs. Dried fish and dried fruits still maintain their ancient place in the food industry.

Recently, a process was invented that freezes the food and then evaporates the water at a temperature below the thawing point so the food is never heated after it is blanched. It is a much more costly process than any of the others, but the product is more like the original in both flavor and texture.

CANNING

Cans of food have been around ever since we can remember, so it is hard to imagine getting along without them. However, the story begins in the year 1795 when the French government offered a prize of 12,000 francs for a new method of food preservation. Nicolas Appert, a confectioner, went to work on the problem and in 1796 announced his success; but for some reason, he did not publish the result until 1810. He packed the food in bottles, corked the bottles tightly, and heated them in boiling water. Some foods were cooked a bit before they were bottled.

Research of the type Appert did is very time consuming. He had to bottle the food, heat it, set it aside for a time, then open a bottle and examine the food. He could see molds and gas bubbles, but he had to depend mainly on odor and taste to measure his success. If the food was still good, he waited another month or so and opened another bottle. In this way he could decide whether the food kept long enough to justify the bother of preserving it. All the testing had to be done separately for each product. Not until around 1860 did Pasteur clarify the matter of spoilage caused by bacteria, yeast, and molds that came with the fresh foods or from the air. Molds were visible, but it took a microscope to reveal the yeasts and bacteria. The heat used in canning killed these plants.

While Appert was working on this food preservation problem, others were working at the same task in England and Holland. Peter Durand took out a patent in England in 1810 for "preserving animal, vegetable, and other foods." His patent also covered the use of vessels made of "glass, pottery, tin, or any other metal or fit material." Durand tried canisters made of sheet steel and plated with tin, which had an advantage over glass or pottery, for the metal was a much better conductor of heat, much lighter and less breakable. His tinplate canisters soon became tin cans, and now in England they eat tinned food while in this country we prefer it canned. The common tin can is about 99% steel and 1% tin, but the name tin is used because it is on the outside where we can see it. Steel is much cheaper than tin and also stiffer and harder, but it rusts quickly and the acids in foods attack it. Tin does not rust and is relatively impervious to attack by acids. However, the tin coating is not as continuous as it looks; a microscope reveals tiny holes in it. When a tin can rusts, the rust starts at these holes and spreads as the iron rust loosens the tin plate. To help prevent this the insides of cans intended for food are coated with a lacquer or a plastic.

The canning industry soon spread from England to the United States. In 1817, William Underwood came over from England, landed at New Orleans, and tried to raise money to start a canning plant. But the citizens of New Orleans were not interested in canning food, and so Underwood walked all the way to Boston where he was more successful. By 1820 his business was in full operation and he was soon exporting canned food to China and to South America.

Canneries began to spring up in a few places where an excess of food was available, but such places were scarce, for food was still grown for family use or to supply a nearby village. About 1853 a man in Maine began canning sweet corn and in 1857 Gail Borden opened the first commercial condensed milk plant in Litchfield County, Conn. But the spread of the canning industry was slow until the Civil War, which boosted canning just as World War II spurred the dehydration process. The early canners had many problems and no IFT or individual scientists to help them. It was not until 1895 that bacteriologists began to work on the spoilage problems of the food canner.

At first the cans were made by hand and a good tinsmith could turn out 100 a day; they are now made by automatic machines at the rate of 300 a minute. The modern canning process varies in procedures and equipment with the size of the cannery and the product to be canned (Fig. 3.4). In general, fruits and vegetables are graded for size, washed, and prepared by women working at tables just as they have always done in the kitchen. The cans are washed and filled by hand or by machine, according to the product, and are closed by automatic machines sometimes in an atmosphere of nitrogen and sometimes in a partial vacuum. The sealed cans go to a pressure cooker retort where the product is cooked with steam at a time and temperature suitable for the product.

Properly canned food will keep for several months but not indefinitely. There are three main causes of spoilage: the can may develop pinholes by the action of the food on the metal or cracks from outside damage; the can may have been poorly sealed; or the food may not have been heated enough to kill all the organisms that cause spoilage. Some bacteria form spores, which correspond to the seeds of flowering plants, and these spores are much harder to kill than the growing plants.

Some bacteria that are extremely resistant to heat grow even in the absence of air, producing a gas that causes the ends of the can to bulge. This proves something is wrong: the swelling might be from hydrogen gas produced by action of the food acids on the metal of the can. If so it doesn't damage the food much, but the consumer has no way of knowing the cause of the gas and should take such a can back to the store and get her money back. The grocer will refund the money; the salesman for the wholesaler will buy the can back and send it to the canner for credit. The whole business

TYPICAL COMMERCIAL CANNING OPERATIONS

Harvesting

Receiving
raw product

Soaking and
Washing

Sorting and
grading

Blanching

Peeling and Coring

Filling

Exhausting

Sealing

Processing

Cooling

Labeling

Warehousing
and Packing

Courtesy of American Can Co.

FIG. 3.4.   CANNING LINE

may be a nuisance to everybody concerned, but it is a regular part
of the food industry, and the canner would rather pay for it than
have the consumer throw it away, because it may supply him with
his first information that all is not well with his product; furthermore,
if the consumer throws it away she may not buy that brand again.
Some spoilage of food is inevitable. All processed foods have a lifetime—less than a year for many products. A code number is stamped
on cans and cartons, telling the processor when and where the package was filled. When the package is returned, the packer can tell
whether it has been in storage too long, or was not properly processed or packaged in the first place.

The worst type of spoilage of canned foods is caused by a bacterium called *Clostridium botulinum*. This organism is present in

most soils and is therefore likely to be present on vegetables. It forms hard-to-kill spores that germinate in the absence of air. It grows best in foods that are not acid, such as snap beans, carrots and beets, and is rarely found in canned tomatoes or canned fruits. Most fruits are acid and are not grown near the soil, however, ripe olives have been found to contain the organism, and in rare cases it occurs in canned meats. As these bacteria grow they produce poisonous substances that have killed many people. The food may develop an odor somewhat like rancid butter, or it may show no signs of spoilage at all. Although the spores are very hard to kill, the toxins are destroyed by cooking for a few minutes.

Botulism is rare in commercially canned foods, but not so rare in home-canned products. The housewife cannot control all the factors in her canning process. The use of a pressure cooker in canning at home is a help because the steam is much hotter than water boiling in an open pan, but the only reliable procedure with home-canned vegetables is cooking them for a few minutes after the jar is opened.

Canned food is about as safe as anything in this perilous world and it does preserve crops, provide fruits and vegetables out of season, and supply first aid to a bride or a busy cook. We eat about 20 billion lb of it annually.

REFRIGERATION AND FREEZING

Refrigeration, which is simply cooling, is used to keep food for a short time either in the kitchen, in the grocery, on a truck or, in a cold-storage warehouse. Freezing is used to keep food fresh for weeks or for months. Freezing meats to preserve them is an ancient process in very cold climates. Many a farmer in our northern states has dressed rabbits, poultry, pork, or beef and hung the meat in an unheated building to freeze. He knew it would keep from December to March unless there was a long winter thaw.

Early in the history of the American colonies every village in the north had an ice house. When the water of a pond or the still water above a mill dam froze to a thickness of 4 in. or more it was sawed into cakes 2 by 3 ft or smaller according to its thickness. These cakes were built into a solid block in an ice house, which was a wooden building with double walls for insulation. Space was left around the ice to be filled with sawdust, and the top of the ice block was covered with a foot or more of the same material. The ice kept through a long, hot summer and sometimes there would still be ice when it was time to fill the house again. How long the supply lasted depended on the demand for ice cream. It was seldom used much for anything else, since ice is not cold enough to freeze any kind of food. Water freezes at 32°F and all foods freeze at a lower temperature—fruits, for example, freeze from about 20 to 28°F.

By 1811 transportation was good enough to permit the shipment of natural ice to the cities. The industry prospered in New England; at one time it was the principal industry in Maine. The ice was cut from the rivers or from ice ponds constructed for the purpose, and and stored in huge ice houses built like the small ones I have just described. These big ice houses were a common sight throughout New England and along the Hudson River. In the summer the ice was shipped to the cities, some of it as far south as the West Indies. The industry lasted over a century, but by the 1920s the big ice houses had almost entirely disappeared.

Doctor Gorrie, a physician in Appalachicola, Fla., invented an ice-making machine in 1851, but the first successful commercial one was not in operation until 1875. From then until after World War I artificial ice gradually displaced the natural product. The ice machine could supply a better grade of ice at less cost than the harvester of natural ice could.

As natural ice and then artificial ice became more plentiful, several uses were found for it. Cold drinks became popular, and restaurants, soda fountains, and bars used great quantities of it. Then the ice box was invented. It was similar to a modern refrigerator with a compartment for storing food and a separate compartment above it for a block of ice. As the ice melted, the water ran down a small pipe to a pan that was set on the floor under the box. The pan always managed to run over at inconvenient times, and by the time the house builders got around to installing a special drain for the icebox, the electric refrigerator had replaced it. But for decades the iceman, with his horse and covered wagon and following of children begging for pieces of ice, was a familiar sight in any city.

In the early 1920s the electric refrigerator was perfected and began to displace the icebox in the home, the butcher shop, and the grocery. A special compartment for making ice in the home refrigerator soon followed, and the iceman was well on his way out. Artificial ice was a thriving industry for less than half a century; only a few small ice plants are in operation today.

As late as the 1920s frozen food, aside from ice cream, consisted of a little frozen meat shipped to dealers in the warmer climates, frozen eggs for the bakers, and fruits frozen to hold until the owner could get around to making them into jams or jellies.

About 1930, Clarence Birdseye invented a process for freezing packaged foods quickly. When a food is frozen, the water in it freezes, and it produces ice crystals with sharp edges. The more

Courtesy of General Foods Corp.
FIG. 3.5.   BIRDSEYE FREEZER

quickly the food freezes the smaller the crystals and the less damage
they do to the tissues of the food. Consequently, when quickly
frozen food is thawed it retains its original form and texture better.
The packaging used by Birdseye has not changed much in the past
40 years and needs no description here, for more people see those
packages than see this book (Fig. 3.5). Commercialization of the
quick freezing process began with fish filets and soon spread to
other products. The business grew slowly because it had to wait
until dealers installed low-temperature storage cabinets, the truckers
got refrigerated trucks, and home refrigerators came equipped with
freezing compartments. In the 1930s, a prosperous grocer in our
town of 40,000 installed a low-temperature cabinet, stocked frozen
foods, and waited. But housewives had not heard of these frozen
foods and did not buy them. The grocer got discouraged and dis-
posed of his cabinet; it was five years before frozen foods were again
available in the city.

In addition to marketing problems and the education of the public,
the industry had many problems to solve. Engineers improved the

freezing machinery, and chemists and bacteriologists tried to find out what the freezing actually did to the food, whether it was free from disease germs, and what temperature changes it would safely tolerate during transportation and storage.

Frozen foods are the most important contribution to convenience since the commercialization of baking and canning, because they transfer a lot of work from the kitchen to the processing plant. The fish are cleaned, the peas are shelled, the fruit peeled, and the spinach washed free from sand. Moreover, since the food is frozen immediately after harvest, it has a more natural flavor and better vitamin content than canned or dried food. In many cases it is better than fresh food on the produce counter, which has been hauled long distances and has been in storage or on display several days before reaching the kitchen. With the exception of bananas and pears, fruits (including tomatoes) do not ripen fully after they have been harvested, but they must be picked while immature so that they will withstand shipment. Since food can be frozen near its source, it need not be harvested until maturity. Unfortunately, most freezing plants are stationary. Fresh foods must be hauled great distances to extend plant operation over a longer season, for the harvest season of fruits and vegetables in any one locality is short.

Unlike canned foods, frozen foods are not sterile. Some fruits and vegetables are blanched to destroy enzymes that cause the fruit to turn dark or overripen, but the bacteria, yeasts, and molds are not all killed. The freezing slows down the rate of spoilage; however, once the food is thawed these organisms speed up their rate of growth and spoil the food rapidly. Frozen food must be kept frozen, used as soon as it is thawed, and never refrozen.

It is impossible to say how long frozen food will keep. Under the best conditions some kinds will keep for two years or longer, others only a few months. The storage temperature must be kept at $0\,^\circ$F or lower to get a long storage life, but the necessary handling between the freezer and the domestic refrigerator makes it impossible to hold it at such a low temperature all the time. At best it is carted out of its original storage room to a truck that must be open for loading, and even if the truck is refrigerated it takes time for it to become cold again. Then comes a wholesaler's warehouse, followed by another truck to the retail store, and perhaps a leisurely transfer of the food to the cold cabinet; and remember the trip home from the store on a hot summer day with perhaps a stop for coffee with a friend.

Despite the difficulties of the industry, over 7 billion lb of food are frozen annually in this country.

CHAPTER 4

Manufactured Foods

Many foods in a grocery may be called manufactured products because they contain only part of a natural food or parts of several natural foods. Confectionery, soft drinks, cookies, jams, jellies, soups, and many other items belong in this group. Most of them are pleasant luxuries and only a few have an essential, established place in a regular diet. Some manufactured products, however, are part of the basic food supply—for example, the dairy products.

MILK

Milk is an ancient natural food and probably the most important single food in the diet, especially to those of us under 25. Unfortunately, it does not keep well—less than a day in hot weather. Nearly all fresh milk sold in the United States today is pasteurized, that is heated enough to kill any disease-producing bacteria, but not those bacteria that cause it to sour. The custom of pasteurization is less than 40 years old, and from the most ancient times until well into the 20th century, men drank sour milk or preserved what they could by making butter or cheese.

BUTTER

The process of butter making is thought to have originated in India about 2000 B.C., and it has been common in Europe for centuries. From Europe the process came to America with the first immigrants.

The dairy maid or the farmer's wife of the American colonies made butter as a matter of course. Immediately after she milked the cows, she strained the milk through a finely woven cloth into earthenware crocks and left it there for several hours, usually overnight. During this standing period the cream rose to the top and formed a distinct layer on the surface. All the fat was in this layer in the form of tiny drops that could be seen individually only with a microscope. She removed the cream with a skimmer, which was a kind of metal saucer with a handle on it like a dipper. She put the cream into a jar that held 2 or 3 gal. In winter it might have taken several days to fill the jar because the cows give less milk then; in summer there was usually more milk, and the jar might have filled up in three or four days. In either case the cream was left in the jar until there was enough of it or until it was sour enough to churn. The acidity was decided by taste or by appearance, for the acid coagulated the casein in the milk, and an experienced butter maker could tell when it was time to churn just by looking at the cream.

Churns were of several types. One popular kind was a wooden keg with a lid that clamped on tightly, and the keg was mounted so it could be turned end over end by means of a crank. This rather gentle agitation caused the droplets of fat to stick together and rise to the surface as clumps of butter.

The housewife transferred the clumps of butter to a large, shallow, wooden bowl and kneeded the plastic mass with a wooden paddle to work out the excess buttermilk. She then added salt, mixed it thoroughly with the butter and formed a "roll" shaped somewhat like a loaf of bread. The characteristic flavor of the butter developed during the souring of the cream; consequently, the flavor of country butter varied with the sourness of the cream, how well the buttermilk was removed, how much salt was added, and with any flavors the butter may have absorbed from onions or other odorous substances to which it had been exposed—fats absorb odors very quickly. The color varied from deep yellow in summer to nearly white in winter. Variation in the natural color of butter was caused by carotene or other yellow pigment, present in the grass the cow ate in summer and absent from the grain and hay she ate in the winter.

In 1881 Alanson Slaughter built a creamery in Orange County, New York. He bought the milk produced by 375 cows and used it to make butter. Before this venture all the butter had been made on individual farms from the milk of a few cows.

The creamery idea spread slowly, but by 1900 a creamery in Vermont was using the milk from 30,000 cows and making over 10 tons of butter a day. Also by 1900 the creameries were making 40% of all the butter in the country, and by 1935 about 75%. Today, country butter has almost disappeared from the market.

The creamery has a big advantage over the housewife as a butter maker. It receives several thousand gallons of milk a day, which it strains and passes through a machine that separates the cream at once. The cream separator was not invented until 1878, which accounts in part for the slow growth of the butter industry.

As soon as it is separated, the cream is pasteurized to kill any bacteria that might cause off-flavors, and then special bacteria are added to sour the cream. The dairy maid had to depend on the bacteria in the milk, but with so much milk, the creamery can afford to grow special bacteria. It also has tanks to hold the cream at the temperature at which it sours in the shortest time and then tests the sourness of the cream by a chemical procedure much more accurate than taste; therefore the cream always has the same acidity.

The creamery has bigger churns than the farmer and manages to draw off the buttermilk and work the butter in the churn itself. Near the end of this working a weighed amount of salt and dye are added so all the butter produced by that creamery has the same color and saltiness.

Finally, the butter is packed into wooden tubs, or into an angular mold to be cut into pound or quarter-pound blocks and wrapped for sale. It then goes to a refrigerated room to wait for a customer.

The butter industry in England and Europe has followed much the same history as just described, but the chief shortcoming of butter everywhere is its cost. Most milk is less than 4% fat and butter contains 80%, the legal minimum in this country. Consequently, it takes about 3 gal. of milk to make 1 lb of butter.

Butter keeps much longer than milk, but unfortunately it constitutes only about 5% of the whole milk, and there is so little demand for buttermilk that most of it goes to feed hogs or other animals.

After the invention of the cream separator the nonfat part of the milk was not sour, but there was no market for this skim milk until recent years when the dairy companies began to dry it; it has now become a regular grocery item.

CHEESE

Making cheese from milk is of prehistoric origin, and it has been an excellent method of preserving the nutrients of the milk. What was at first a family project soon became commercialized. The farmers of Europe, for example, live in villages and farm and pasture the land for miles around. Consequently, the excess milk produced by all the farmers of the village soon gave rise to a community factory for the manufacture of cheese. The cheese has always been known by the name of the village or immediate region where it is made, and so we have Cheddar, Edam, Camembert, Roquefort, Gorgonzola, Limburger, and a host of others with names of geographical origin. Such names as brick, pineapple, and blue are recent inventions.

The nature of the original cheese industry and its nomenclature makes it impossible to tell how many kinds of cheese there are. A bulletin published by the USDA several years ago listed over 800 varieties, a specialty food store in our city now lists 128 kinds, and the standards of the Food and Drug Administration define 30 different kinds.

As methods of transportation and communication improved, some cheese factories grew and branches were established in other localities so the name of the cheese lost its local significance and became the name of a type of cheese. Camembert cheese, for example, is not all made in the village of Camembert; it is made in this country and elsewhere, and even that made in France is not all made in Camembert; in fact, most of it is not. The production of Cheddar, Swiss, Limburger, and other kinds of cheese has spread throughout the world and the result is such incongruous names as Wisconsin Swiss and New York State Cheddar.

Different kinds of cheese differ in color, texture, appearance, flavor, and composition; but the general process for making them always begins the same way. The milk is strained to remove foreign matter. Some manufacturers pasteurize the milk and some countries require them to. In the United States the milk must be pasteurized if the cheese is to be sold within 60 days after its manufacture.

The old village cheese maker allowed the milk to stand in a tub or tank until it soured naturally, but the modern manufacturer, with several tons of milk on hand, doesn't risk that, for the milk may contain bacteria that will produce a disagreeable flavor in the cheese. So he generally pasteurizes the milk and adds a kind of bacteria he knows will convert the lactose (milk sugar) into lactic acid. Herein lies part of the art of the cheese maker. Milk contains about 5% lactose and if all that were converted to lactic acid the milk would be much too sour. The old cheese maker decided when the milk was sour enough by tasting it, but the modern manufacturer, after he has tried out several different acidities, selects one and determines when that has been reached by chemical analysis. The acidity generally used is 0.2% lactic acid. The vats in which the milk is soured are now made of metal—stainless steel mostly. They are rectangular, about 2 ft deep, 5 ft wide, and long enough to hold the volume of milk usually received (that is, 10 to 40 ft). They have double walls so they can be heated or cooled by steam or water. A large factory has several such vats.

The milk is heated to 85°F and rennet is thoroughly mixed with it as soon as the proper acidity is reached. Rennet is an enzyme (see Chap. 12) obtained from the stomachs of calves and is used to coagulate the casein of the milk. Very little rennet is required; 1 lb will coagulate 2 million lb of milk. Within $\frac{1}{2}$ hr after the rennet is added the milk has coagulated to a solid mass of the consistency of

From Potter (1973)

FIG. 4.1. CUTTING CURD OF CHEDDAR CHEESE

a gelatin or a cornstarch pudding. The enzyme is familiar to house-wives as the proprietary Junket powder used to make puddings.

After the milk has coagulated, the curd is cut into cubes about ½ in. on an edge with curd knives that bear a crude resemblance to tennis rackets. There are 2 of them; each consists of a rectangular steel frame about 8 by 20 in., strung with steel wires ½ in. apart. The wires on one knife are vertical and the other horizontal. These knives are drawn through the curd by hand; the one with the vertical wires in both directions to cut the curd into ½-in. columns and the other need be used only once to cut the columns into cubes (Fig. 4.1). The size of a knife that a man can handle and the length of his arm determine the width of the vat and the depth of the milk in it.

After the curd is cut, it is stirred with a wooden rake, and the cubes contract and squeeze out a whey, which is drained off through a screened opening at the bottom of the vat. If the curds are now mixed with salt and pressed into a block or packed into a container, the product is cream cheese if whole milk was used, or cottage cheese if it was made from skim milk. Incidentally, skim milk and nonfat milk are the same thing and neither name is appropriate; the dairy maid's skimmer is a thing of the past and the separator is not 100% efficient.

The process just described is used for practically all kinds of cheese up to this point, but if the product is to be a ripened cheese there is

Courtesy of Danish Dairy Assoc., Aarhus, Denmark

FIG. 4.2. BLUE CHEESE

much more to be done. Space does not permit description of the manufacture of many kinds of cheese, but the processes used for blue and Cheddar are typical of most of them.

Blue cheese (Fig. 4.2) is ripened by the growth of the mold *Penicillium roqueforti*. The mold is grown on bread, which is then dried and ground to a powder. The drained curd is packed by hand into cylindrical metal forms about $7\frac{1}{2}$ in. in diameter and 6 in. high. The sides of the cylinder contain small holes, and both ends are open. The form is set on a board laid across a vat, and, as the curd is added to the form by hand, the mold is sifted in between layers of the curd. Some processors mix the mold with the curd along with the salt. The curd is heaped up above the top of the form and some whey is pressed out as the form is filled. The forms are inverted at intervals and the thickness of the cheese shrinks to about 5 in. because of the drainage of whey.

Molds will not grow in the absence of air, which is the reason the cakes of blue cheese are so small—about 5 to 6 lb. After the whey has ceased to drain, the cake is removed from the form and perforated from top to bottom by a machine with 50 or more long steel needles $\frac{1}{8}$ in. in diameter to admit air into the interior of the cheese. The cake is then placed on edge with space between the racks so that each cheese gets plenty of air.

The cheese remains on these racks for from 6 weeks to 3 months according to the requirements of the different markets, and is then "put to sleep" as the French say it. The outside of the cheese is scraped to remove excess salt and mold and wrapped in metal foil to exclude the air and thus stop, or at least retard, the mold growth. It is then stored below 32°F which also helps to prevent any further ripening.

In the manufacture of Cheddar cheese, which is the common American variety, the procedure differs considerably from that of the blue cheese. The first departure is the addition of an orange dye to the milk with the rennet. But when coagulation is complete the curd is cut and the whey drained off in the usual way. The temperature is then raised to about 100°F and the cubes of curd fuse into a solid mass. The mass is cut into coarse strips to facilitate handling and to encourage further draining. After draining they are again piled up and fused. This process is called cheddaring. As soon as the cheddaring is completed the cheese is put through a mill that cuts it into small pieces. Salt is added and the cheese is transferred to cheese hoops, which are cylindrical with open ends and lined with cheese cloth to be folded over the curd when the hoop becomes full.

The filled hoops are placed on edge in a horizontal press with circular blocks of wood between them. Pressure is applied gradually from one end of a row of several hoops and is gradually increased over 24 hours or longer, and each cheese is reduced in thickness by the loss of whey. American cheese is now made into several forms by different types of press.

When the cheese is removed from the press it is often coated with paraffin to prevent drying out and the growth of molds on the surface. In the normal course of events the cheese goes to a room for ripening where it is held at 40° to 50°F for 2 months or more and then to storage at near the freezing temperature. During World War II there was such a great demand for cheese because of the meat rationing that storage was omitted and the ripening was expected to occur while the cheese was on its way to the consumer. As a result, the government ruled that a cheese shipped in less than 60 days from the time it was made must be made from pasteurized milk. Lactic acid will kill pathogenic bacteria, but it takes time.

The fresh cheese is rubbery in consistency and very bland in flavor. During the ripening the protein is broken down somewhat and the texture becomes more brittle, while the bacteria from the original milk produce the flavor characteristic of Cheddar cheese. The mild, medium, and sharp cheeses on the grocer's shelf represent different periods of curing.

ECONOMY OF BUTTER AND CHEESE

Butter and cheese making have been the chief methods of preserving the nutrients of milk for centuries, and, meanwhile, these products have earned places in the family menu. Unfortunately, neither product contains all the food value in the fresh milk. Butter preserves the fat and little else since it is 80% fat. Most of the sugar, protein, and minerals are left in the buttermilk, which does not keep long and never has become a popular food except with the hogs.

Cheese preserves more of the milk than butter does, but it is estimated that about 70% of the nutrients of the milk remain in the whey, for it contains 20% of the protein and nearly all of the minerals and water soluble vitamins. Two gallons of milk (17 lb) make 1 lb of cheese, and if the whey is evaporated, 1 lb of milk solids is left.

It is estimated that 70% of the country's 20 billion lb of whey is wasted; most of it goes into the sewers. It is expensive to recover whey solids because of the enormous amount of water to be evaporated. Some whey is used as animal feed and some is dried and added to cheese spreads, salad dressings, and other composite foods. The present furor over stream pollution will probably increase the recovery of more of this valuable food.

CONCENTRATED MILKS

In 1813, Edward Howard invented the "vacuum" pan, and about 40 years later it occurred to Gail Borden that this would be a useful device for the preservation of milk. He received a patent for a condensed milk process in 1856 and opened a plant to produce the product in Litchfield County, Conn. That the industry has grown is indicated by the fact that there are now 500 plants in the United States that condense milk, and they produce about half the world supply of it.

There are several concentrated milks, but the most common ones in the retail trade are evaporated milk and sweetened condensed milk.

Evaporated Milk

This product is made from whole milk that is strained, analyzed for fat content, and examined for any off-flavor it might have taken up. There are both State and Federal standards for the concentrated milks and so the quality and composition of the fresh milk is very important. Moreover, since condensed milks are sold under brand names, uniformity of quality must be under control.

After the raw milk has been examined and approved, it is heated briefly to 212°F and then passed into a vacuum pan from which about $\frac{5}{6}$ of the air has been removed. A vacuum pan never contains a vacuum, but only a low pressure of air, water vapor, or any other gas that it may happen to contain. In the evaporation of milk, the air is soon removed and the pressure is that of the water vapor. The advantage of the vacuum pan is that a low temperature can be used and the water will evaporate as fast as it would at a much higher temperature in an open pan. The milk is evaporated at about 130°F.

The Federal standard and that of most States requires evaporated milk to contain 7.9% milk fat and 25.9% total milk solids. The standard determines when the evaporation has gone far enough because the milk still contains nearly 75% water. A pound of evaporated milk represents 2.2 lb of fresh milk.

After the evaporation has produced the proper concentration, the milk is canned and processed at 240°F for about 15 min. Milk is very easily damaged and the skill with which the several stages in the process are carried out determines the quality of the evaporated milk.

Condensed Milk

The other common concentrated milk is sweetened condensed milk, which was the product that Borden began to manufacture in 1857. The milk receives the usual preliminary tests and treatment and then the operator adds 18 lb of sugar, glucose, or a mixture of the two for each 100 lb of milk. The preheating follows, but only to 140°–150°F. The milk is then evaporated in vacuum pans and canned. The cans are not heat processed and so the milk is not sterile; the sugar acts as the preservative.

The Federal standard for sweetened condensed milk requires at least 8.5% milk fat, 28% total milk solids, and enough sugar to prevent spoilage. A typical analysis is: water 27.1%, protein 8.1%, fat 8.7%, and sugars 54.3%. The least amount of sugar that will prevent the spoilage of most foods is around 50%.

OTHER CONCENTRATED PRODUCTS

In Chap. 3, I have mentioned dehydrated milk and dehydrated skim milk, products now produced in large quantity. There are several other concentrated milk products, such as malted milk, plain condensed skim milk, sweetened condensed skim milk, and others. Most of these products go to bakers, confectioners, or other food manufacturers along with large quantities of the more familiar evaporated and condensed milks.

ICE CREAM

The commercial manufacture of ice cream was begun by a dairyman in 1851. Before 1900 most of the ice cream was made in the home using the following principle. If salt is added to water, the

FIG. 4.3. ICE CREAM FREEZER

freezing point of the water drops; and if we dissolve all the salt possible, the temperature of freezing falls to 0°F. Likewise, if salt is added to ice, the melting point becomes lower. The melting point of ice and the freezing point of water are the same for the same amount of salt.

This was the method of getting a low temperature before the invention of mechanical refrigeration and was employed by Nancy Johnson, who invented the freezer for making ice cream (Fig. 4.3). It consisted of a metal can with a stirrer inside designed to stir the ice cream mix and scrape the sides of the can. The can with its stirrer was mounted inside a wooden tub and equipped with gears and a crank to rotate the can while the stirrer remained stationary. Ice and salt were packed between the can and the tub. The freezer was turned to beat air into the mixture and to prevent the formation of large ice crystals or solid ice on the wall of the can. Cream is a poor conductor of heat and the stirring brings all parts of it into contact with the wall of the can and thus speeds the freezing.

The manufacture of ice cream increased considerably in 1870 when a steam engine was first used to turn the large freezers used in the factories. Electricity replaced steam in 1885, and in 1900 the ice and salt freezer gave way to one that was cooled by brine from a refrigerating machine. The production of ice cream reached 80

million gal. by 1909 and has since grown to 400 million gal. a year.
We consume an average of 17.7 lb per capita in a year.

MARGARINE

America, with lots of pasture land at its disposal, produced milk
and butter cheaply. Europe, on the other hand, produced these at a
high cost—a heavy burden on those with low income, which was
most of the population. This and a prize offered by the government
led the Frenchman, Mege-Mouries, to invent a substitute for butter.
By 1873 the process was patented in the United States. Production
in this country began in New York City about three years later. The
product was called oleomargarine in France, Germany, and the
United States and margarine in England. Both names are now official
in this country.

Mege-Mouries idea was very simple; he made a mixture of fats
with the consistency and melting point of butterfat and then gave
it a flavor of butter. The fat, of course, had to be cheaper than butter.

For more than 30 years the fat used was mainly beef fat, that is,
tallow. Tallow is a mixture of several glycerides (see Chap. 11) of
different melting points and the mixture is such that its melting
point is much higher than that of butterfat. The Frenchman warmed
the tallow and pressed it, so the glycerides that had melted ran out
and the solids remained in the press. The liquid portion was called
oleo oil and the solid portion, *stearine*. Now that he had a solid and
a liquid fat, he could mix them in any proportion he chose. He experimented until he got a mixture with the consistency and melting
point of butterfat. Sometimes he added lard when it was cheap
enough and free from odor; beef fat is odorless and flavorless.

Now that the fat problem was solved, how about the butter flavor?
The answer was obvious. He got some milk and soured it, just as the
butter maker soured his cream. The fat mixture was churned with
the sour milk until the fat had absorbed the flavor; then the excess
milk was worked out, just as the butter maker worked his butter.
Salt and a dye were added, and the resulting product was a fair
imitation of butter—but much cheaper.

To say the manufacture and sale of margarine met with strenuous
opposition from the dairymen and others is an understatement.
Consequently, many laws and health department regulations were
designed to discourage the sale of oleomargarine. Two of our dairy
states passed laws requiring oleomargarine to be colored pink or
green, but the manufacturers contested those stupidities in the
courts, and the Supreme Court pronounced the laws unconstitutional. City authorities often required a restaurant that served

margarine to post a sign in a prominent place to announce that fact. In 1902 uncolored margarine was taxed at ¼¢ per lb, and colored margarine at 10¢. The manufacturers met this obstacle by including a gelatin capsule of dye with each pound of margarine so the housewife could color it before serving it to the family or guests. Space does not permit a full listing of the obstacles put in the path of the margarine business, for they were a multitude.

Another event had a profound effect on the future of margarine. In 1902 Professor Paul Sabatier, of the French University of Tolouse, discovered a way to convert an oil, such as cottonseed, peanut, and corn oil, into a fat of any consistency—from that of the oil to that of hard candle wax.

The process depended on the fact that the glycerides (see Chap. 11) of the unsaturated acids are liquids, but those of the saturated acids are solids. Oleic acid $(C_{17}H_{33}COOH)$ is a liquid and so are its glycerides; stearic acid $(C_{17}H_{35}COOH)$ and its glycerides are solids. From these formulas it is obvious that if two hydrogen atoms could be added to each oleic molecule it would become a stearic molecule and the fat would be solid. Sabatier's discovery was how to add these hydrogen atoms. He used finely divided nickel as a catalyst and supported it on pumice or another solid so he could remove it from the oil after the reaction was over. He suspended this catalyst in a closed tank of oil and bubbled hydrogen through the oil. The hydrogen combined with the unsaturated molecules of the liquid olein to produce solid stearin. The consistency of the final product depended on how much olein had been changed to stearin. The process was soon developed commercially in both Europe and the United States. It was called by the obvious name, *hydrogenation.*

The importance of the hydrogenation process lies in the fact that the three main uses of food fats are: shortening for various bakery products, to spread on bread, and to make soap. All three require solid or semisolid fats, and the vegetable oils are very much cheaper than the natural solid fats such as butter, lard, and tallow.

Cottonseed oil was the first vegetable oil produced in the United States. The first mill for the purpose was built in the 1860s, but by 1890 190 such mills were in operation. Production increased from 20 million lb in 1875 to 1 billion lb in 1905.

Just as butter was the main spread for bread, lard was the main shortening used in baking. When stearine and cottonseed oil were added to lard or were used alone the mixture was called "shortening compound." It was usually 20% stearine and 80% cottonseed oil. By 1887 the shortening industry used nearly all the cottonseed oil.

TABLE 4.1

FATS USED IN MAKING MARGARINE

Fat	Millions Lb			
	1917	1932	1942	1969
Oleo oil	96.7	12.5	22.5	12
Lard	42.4	9.4	8.1	86
Stearine	2.5	3.7	2.9	—
Other animal fats, mostly butter	3.5	0.5	4.1	18
Coconut oil	19.8	123.2	3.5	—
Cottonseed oil	63.7	15.1	166.4	75
Peanut oil	10.5	2.5	0.9	3
Soybean oil	—	—	133.3	1334
Corn oil	—	—	—	172
Safflower oil	—	—	—	43

In 1910 the consumption of lard was 12 lb per capita and that of the compound 9 lb.

Before 1900 a little cottonseed oil was used in the manufacture of margarine, but early in the new century the fats used in that industry began to change rapidly. With the change in fats, coconut oil came into use because its acids are much the same as those in butter and the two fats melt at about the same temperature.

Coconuts are grown in tropical countries where the nuts are broken open and the layer of "meat" removed and dried in the sun. This dried coconut is called "copra" and contains 60% fat. It is usually shipped to the country where the oil is to be used, and there the oil is pressed out and refined.

In 1934 the United States imposed a processing tax of 3¢ a pound on coconut oil from the Phillipines and 5¢ on oil made from copra from any other country. This raised the cost of the oil so much that the margarine makers began to look for other fats.

The depression of the 1930s and the government's efforts to aid the farmers increased the production of peanut oil and brought soybean oil into the market. A little soybean oil was made in the early 1920s, but the real production began with the farm aid of the 1930s when 35 million lb were produced in a single year. Production increased rapidly to 3500 million pounds in 1955. It has now become the principal oil hydrogenated for use in margarine and shortening. Table 4.1 indicates the changes in margarine in the past half century.

The prohibitive 10% tax on colored margarine was removed in 1950, and the use of margarine increased suddenly, although there had already been some increase during the war years. In 1940 the per capita consumption was about 2 lb, in 1950 it was 6 lb, and in 1970, 11 lb. The use of butter, meanwhile, dropped from over 16 lb in 1940 to 5.2 lb in 1970.

Margarine is the only food specifically regulated by the Federal Food, Drug and Cosmetic Act. Congress passed a special law that has been incorporated into the food law as Section 407. One astounding provision of the regulation is that colored margarine or colored oleomargarine sold in the state in which it is produced shall come under the same regulations as those in interstate commerce. No other food is so regulated. The regulation continues:

(b) No person shall sell or offer for sale, colored margarine or colored oleomargarine unless—

(1) Such oleomargarine or margarine is packaged.

(2) The net weight of the contents of any package sold in a retail establishment is 1 lb or less.

(3) There appears on the label of the package:

(A) the word "oleomargarine" or "margarine" in type lettering at least as large as any other type or lettering on such label, and

(B) a full and accurate statement of all the ingredients contained in such oleomargarine or margarine, and—

(4) each part of the contents of the package is contained in a wrapper which bears the word "oleomargarine" or "margarine" in type or lettering not smaller than 20 point type.

(c) No person shall possess in a form ready for serving colored oleomargarine or colored margarine at a public eating place unless a notice that oleomargarine or margarine is served is displayed prominently and conspicuously in such place and in such manner as to render it likely to be read and understood by the ordinary individual being served in such eating place or is printed or is otherwise set forth on the menu in type or lettering not smaller than that normally used to designate the serving of other food items. No person shall serve colored oleomargarine or colored margarine at a public eating place whether or not any charge is made therefore, unless—

(1) each separate serving bears or is accompanied by labeling identifying it as oleomargarine or margarine, or—

(2) each separate serving thereof is triangular in shape.

There are two more subsections, but they are of interest only to the manufacturer or law enforcing officer. The cow is still sacred.

OTHER FOOD PROCESSES

Many other food processes prepare the natural food for the kitchen or even for the table. Among them are refining of vegetable oils; making candy, jams, jellies, and pickles; and even manufacturing cat and dog food to deliver Fido and Tommy from the scarcity of table scraps.

CHAPTER 5

Imports

Although we produce huge quantities of food in the United States, we still find it necessary to import a great variety of foods—mostly products that will not grow in our climate.

SUGAR

Of the foreign products we import, probably the most important is sugar, which is extracted from sugar cane and the sugar beet. Sugar beets are natives of the temperate zone and consequently, are raised in Europe and in about 20 of our states. Sugar cane is tropical, although Florida and Louisiana do manage to grow some with the aid of a substantial subsidy, which the beet growers also enjoy. The cane growers in the 2 states produce over a million tons of sugar a year and the beet growers 3 million tons; the combined subsidy is over $70 million. Four million tons seem like a lot of sugar, but it is less than 5% of our total consumption. We import from offshore, over $1 billion worth of raw sugar annually—we must each have our 100 lb. The cane sugar imported into the continental United States comes mainly from Hawaii, Puerto Rico, the other islands of the Caribbean, and the countries of Central and South America.

The production of cane sugar involves three stages: the cane must be grown, the sugar extracted, and then refined. The sugar factory is generally near the cane fields because the margin of profit at the several stages is small and the cost of transporting the cane must be kept low. The amount of sugar in the cane varies from 10 to 15% according to climate and other factors.

The manufacture of sugar is simple in principle but very complicated in practice. I can explain this anomaly by describing two factories I visited. The first was in an underdeveloped country and consisted of a cane mill made up of two vertical steel rollers rotated by an ox walking in a circle while a man fed the cane between the rolls a stalk at a time. The juice from the crushed cane was caught in a barrel, transferred to two big iron kettles, and boiled down over a wood fire. After the sugar began to crystallize, the boiling was stopped and the kettles emptied into molds that held 1, 2, or 5 lb. When cooled, it set to a solid mass like a lump of sugar and consisted of sugar, molasses, and bits of cane that had not been strained out. In this form it went to a large public market in the nearby capital city.

The other mill I visited is a much more common type in the sugar industry. Cane was brought to the mill in trucks or railroad cars and dumped into a pit from which a conveyor carried it to a mill that consisted of several sets of horizontal steel rollers driven by electric motors. When the cane passed through the first set of rollers, it was shredded and some juice was squeezed out. However, the cane still contained some of its own sap, and so it was sprinkled with water and passed through the second set of rolls. This process was repeated with each succeeding set of rolls. The idea was to get all the sugar out of the cane and the principle was that of washing soap out of a sponge: wet it, squeeze it; wet it again, squeeze it; and repeat as often as necessary.

The cane juice, somewhat diluted with water, was carefully clarified by a complicated procedure. The clarified juice went to vacuum pans where it was evaporated until crystals formed, then to another set of pans to evaporate some more. When the operator decided that the evaporation had gone far enough, he discharged the evaporator into a large horizontal trough somewhat like a bath tub with a horizontal stirrer rotating in it. The sugar crystallized as the mixture cooled. When the crystallization was complete the mixture went to a centrifuge that threw the molasses off and retained the sugar crystals.

Some molasses is refined for the grocery trade; but we do not care much for molasses, and so most of the crude product goes into cattle feed or to making industrial alcohol or rum.

The raw sugar consists of fine brown crystals. It is put into 300-lb jute bags and shipped to the continental United States for refining. The refineries are in Boston, New York, Philadelphia, Baltimore, or other cities on the east or west coast. Even most of the raw sugar from Florida is shipped to Savannah for refining.

At the refinery the sugar goes through something of a repetition of the manufacturing process. The grinding, of course, is omitted, but one additional step is added. The raw sugar is dissolved in water, and the solution filtered through a charcoal made from bones (bone-black or animal charcoal), which absorbs the coloring matter and some of the other impurities. The colorless solution is then evaporated until the sugar crystallizes. Here the size of the crystals is more important than it is at the factory, for this is the sugar that appears on the dinner table. The crystals are screened into granulated sugar of different coarseness. Some of the crystals are ground into powdered sugar, and some of the solution that has not been completely decolorized is used to make brown sugar.

BANANAS

It is about as easy to imagine this country without automobiles as it is to imagine the food stores without bananas. Although the banana does not make up a great part of the national diet, it is one of our cheapest luxuries.

Apparently the banana is a native of India—the army of Alexander the Great found it in the valley of the Indus in 327 B.C. People migrating, probably the Arabs, carried the fruit to the Near East and Egypt by the year 600 and then continued to advance its propagation westward as they moved across the north of Africa and into Spain. The Spanish took it to the Canary Islands and from there to Santo Domingo by the year 1516. The Spanish and Portuguese explorations and settlements of the 16th century, soon spread the banana throughout the islands and along the shores of the Caribbean, a region that now supplies the United States and part of Europe with the fruit.

Eighteen centuries from India to the new world seems like a long time, but part of the delay was caused by the way in which the banana is propagated. Seeds are easy to carry and plant, but the banana has no seeds and must be propagated by planting pieces of the root, like sweet potatoes are planted. After the banana did reach the Western Hemisphere, another three centuries passed before it became a commercial food crop.

Bananas began to appear in this country about the time of the Civil War. I once knew an elderly lady in western Pennsylvania who told me she was engaged to marry a soldier who was discharged from the Union Army in Baltimore. He bought some bananas for her and carried them all the 400 miles to Grove City. After all his bother, she didn't like them, but he married her anyway. The first full shipload of bananas arrived in Boston in 1872 when a Cape Cod sea captain landed a cargo from Jamaica.

One may see fields of bananas on any island with a warm climate from Bermuda south into the Caribbean or elsewhere in tropical or subtropical areas. There are no fields of bananas in the continental United States, although botanical gardens and several back yards in Florida have some banana plants on display. From August to November these plants may have fruit on them; but they do not tolerate frost and from December to April the Florida plants are apt to look brown and dejected.

A banana tree is not a tree by most standards but more like a sugar cane or a cornstalk. A newly planted field will produce fruit in about a year. By the time the first fruit is mature the tree may be 15 ft tall and 6 in. in diameter; the stem or bunch of bananas hangs higher than a man's head. When the fruit reaches the supermarket it is in hands of a dozen or more individual bananas (fingers), or in parts of hands so the customer can buy a smaller number than a full hand. On the tree the stem contains 6 to 9 of these hands, so it is heavy and two men are required to harvest it. A surprising feature of a stem of bananas is that the stem hangs down but the bananas point up.

The fruit bruises easily and so a cutter notches a tree below the stem with a knife on a long pole and bends the top of the tree over to deposit the stem on the shoulder of another man, He then cuts the stem free from the tree with a machete. The shoulder man carries the stem to the nearest road or railroad and loads it on a truck or a railroad car. The cutter cuts the tree down and leaves it to decay and fertilize the soil.

One tree never produces more than one bunch of bananas, but sprouts come up from the spreading banana roots and so production is continuous. In a few years the original rows in which the bananas were planted disappear and a veritable jungle develops. The plants are not cultivated, but some of the sprouts and other tropical growth that springs up must be cut or the jungle will become too dense to produce any fruit. A visit to a banana plantation is an interesting experience laced with logs and 6-in. banana trees to clamber over, mud to step into, and the climate of a steam bath.

Cuba, Jamaica, Guatemala, Honduras, Costa Rica, Nicaragua, Panama, Columbia, Venezuela, and Ecuador have been our main suppliers of bananas and some of them are still our major sources of the fruit. Several shipping companies land bananas at Tampa, Mobile, New Orleans, and the bigger ports of the Atlantic and Pacific.

The banana is never allowed to ripen on the tree. It averages one day getting from the plantation to the port, a week on a ship, another week in a wholesaler's warehouse where it is partly ripened. Then the retailer gets it and hopes to dispose of it in a day or two. Consequently, the ripening is usually completed in the consumer's kitchen. A ripe banana is too soft to stand much handling. The best temperature for ripening is around 70°F and that temperature should be maintained until the fruit is used.

One species of banana is called a plantain. A common vegetable in the tropics, it appears in our larger markets only now and then. The fruit is bigger and more angular than the familiar banana. It is sliced and fried or otherwise cooked while it is still green and starchy rather than sweet.

CHOCOLATE

I suppose getting along without chocolate would be as distressing as the absence of bananas. It has been with us since the oldest citizen can remember, and before. In fact, the first chocolate mill within our borders was built in Massachusetts in 1765. In all the years since then, it has become the fourth best-liked flavor after salt, sugar, and vanilla. It is not only a favorite flavor; it also has a high food value.

The "chocolate" tree is a native of tropical South America (Fig. 5.1). The real name of the tree is *Theobroma*, which means "food for the Gods"; the Swedish botanist who named it also liked chocolate. There are several species of the tree, but the one that is cultivated is *Theobroma cacao* and its seeds are called cacao beans. Grown commercially in the Caribbean, South America, west Africa, and Indonesia, this tree will not withstand cold weather. It requires a rich soil, plenty of rain, and temperatures of 80° to 90°F. Because of the temperature requirement it is grown in the shade of taller trees. The cacao trees are usually 10 to 15 ft tall—much the size of our common peach tree. Sometimes bananas are planted in the cacao groves for shade. Although banana trees are not much taller than the cacao trees, they do produce bananas whereas the taller hardwoods furnish only shade.

The cacao tree is unique in several respects. The blossom is a tiny pink flower that appears in clusters at different places on the bark of the tree, almost anywhere from the trunk within 2 ft of the ground to within that distance of the tip of a branch. From these clusters of tiny flowers develop pods on a short stem. The pods mature at a length of 5 to 10 in. and are shaped somewhat like an underinflated football (Fig. 5.2); some varieties are pointed at the ends. A flowering area on the tree is only 2 in. or so in diameter and it must be protected, for these spots are the only source of fruit, and one may have flowers, little pods, pods the size of okra, and mature pods all in one cluster at the same time. The pods are harvested by a man who goes along with a burlap bag and a sharp knife and cuts the pod from the tree. Sometimes a man in a hurry may grasp a pod and yank it off. If he does, he may loosen the bark and destroy the flower cushion completely, and the tree will produce no more pods at that location. When the harvester gets the bag full he carries it to the nearest road or railroad where other workers break the pods open and claw out the 25 to 50 "beans."

The hull of the cacao pod is hard and brittle but not woody like the hull of a walnut. About the size of the first joint of a man's finger, the seeds have a brown seed coat like an apple seed. The

Courtesy of Cadbury Brothers Ltd.

FIG. 5.1. CACAO TREES

seeds are embedded in a gelatinous material somewhat like the seeds of a watermelon, but the cacao pod has many more seeds and less pulp than a watermelon, and the gelatinous material is much more adhesive. As the seeds are removed from the pods they are put into boxes to be dumped into a truck or railroad car. If one becomes curious and tastes a bean he finds it tastes much like any other raw bean, with no hint of the flavor of chocolate.

The beans go next to a plant for processing where they are put into a bin to ferment. The slimy pulp, which still adheres to the beans, is mostly carbohydrates of complex composition. The fermentation first breaks it down to sugars and then converts the sugars to alcohol. Finally, the alcohol is converted to acetic acid and so the bin smells strongly of vinegar. The fermentation process must be closely controlled because changes inside the bean are going on at the same time that the outside pulp is fermenting. The fermentation produces heat; therefore, the main problem is to control the temperature. The bin may be of wood or concrete, and control is determined by experience with the depth of beans in the bin and how

FIG. 5.2. CACAO POD

often and how well they are stirred. After 5 or 6 days the fermentation is complete and the beans are removed from the bin, washed, dried, and bagged for shipment.

Raw cacao beans contain about 5% water, 2 to 3.5% mineral matter, 4 to 5% sugars, 50% fat, and 15 to 20% starch. The public seldom hears the name *cacao*, for when the beans reach this country they soon go to a factory where they are made into chocolate and cocoa. The chocolate companies with brand names and wide distribution buy cacao beans from several sources and mix them. The flavor of the finished chocolate depends on the source and variety of the beans, the fermentation, the manner and extent of the roasting, and the addition of sugar or other flavor to the finished product.

The manufacture of chocolate products requires considerable attention to detail. Most of the characteristic chocolate flavor develops during the roasting and is affected by the time and temperature of this process. A "heavy" roast produces a strong, bitter flavor.

Roasting makes the hull of the bean very brittle, and so the beans are passed between rollers that crack them and loosen the hull, which is blown away by a blast of air. However, some hull still adheres to the endosperm and is very hard to remove. The legal definitions of chocolate take this difficulty into account by allowing a small amount of hull in the finished product. The cracked beans are called cocoa nibs, and must not contain more than 1.75% cacao shell.

The nibs are ground on a stone mill. The heat of the grinding melts the fat and this liquid chocolate that flows over the edge of the stone is called chocolate liquor; when it cools it sets to a solid but it still retains its name. The government doesn't want to miss anything, so the official definition of this product also calls it chocolate, baking chocolate, bitter chocolate, cooking chocolate, chocolate coating, and bitter chocolate coating. By whichever name it is called the product must contain at least 50% and not more than 58% cacao fat. All the details of the standard fill a large page of small type, and interest mostly manufacturers and the government inspectors. But the consumer might like to know that the manufacturer may add ground spice, ground vanilla beans (or their extract), artificial flavor, butter, milk fat, dried malted cereal extract, ground coffee, ground nut meats, and a few kinds of salts. If the manufacturer does add any of these things, he must say so on the label.

Besides the cocoa nibs and the chocolate liquor, the government has set standards for the six kinds of chocolate and four kinds of cocoa. The most familiar kinds of chocolate are sweet chocolate and milk chocolate. Sweet chocolate must contain not less than 15% chocolate liquor and may be sweetened with sugar, glucose, corn syrup, honey, maple sugar, or molasses. It may also contain any of the additives permitted in the chocolate liquor.

Milk chocolate contains much the same ingredients as sweet chocolate, but the proportions are different and the amounts are specified. It must contain at least 3.66% milk fat, 12% milk solids, and 10% chocolate liquor.

Cocoa

When chocolate liquor is warmed it becomes a plastic mass. In this state the manufacturer presses it, and the melted fat runs out. The fat solidifies when it cools; it is called cocoa butter. A pale yellow color, it is used in confectionery, cosmetic, and pharmaceutical products. The residue from which the fat is removed is called cocoa.

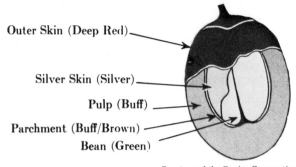

Outer Skin (Deep Red)

Silver Skin (Silver)

Pulp (Buff)

Parchment (Buff/Brown)

Bean (Green)

Courtesy of the Squier Corporation

FIG. 5.3. COFFEE BERRY

The roasted beans may contain over 50% fat, so the cocoa could contain anything less than that. Consequently, it is necessary to have standards. The government has set such standards and three kinds of cocoa appear in the grocery: (1) Breakfast cocoa (high fat cocoa) must contain not less than 22% cacao fat and may contain the usual spices, flavorings, and salts allowed the chocolates. (2) Cocoa (medium fat cocoa) must contain less than 22% cacao fat, but not less than 10%. (3) Low fat cocoa contains less than 10% fat and either of these may contain the same additives as the breakfast cocoa.

COFFEE

Not far behind sugar and cacao in importance is coffee. Not a food, it probably takes its place in as many meals as any single food does, not to mention the morning and afternoon breaks so religiously observed by office workers, housewives, and many others.

Coffee is the seed of the fruit of a tropical tree that grows to a height of 10 to 15 ft; many of us would be inclined to call it a bush. The fruit resembles a red cherry and contains two seeds that are flat on one side and fit together to form a round center in the fruit. The seeds are surrounded by a white flesh somewhat like that of a cranberry (Fig. 5.3).

The fruit is crushed between rollers set far enough apart to avoid crushing the seed. The crushed fruit goes into a tank of water for fermentation, which loosens the seeds from the flesh. The seeds are heavier than water and sink, but the pulp floats. The seeds are removed from the tank and spread out on a large wooden or concrete platform to dry in the sun. This raw coffee is a gray-green color and has very little taste. It is shipped in burlap bags to the various countries of the world.

Coffee is grown in many tropical countries. We import nearly 3 billion lb from more than 50 countries. Brazil supplies about 30% of the total followed respectively by Colombia, the Ivory Coast, Uganda, Angola, Guatemala, Mexico, Indonesia, and Ethiopia.

Most of the imported coffee is the raw bean, but we also import 4 million lb of roasted coffee from Panama, Mexico, Colombia, Brazil, and 11 other countries. More surprising still, we import 10 million lb of soluble (instant) coffee from Brazil, Guatemala, Mexico, Nicaragua, and 11 other countries.

There are different varieties of coffee just as there are different kinds of apples. The character of it differs with both the variety and the geographical source; consequently, the companies that sell widely known brands of coffee buy coffee from several sources and mix it to have the same flavor in each package. Most of the flavor and all the color develop during the roasting and are a complex mixture of many chemical substances.

OTHER IMPORTS

Space does not permit discussion of such imported foods as Brazil, macadamia and cashew nuts, pineapples, coconuts, olives, olive oil, or of tea, vanilla, and spices—not to mention wines and liquors. Most of them are better classed as luxuries than as essential foods.

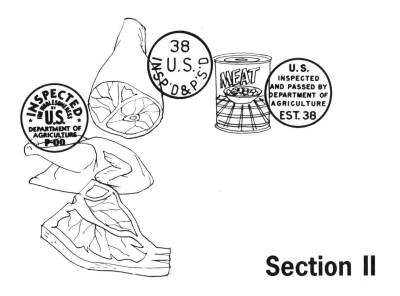

Section II

Legal Regulations

CHAPTER 6

There Ought to Be a Law

In the previous chapters I have attempted to show that the food supply today is far different from what it was at any time in the past. In fact it has gone through four stages. First, humanity obtained its food by hunting, fishing, and migration. Next, man settled down and began to produce his food through the practice of agriculture, with far less effort than the hunting, fishing, and migration required. In both these stages all the food was quite fresh. In the third stage the growth of cities made it necessary and profitable for the neighboring farmers to supply their city cousins with food, and freshness declined. There finally arrived the complete commercialization of the food industry in which local supplies almost completely disappeared. Grains, fruits, and vegetables are grown in areas most suitable for each and carried long distances to the consumer. This became possible because of the improvement in transportation and preservation, and so the food industries became big business. To complete the picture, the food processor has found it profitable to do more and more of the work of the kitchen and many foods became highly refined.

This final stage gradually led to abuses. The industry has become impersonal; no processor knows who will eat his food and no consumer knows who produced or processed any important part of it. The abuses invited legal control.

FOOD IN 1900

Before 1900 the consumer knew the farmer, the butcher, and the baker personally. If anything was wrong with the food (such as short weight, small eggs, sour milk, or stale bread), the purchaser complained to headquarters, and the vendor had to satisfy the customer or lose his business.

The cold storage warehouse appeared about 1865 and the railroads began to offer refrigeration in the 1880s. These developments made it possible to ship fresh food long distances and hold it until the market could absorb it at a good price. By 1890 the cold storage warehouse was a fixed part of the food industry.

Financial loss from spoilage has always plagued the food industry. In 1900, the preservation of food from the time it was processed to the time of its consumption was a serious problem. Keeping flour, coffee, and sugar was relatively easy; just keep them dry and away from mice and rats. Dried fruits were treated with sulfur dioxide, which preserved them for a long time. Dried fish were salted. But fresh meat, butter and eggs had to be shipped and stored cold, which retarded, but did not stop, the rate of spoilage. The correct use of heat in canning was not well understood and so there was spoilage in canned goods, especially after tomato ketchup and other such mixtures came on the market. Milk could turn sour during the daily delivery in hot weather, and any surplus was sure to sour before the next day. Spoiled food was a constant source of loss to somebody along the line from the producer of the food to the consumer of it.

PRESERVATIVES

The science of chemistry concerns itself with the decomposition as well as the composition of matter. It was natural for the food processor to turn to the chemist for the solution of his spoilage problems. The chemists knew, or soon learned, that certain chemical substances slow down or stop the activity of the microorganisms that cause spoilage. Sugar, salt, vinegar, and wood smoke had been used as preservatives for centuries; but the new problems required more powerful ones, and they were soon forthcoming. Chief among them were sulfur dioxide, formaldehyde, benzoic acid, boric acid, and salicylic acid.

None of these substances is extremely poisonous, like arsenic or strychnine, and they were used in such small amounts that the chemist considered any possible health hazard as highly unlikely. One complication was the invention of new preservatives; there were more than 150 patented. Many were in use and still turn up now and then. In the late 1930s I taught a course in chemistry that included food analysis. For milk analysis the laboratory instructor bought some bottles of milk from the college cafeteria. Formaldehyde in milk had been illegal for years and the official method of analysis included two tests for it. The students were directed to remove a small sample of the milk, and add formaldehyde to see what a positive test looked like, and then test the milk. One afternoon the laboratory supervisor came into my office and announced that the students were getting a positive test for formaldehyde in the milk. I told her they were probably adding it to the bottle instead of to a small portion; but she said the whole 20 of them were not that dumb, and besides she had made the test herself. I promised to look into the matter, bought a bottle of the same milk, and tested it in my private laboratory where I knew there was

no formaldehyde anywhere about. The milk did contain formaldehyde—22 of us had found it by two official tests.

The assistant broke the news to the woman who ran the cafeteria,
and she changed dealers within the hour. The dealer, a local poli-
tician who was distributing the milk from a large dairy farm a few
miles away, immediately came to the cafeteria to learn why he had
lost the business. The cafeteria manager announced bluntly that the
milk contained too much formaldehyde. How did she know? The
chemistry department had analyzed it. This information brought
him to my office with blood in his eye. After a few stormy remarks
he asked whether I had analyzed the milk or had it been done by a
student. I told him the circumstances of the discovery and that I
had made a thorough test myself. All this information had a cooling
effect, because formaldehyde was prohibited in milk, and the State
had a good enforcing agency. Furthermore, 22 people could testify
to its presence. He made a defiant exit with the announcement that
he would look into it; and if he found I was wrong, I would hear from
him. That was over 40 years ago, and I have yet to hear from him.
I never knew what had happened, but the dairy was selling raw
milk and I suspected that a salesman had sold the manager a patent
preparation with the assurance that it was legal, and that neither
of them knew that it reacted with the water in the milk to produce
formaldehyde. Whatever the cause of the debacle, the dairy soon
began to pasteurize its milk.

The impersonal nature of food also led to outright fraud. Meats
were dyed red to make them look fresher than they were, and
copper salts were added to canned peas to make them appear young
and tender. Substitutions were common. Water was added to milk
although that was not a new idea. Corn meal or flour was added to
sausage because it was cheaper than meat. Buttermilk was left in
butter because it was cheaper than the fat it replaced. Flour was
added to expensive ground spices and many other substitutions
became common.

PATENT MEDICINE

While various fraudulent practices were increasing in the food
industry, a related industry was becoming a far greater menace to
health—the patent medicine industry. These nostrums were sold
from door to door, at medicine shows held in tents or local "opera
houses," in drug stores and general stores, or advertised in newspapers and magazines and sold by mail. The medicine was sometimes complicated in composition; alcohol, pine tar, opium, and
other drugs were widely used. The biggest sales were in the rural

areas where doctors were scarce and ills, both real and imaginary, were abundant. Prohibition areas were also good markets for Peruna, Jamaica Ginger, and other products that were rich in alcohol.

In the year 1900 the patent medicine business was the biggest national advertiser in the newspapers and sales amounted to nearly $60 million, which did not include the sales of the small operators. The advertising was a combination of psychology and fraud. It described vividly and in detail the symptoms of many diseases including cancer, consumption, and old age. Anyone who read these descriptions of the symptoms was sure that he had the illness described and answered the ad, which generally promised and provided further information. This information was usually so convincing that it brought forth the necessary dollar for a bottle of the magic remedy. The victim's name then went on a sucker list that was sold to other medicine men. The patients seldom had anything wrong with them except the aches, pains, and weariness common to most of us, therefore the alcohol or the opium did relieve many of them and often produced a glowing testimonial.

In 1904 and 1905, Edward W. Bok, Editor of *Ladies Home Journal*, had several patent medicines analyzed and published a series of articles exposing the advertising and pharmacological fraud in the industry. One ad contained the statement: "Mrs. Pinkham in her laboratory at Lynn, Massachusetts, is able to do more for the ailing women of America than the family physician." Bok published this advertisement and alongside it a picture of Mrs. Pinkham's tombstone, which showed that she had been dead for over 20 years.

Other magazines joined in an exposé of the patent medicine industry. *Collier's Weekly* ran a series of articles by Samuel Hopkins Adams entitled *The Great American Fraud*. He illustrated his articles with pictures of the advertisements, coroner's reports of deaths, newspaper stories, and other items. The industry was attracting considerable attention.

STATE ACTIVITIES

By the early years of the 20th century, the food, drug, and liquor situation was so bad that public officials were beginning to be concerned about it. Several States had Departments of Agriculture or Boards of Health or both, and these agencies had laboratories to analyze products that were for sale in the state.

The part played by the farmers in the establishment of these laboratories in the State departments of agriculture is indicated by the early activities of the state chemists. On September 9, 1884, two

chemists from the USDA and several state chemists met in Philadelphia to discuss their problems in analytical chemistry. In the
group were State chemists from Connecticut, Georgia, Mississippi,
North Carolina, South Carolina, and Virginia. They formed a
society which they called the Association of Official Agricultural
Chemists, and adopted a constitution that indicates the nature of
their work. The preamble reads:

> Membership in the Association is institutional and includes the
> State Departments of Agriculture, the State Agricultural Colleges
> and Experiment Stations, the Federal Department of Agriculture
> and the federal, state and city officers charged with the enforcement
> of food, feed, drug, fertilizer, insecticide, and fungicide control laws.

The Association devised an elaborate plan for testing an analytical
method before they adopted it as official. There was really nothing
"official" about the Official Methods before 1906; they were simply
the methods adopted and used by chemists in official positions in
city, State, or Federal laboratories.

The Association began with methods for the analysis of fertilizer,
but within the first four years it adopted methods for the analysis of
cattle feeds and dairy products. Several State and Federal chemists
soon became active in analyzing feeds, fertilizers, and dairy products
that were regulated by law, but also other foods and drugs they
thought might need legal regulation. These explorers soon began to
find some interesting conditions.

In 1898, the State food commissioners and chemists formed
another association, which they called the National Association of
Dairy and Food Departments. While the older AOAC dealt only
with methods of chemical analysis, the newer one had broader
interests, such as problems of law enforcement, what other commodities needed regulation, and other matters of concern to the State
commissioners. The Association met annually with numerous topics
as subjects of the speeches and discussions at the meetings.

At the meeting held in St. Paul in 1903, James H. Shepard of
South Dakota reported the presence of a great variety of dyes and
preservatives in several foods and presented a menu to show the
amount of these substances one might consume in a day.

The Ohio Commissioner said that even if every farmer in Ohio
had a sugar orchard they could not supply all the maple sugar sold
in the state.

At the meeting in St. Louis in 1904, Commissioner Edwin F.
Ladd of North Dakota said that 90% of the butchers in his state
were using preservatives for their meat; 70% of the chocolates

Courtesy of FDA

FIG. 6.1. DR. HARVEY W. WILEY

examined were adulterated; 90% of the French peas sold in the state were colored with copper salts; 84% of the canned mushrooms were bleached with sulfur dioxide; and only one brand of tomato ketchup was pure. He also said that potted chicken and potted turkey were sold widely in the state, but he had not found a can so labeled that contained either.

From time to time others reported nutmegs made of wood, alfalfa seeds in raspberry jam, Plaster of Paris in candy, ground wood in ground pepper, and flour in ground mustard.

Such was the state of affairs in the early years of this century. California had passed a law in 1872 to regulate foods and a few other States did so before 1900. In 1848 Congress had passed a law prohibiting the importation of "spurious or adulterated drugs and medicines," and in 1890 it passed a more inclusive one to prohibit the importation of "adulterated and unwholesome food, drugs or liquor." We were then protected from the insidious foreigner, but not from our fellow citizens.

HARVEY W. WILEY

The most active and ardent advocate of Federal regulation was Harvey W. Wiley (Fig. 6.1). He was a huge man with a keen wit and enormous energy that lasted until his death in 1930 at the age of 86. Graduated from Hanover College in Indiana in 1867, he received an M.D. from the Indiana Medical College in 1871 and a B.S. degree from Harvard in 1873.

When Purdue University was founded in 1874 he became its first chemistry teacher and was soon appointed Indiana State Chemist. In 1883 he was appointed Chief of the Bureau of Chemistry of the USDA, a post that he held for 29 years.

From the time of his appointment in 1883, Wiley kept urging Congress to pass a law regulating the quality of food and drugs, but made little impression on that body. Some Congressmen were also food processors who didn't care to be regulated, some were influenced by food processors who had powerful lobbyists in Washington, and some treated Wiley with the usual indifference bestowed on a reformer. Consequently, Wiley decided that an aroused public was the only answer and proceeded to tell the people about the shortcomings of the foods and drugs they bought. He was a persuasive speaker and accepted every invitation he possibly could to speak on his favorite subject. A speech in New Jersey made a convert of Miss Alice Lakey who informed herself on the subject and began speaking before the women's clubs of the New Jersey State Federation, and then extended her activities to clubs beyond the borders of her state.

AGITATION AND TURMOIL

Wiley also had other allies; here and there a speaker became enamored of the subject. Several State commissioners were publicizing the evils they encountered to spur their legislatures to activity. Articles appeared in the *Ladies Home Journal* and other magazines. The newspapers and some of the magazines were a bit shy of such articles because of the advertising space the food and drug industries bought. In fact, some of the industries made it plain to these periodicals that if they took up the crusade they could count on the loss of their advertising.

By the fall of 1902 the crusaders had made some impression on Congress. The House passed a bill providing for a mild form of regulation, and senators from Idaho and North Dakota, presented a similar bill to the Senate. But, alas, their bill didn't even come to a vote and neither did the other bills that were presented to the Senate over the next four years.

The details of regulation proposed by these bills did not cause their failure to pass—the main cause was the political set-up of the times. Mark Sullivan in *Our Times*, which was written in the 1920s, expresses it very clearly. He points out that the Republicans were in control of Congress and that the party was the traditional party of big business, which supplied liberal campaign funds for elections and reelections. Senator Hanna, himself, was head of the iron industry and Senator Elkins of coal. Senator Depew was the lawyer for the railroads and Senator Foraker for Standard Oil. Several lines of food processing, such as meat packing, had become big business and trade associations were growing in the food, drug, and liquor fields. One of these, the National Wholesale Liquor Dealers Association, was one of the most powerful opponents of the bills; at least it claimed to be and everybody was inclined to agree.

In spite of Wiley's long fight, and the efforts of others, no progress was made unless the presentation of bills to Congress is progress. But the crusaders didn't give up. Constituents began writing to congressmen and the State commissioners kept on trying.

At the St. Louis World's Fair in 1904 the food processors had a big display of their packaged goods. Nearby, the food officials of about a dozen states rented space and arranged an exhibit of foods that were not just as they should be, and several packages appeared in both exhibits. The food officials made their exhibit more dramatic by extracting the dye from some of the foods, dyeing pieces of silk or wool with them and exhibiting the dyed cloth along with the food from which the dye had come. These dyes may or may not have been harmful, but in either case the public was impressed.

The Proprietary Medicine Association did not confine its activity to publicity. Somehow or other, *Collier's Weekly* acquired the minutes of a meeting of this association and published some interesting extracts from them. The members were discussing ways to prevent adverse legislation. The president said his practice was to put a clause in his advertising contracts with newspapers to the effect that the contract became void "if any law is passed in your state, which is adverse to my business." Then if a bill came up before a State legislature he sent a letter or telegram to every newspaper in the State pointing out that if such a law passed, he would be forced to cancel his advertising in that State. Other members of the association inserted similar or even stronger statements into their advertising contracts.

ENTER PRESIDENT ROOSEVELT

In 1905 a group of reformers decided to enlist a powerful ally—the President. In the group were the secretary of the National Association of Dairy and Food Departments, commissioners from Ohio and

Connecticut, a representative of the national organization of retail grocers, a man from the H. J. Heinz Company, and Miss Alice Lakey. When these six people called on Roosevelt in February he listened to them, promised to look into the matter, and told them to come back in the fall. During the summer he talked with Wiley, his personal physician, and several others about the subject. When the visitors returned in November he promised to recommend the passage of a law. He kept his promise.

In a message to Congress on December 5, 1905, Roosevelt said:

> I recommend that a law be enacted to regulate interstate commerce in misbranded and adulterated foods, drinks, and drugs. Such law would protect legitimate manufacture and commerce, and would tend to secure the health and welfare of the consuming public. Traffic in foodstuffs which have been debased or adulterated so as to deceive purchasers or injure health should be forbidden.

Before the month was out the senator from Idaho reintroduced his bill, which was now supported by the President, and it threw the Senate into confusion. Pro and con speeches were bitter and everybody concerned was in a flutter. Then, suddenly, the opposition gave up. Why, has never been explained, but it was undoubtedly a political maneuver of some kind that failed to work as planned. The bill passed the Senate by a vote of 63 to 4.

The bill then went to the House and was referred to a committee where it was laid to rest. The leaders thought that with all the business interests opposing the bill there would to too much controversy and decided not to bring it before the House that session. This was a blow to the advocates, because such a bill had passed the House more than once in earlier sessions.

THE JUNGLE

At this point a bomb fell on the opposition. In February 1906 Upton Sinclair published a novel, *The Jungle*, which told the story of Jurgis, a Lithuanian peasant, and some of his relatives and friends who came to this country and went to work in a packing house in Chicago. Sinclair was a socialist who was interested in the conditions of the workers. He went to Chicago and lived for seven weeks among those who worked in the packing houses. In the process of describing the conditions of the workers, he also described the methods used to butcher cattle and hogs and the handling and processing of the meat. There were government inspectors of the live animals, but none to inspect the carcasses after the animals were killed. Consequently, tubercular animals would be rejected by the inspectors and then somehow find their way back into the packing line. Other practices, or rather malpractices, were described quite vividly in the pages of *The Jungle*.

The book at once became a sensation and went on to become a best seller. Sinclair, however, was disappointed, for he was interested in the wretched labor conditions; but the readers were more interested in the condition of the meat supply. As Sinclair expressed it: "I aimed at their hearts and hit their stomachs."

Roosevelt read the book and was considerably upset by it, especially because it reflected on government inspection. He called in James Wilson, the Secretary of Agriculture, because the animal inspection service was in his department. The president realized the book was fiction and probably considerably exaggerated. The publisher, Doubleday, Page and Company, also had misgivings when Sinclair submitted the manuscript, and had sent lawyers to Chicago to check on the facts. The facts turned out to be even worse than Sinclair had indicated. Doubleday decided to publish them in a magazine the firm owned, called the *World's Work*. The publisher sent copies of the articles to the President before they were published.

The Secretary of Agriculture, of course, appointed a committee to "investigate" the meat inspection, but when the President read the magazine articles, which were not fiction, he appointed an investigating committee of his own. The report of his committee was so bad that he hesitated to publish it for fear of ruining the meat packers completely. Meantime, Sinclair was publishing newspaper articles to tell some things he had left out of the book.

Roosevelt influenced Senator Beverage of Indiana to introduce a meat inspection act. Introduced on May 22, 1906, the act passed the Senate on May 25, whereupon the packers lost their heads completely. They came to Washington; they had over a thousand telegrams sent to Roosevelt protesting the publication of his committee report; they threatened the stock raisers unless they joined in the protests; they even tried to intimidate both the President and his committee.

THE PURE FOOD LAW

The bill still had to pass the House against all this opposition. On June 2, Roosevelt urged the House to pass it and sent along part of the committee report. Someone got hold of this part of the report and sent it to the press. Coming after the Sinclair book and the *World's Work* articles, it created a furor throughout the country. Meat sales declined; one packer said his sales were cut in half. This decline in business profoundly impressed packers and led some of them to think that perhaps a tougher inspection might help bail them out of their evil reputation. Consequently, they eased off a bit in their opposition.

The Meat Inspection Act passed both houses of Congress and carried the Pure Food Law along with it. The latter had been sleeping in committee until the Meat Inspection Act brought it to life. The President signed both bills on June 30, 1906. The Meat Inspection Act became effective the next day, July 1, 1906, but the Food Law not until January 1, 1907.

The Meat Inspection Act provided inspection of red meat (namely, cattle, hogs, sheep, goats, and horses) from the live animals to the final processing of the meat. However, both laws had a constitutional limitation; they applied only to food in interstate commerce, to exports and imports, and to food processed or sold in the Territories or the District of Columbia. If meat, milk, or other food were produced by someone who did not sell any of it outside the State, he was not concerned with either law; he was subject only to the laws of his own State.

CHAPTER 7

There Is a Law

After more than 20 years of struggle led by Wiley, the people had a law to regulate the quality of their food and drugs. The full title of the law was: "An Act for preventing the manufacture, sale or transportation of adulterated or misbranded or poisonous or deleterious foods, drugs, medicines and liquors, and for regulating trade therein and for other purposes."

The law specified that it was to be enforced by the Secretary of Agriculture, the Secretary of the Treasury, and the Secretary of Commerce and Labor. These were the three Departments most concerned; the Department of Agriculture was concerned with the production of food, the Treasury Department collected duties on imports and taxes on liquors, and the Department of Commerce regulated transportation. The three Secretaries were to make regulations for the enforcement of the Act; however, the heaviest duty fell on the Secretary of Agriculture. The Bureau of Chemistry was in his Department, and was assigned the job of finding whether a food or a drug was adulterated or misbranded under the law. The Secretary appointed inspectors who bought samples of suspect food and drugs that could be proven as items in interstate commerce. These samples came to the laboratories of the Bureau where they were analyzed; if they were in violation of the law, the results were reported to the Secretary of Agriculture who was required to refer the matter to the Federal district attorney for the proper action.

The Secretaries had six months in which to make the regulations for the enforcement of the law, which did not go into effect until January 1, 1907.

THE POISON SQUAD

A start had already been made on the problems of enforcement because of the Import Act of 1890; also Wiley anticipated the passage of a general law and began to plan its enforcement. In 1902 he obtained permission of Congress to test the harmfulness of certain preservatives used in foods. He selected 12 healthy young men who volunteered for the work. Most of them were employees of the Department of Agriculture. The chemical to be tested was added to their food, and they were examined frequently for any ill effects. The experiments continued for five years, but few of the men served more than one year.

The work drew enormous publicity and reporters haunted the place. One of them called the group "the poison squad" and the Poison Squad it has been ever since. They tested seven common additives: benzoic acid and its salts, boric acid and the borates, salicylic acid and the salicylates, sulfur dioxide and the sulfites, formaldehyde, copper sulfate, and potassium nitrate (saltpeter). The results were not very conclusive because the ill effects on these men were too slight to detect with assurance.

FOOD STANDARDS

In 1900 there were practically no standards for foods; but in 1902 Congress authorized a committee in the USDA to set food standards, and the Secretary appointed a committee of five of which Wiley was Chairman.

Definitions and standards are necessary for the enforcement of a law to regulate foods. For example, maple syrup is made by evaporating the sap of the sugar maple tree. The sap contains 2 to 4% sugar and as the water boils away the percentage of sugar increases. When do we stop the boiling and call the product maple syrup? As the amount of sugar in syrup increases the density increases and the standard was set at the point where a gallon of the syrup weighs 11 lb; it is about 70% sugar. The standards were not purely arbitrary; they were set to correspond to the best manufacturing practice of the day. If maple syrup is boiled down until it weighs 12 lb to the gallon, sugar crystallizes out in a hard mass when it cools, and if the boiling is stopped at 10 lb to the gallon, the syrup does not keep well.

Many other foods presented problems of standards of composition, both for protection of the consumer and as a guide to the manufacturers who are in competition within the industry. Although the committee set standards for many foods, they were only advisory standards unless they were signed by all three of the Secretaries, whereupon they became part of the law. Advisory standards, however, were very useful for they were the opinion of several experts on what the food should be, and therefore served as a guide to food processors. Moreover, the producer knew that below-standard products invited prosecution.

Congress helped out in the matter of standards in 1923 by passing two laws. One defines butter and the other defines and prohibits the sale of filled milk. The Filled Milk Act declares:

The term "filled milk" means any milk or cream or skimmed milk, whether or not condensed, evaporated, concentrated, powdered, dried or desiccated, to which has been added, or which has been blended or compounded with, any fat or oil other than milk fat, so that the resulting product is in imitation or semblance of milk, cream, skimmed milk, whether or not condensed, evaporated, concentrated, powdered, dried or desiccated.

The law then prohibits the sale of filled milk.

According to the Act of Congress of March 4, 1923: "Butter . . . is made exclusively from milk or cream or both, with or without common salt and with or without additional coloring matter, and contains not less than 80 per centum by weight of milk fat all tolerances being allowed for." The fat was specified as milk fat in order to prevent the addition to butter of a cheaper fat, such as coconut oil, hydrogenated cottonseed oil, or lard.

The price of butter made it very profitable to remove the butterfat from milk, add a cheap vegetable fat to the skim milk, and sell the product for whole milk. This was what the Filled Milk Act sought to prevent, and it has always been effective. Recent dietary research on fats has shown that milk made with one of the highly unsaturated oils has a greater dietary value than natural milk; the Filled Milk Act was declared unconstitutional November 9, 1972.

Congress did not define any other food until 1950, after a new law had been enacted.

ENFORCEMENT

In accord with a provision of the law, the three Secretaries each appointed a member of a committee to make regulations for its enforcement. Wiley was appointed chairman and during the summer of 1906 the committee met in Chicago, New York, and Washington. Anyone who was interested was invited to attend and express his views. With no precedent to follow, the work of the committee was a tremendous task and a full-time job for the three months. Nevertheless, they succeeded in drawing up 40 regulations which the three Secretaries signed. By October 17 the regulations were published. Some of them, however, were amended later.

The official title of the Act was too long for use in conversation, speeches, or printed documents, and so Regulation 1 gave it a shorter title: "The Food and Drugs Act of June 30, 1906." Popular usage improved Regulation 1 and called it the "Pure Food Law."

The law contained the expression "original unbroken package," and Regulation 2 decided this referred to both the wholesale and retail package. Regulation 3 described the method to be used to

collect samples. Regulation 4 prescribed the use of the analytical
methods of the AOAC for the analysis of foods and the methods of
the U.S. Pharmacopoeia for the analysis of drugs. These official
methods are revised every five years.

The United States Pharmacopeia and the National Formulary are
published under the direction of the American Pharmaceutical
Association and describe drugs, set standards for many of them, and
prescribe the methods of analysis to be used in the drug trade. The
Secretaries not only adopted these methods of analysis, but in
Regulation 7 they adopted the drug standards also.

The other 35 regulations dealt with hearings, the publication
of the results of analysis and of court action, and other details of
administration.

DIFFICULTIES

Food producers, processors, and distributors had copies of the
law and the Regulations, but the Secretary of Agriculture was
besieged with questions that neither the law nor the Regulations
answered. Instead of answering each inquiry individually the
Secretary published the answers in a long list of *Food Inspection
Decisions* (FID), because in many cases the answer was of interest
to a whole industry. The Decisions were numbered for reference.
By the end of December 1906, 48 Decisions had been issued. The
decisions were not mentioned in the law, but were a personal inter-
pretation by the Secretary of Agriculture. All the decisions made
before the law became effective were prepared by the Bureau of
Chemistry, mainly by Wiley, and signed by the Secretary of Agriculture. Wiley in his book, *The History of a Crime Against the Food
Law*, says:

> For a few days after January 1, 1907, the Bureau of Chemistry
> was unrestricted in its first steps to carry the law into effect. Al-
> though all matters relating to adulteration or misbranding were now
> solely to be adjudicated by the Bureau, it was decided to continue
> to have these opinions, as heretofore, signed by the Secretary.
> The first decision under the new regime was signed by the Secretary
> January 8, 1907. It discussed the time required to render decisions.
> It was prepared because many persons presenting problems were
> complaining of delay.
>
> An open break in the plan of preparing decisions by the Bureau
> of Chemistry for the Secretary came in the case of FID 64 signed by
> the Secretary March 29, 1907. The question was: "What is a sar-
> dine?" The Bureau of Chemistry prepared a decision that only the
> genuine sardine prepared on the coast of Spain, France, and the
> Mediterranean Islands was entitled to the name.

Then the fun began. The Food Inspection Decisions were not Regulations unless they were signed by all three Secretaries, but they did indicate the Department's attitude. If the decisions were violated, the violation might be carried to the courts where the decision in the highest court that passed on the question would become law. Consequently, the decision itself had the effect of a law as far as the distributor or processor was concerned, for he could be hailed into court for violating it. The USDA published the court decisions as a third publication series under the title *Notices of Judgment.*

The sardine packers in Maine were the first to complain about FID 64. The Secretary referred the matter to the Fish Commission of the Department of Commerce, which seemed the logical thing to do, but it infuriated Wiley who insisted that the Bureau of Chemistry was the only agency appointed by the law to determine what constituted a violation until the matter was decided by a court. The law read:

> Sec. 4. That the examination of specimens of foods and drugs shall be made in the Bureau of Chemistry of the Department of Agriculture or under the direction and supervision of such Bureau, for the purpose of determining from such examinations whether such articles are adulterated or misbranded within the meaning of the Act; and if it shall appear from any such examination that any of such specimens is adulterated or misbranded within the meaning of the Act, the Secretary of Agriculture shall cause notice thereof to be given to the party from whom such sample was obtained.

Herein lay the source of the disagreement between Wiley and Secretary Wilson. The law designated the Bureau of Chemistry as the analyzing agency and the Secretary as the one to notify the owner, but it did not specify who was to interpret the analysis and decide the matter of violation. The Secretary, of course, felt that the decision was his since he was the one designated to notify the owner. Wiley maintained that the Chief of the Bureau of Chemistry should make the decision.

The opinion from the Bureau of Fisheries was: "Commercially, the name sardine has come to signify any small canned clupeoid fish;" and then went on to make some suggestions. A clupeoid fish, incidentally, is any fish resembling the herring family.

Over Wiley's protest the Secretary adopted the definition and specified that the label must also carry the name of the State or country in which the sardines are canned—such as Maine Sardines, Portuguese Sardines, etc. The decision seems fair enough, but it brought a protest from the French Ambassador.

The objection of the French was not the only result of the sardine controversy; it had far-reaching effects on the future of the Pure Food Law. The law was to a considerable degree the creation of Wiley who had struggled for a quarter of a century to have it passed. But Wiley was a reformer and reformers are seldom popular, especially with those whom they are trying to reform. Wiley had opposed Roosevelt on a question of the tariff on Cuban sugar, and thereafter the President seemed doubtful of Wiley's actions. Around the first of March 1907 he had Secretary Wilson appoint an Associate Chief of the Bureau of Chemistry, who was to be independent of Wiley and reported directly to the Secretary. He appointed Dr. Frederick L. Dunlap. The duties of the Associate Chief were never clearly specified, but one of them was soon apparent. On April 25, 1907 the Secretary appointed a Board of Food and Drug Inspection to prepare the FID. Wiley was appointed as Chairman, and the other two members were Dunlap and the Solicitor of the USDA, George P. McCabe. At least two of the Board had to sign each decision they presented to the Secretary. This provision could eliminate Wiley's opinion because the other two were direct representatives of the Secretary and not of the Bureau of Chemistry. However, Wiley did sign most of the decisions. The last FID that Wiley signed was number 141, February 17, 1912. On March 15 of that year he resigned as Chief of the Bureau of Chemistry. With changes in personnel, the Board continued for several years.

THE WHISKEY DECISION

Some of the whiskey distillers were the most powerful opponents of the Pure Food Bill, and after it was passed they continued to try to get approval for their most profitable practice—blending. Whiskey is a native of Great Britain; it had been made in England, Scotland, and Ireland for centuries. Since the American colonists were mostly British, it was quite natural for them to make whiskey. Corn, rye, barley, or wheat (whichever was the cheapest) was ground to a meal and cooked to make the starch soluble in water. Malt was made by wetting barley and keeping it warm until sprouting was well under way. The sprouting produces an enzyme that changes starch to sugar. The malt was then dried and ground.

Malt and water were added to the cooked meal to make a *mash*. After standing for a few days all the starch changed to sugar and then yeast was added. The yeast produces another enzyme that changes sugar to alcohol. When this change was complete, the mash was distilled in a pot still, and the distillate contained the alcohol and water and a little flavor from the grain and some that was formed during fermentation. After the alcoholic content was adjusted to about 50% by volume, the distillate was put into an oak barrel that had been charred on the inside. There it soaked color and flavor from the charred wood. All these flavoring substances are called *congeners*. From beginning to end it was a long process, for in 1906 the minimum aging time was four years.

A new type of still made it easy to produce 95% alcohol from grain or molasses, but without any congeners; in the liquor trade this product was called "neutral spirits." This development was the main cause of the trouble. To a barrel of aged whiskey, was added a barrel of alcohol and a barrel of water. The result was three barrels of whiskey of which two did not have to go through the long aging process. Of course, the alcohol and water were colorless, but a little caramel or prune juice took care of that. The product was called "blended" or "rectified" whiskey.

In 1898 Congress passed two laws on the subject of whiskey. One of them legalized blended or rectified whiskey; the other was the "bottled in bond" law. The latter was to protect the producer of straight whiskey from the blenders. It provided that whiskey could be bottled in bonded warehouses under the eyes of government inspectors, that it must be 100 proof (50% alcohol by volume), and all of it had to be aged four years.

Such was the liquor industry when the Pure Food Law was passed. The rectifiers had been apprehensive all along about the effect on their business if the Bill passed, and that is why they opposed it so strongly. But it passed in spite of their best efforts, and they at once began to flood the Secretary with Letters inquiring how whiskey was going to be defined. On December 1, 1906, the blow fell when FID 45 defined whiskey for them. Wiley wrote the decision and the Secretary signed it. Accordingly:

> Whiskey is a distillate, in a pot still, of the fermented mash of a cereal or mixture of cereals, containing all the natural elements of the grain and the ethyl alcohol and its congeners, volatile at the temperature of the distillation. It contains also the coloring matters and other soluble products extracted from the wood (oak) in which it is stored and any new compounds arising during storage. Potable whiskey is kept in storage for four years.

The liquor interest's worst fears were realized for blending now constituted the adulteration of whiskey.

The blenders went directly to headquarters. Senators began taking interested constituents to see the President. At this point the Secretary weakened and reversed Wiley's decision, whereupon

Wiley made an appointment to see President Roosevelt and explained the matter in great detail—he even demonstrated how the blending was done. Roosevelt was never one to delay action and so he sent the matter at once to his Attorney General for an opinion. The Attorney General, Charles J. Bonaparte, promptly decided that Wiley's Definition was correct, and it remained until the end of the Roosevelt administration.

The courts, which are the final arbiters in such matters, got a chance for a decision in seven cases, for the liquor people contested the definition in seven Federal courts and lost all the decisions.

On March 4, 1909, President Taft was inaugurated and was at once besieged by the liquor rectifiers. He assigned the Solicitor General to hold a hearing at which both sides presented their arguments. The Solicitor General's decision supported FID 45 just as the Roosevelt administration and the courts had done. But the liquor interests were not satisfied, and so Taft held a hearing of his own. It was attended by the Attorney General, the Secretary of Agriculture, who was still James W. Wilson, lawyers for the liquor companies and some others. After the hearing Taft gave a long judicial opinion, in fact, one member of the Supreme Court said later that the President had usurped their function, for the matter was already on its way up to that court. But Taft settled the matter by liberalizing the use of the word "whiskey." On December 27, 1909, he issued an executive order to the three Secretaries to issue a decision in accord with his opinion. They issued FID 113, which was even more liberal than Taft's opinion demanded. It said in part:

> All unmixed distilled spirits from grain, colored and flavored with harmless color and flavor in the customary ways, either by the charred barrel process, or by the addition of caramel and harmless flavor, if of potable strength and not less than 80 proof, are entitled to the name whiskey without qualification.

The Decision also permitted the use of alcohol from molasses in the blends. The decision stood for ten years when the Volstead Act ended the legal liquor business.

Wiley, in his *History of a Crime Against the Food Law*, calls the Taft decision the first of several crimes against the Food Law. It certainly did weaken enforcement and respect for the law.

THE REMSEN BOARD

The liquor interests were not the only ones to contest the enforcement of the Food and Drug Act. Some food processors who were using sodium benzoate to preserve tomato ketchup, and some who were using saccharin to sweeten canned sweet corn, visited President Roosevelt, who called in Secretary Wilson and Wiley for a conference. On this occasion Wiley was victorious. His Poison Squad had found sodium benzoate harmful. After the ketchup manufacturers had stated that ketchup would not keep without it, Wiley reported the results of the poison squad experiments at Roosevelt's request. The President then approved the Decision that had been issued to prohibit the use of this preservative.

The corn canners were represented at the conference by James S. Sherman who was then a member of Congress. He testified: "My firm last year saved $4000 by sweetening canned corn with saccharin instead of sugar." At this, Wiley didn't wait for the President to ask his opinion but blurted out: "Everyone who ate that sweetcorn was deceived. He thought he was eating sugar, when in point of fact, he was eating a coal-tar product totally devoid of food value and extremely injurious to health."

With the first part of this statement, Wiley was on solid ground for saccharin has no food value. The use of saccharin in food was adulteration for that reason. But with the last statement, he stepped into quicksand. The Poison Squad had not tested the poisonous properties of saccharin; nor had anybody else at that time, and the result of this statement of Wiley's was a surprise to everybody present. According to Wiley, the following colloquy followed:

"You tell me that saccharin is injurious to health?"

"Yes, Mr. President, I do tell you that."

"Dr. Rixey gives it to me every day."

"Mr. President, he probably thinks you may be threatened with diabetes."

"Anybody who says saccharin is injurious is an idiot."

This exchange broke up the conference.

Despite his fervor for the enforcement of the Pure Food Law, Wiley had a keen sense of humor and commenting on Roosevelt's closing remark he said: "That distinction has not departed from me to this day (1929). The thing that hurts most is that in the light of my long career, I fear I deserved it."

The day following this conference on sodium benzoate and saccharin the President issued an order establishing the Referee Board of Consulting Scientific Experts. Neither toxicology nor physiological chemistry was a highly developed science at the time and it was difficult to find any "experts" who knew anything about the harmfulness of saccharin or of any of the dyes and preservatives used in the food industry. Dr. Ira Remsen was appointed Chairman of the Board and it soon became known as the Remsen Board. He was an organic chemist who had established the graduate school of chemistry at the Johns Hopkins University, and probably the best known chemist in the country at the time, but neither his training nor his experience was particularly useful for the determination of the harmfulness of chemicals. However, the other four members of the Board did have experience and training that enabled them to plan and carry out experiments to learn the effect of chemicals on the human body.

The Board reversed Roosevelt's decision and permitted the use of sodium benzoate. It also permitted the use of saccharin as a sweetener and the use of sulfur dioxide for the preservation of dried fruit. The Board soon became highly controversial. Roosevelt, Wilson and the food processors supported it. Wiley, the state food officials, and the public were generally against it. An Assistant Attorney General in the Taft Administration declared the board illegal and pointed out that the original Bill had contained a provision for such a board, but that it had been eliminated in the House-Senate conference that submitted the Bill for final action.

The vicissitudes of the Pure Food Law may lead the reader to think the law was useless. This is far from the truth. Its biggest blows were the definition of whiskey and the liberality permitted in the use of chemicals in food. As for the whiskey, the artificial product was probably less harmful than the real one and anybody was free to buy any brand that he chose—whiskey, bottled in bond was still available. The worst losers from this source were the manufacturers of straight whiskey; the rectifiers could undersell them because many customers didn't know one kind of whiskey from another.

Aside from the effect on various food industries, the controversy over the use of saccharin, preservatives, and dyes in foods had its real pros and cons. The law prohibited: "...the addition of any poisonous or deleterious substance..." to food. The users of chemicals argued that even though a big dose of a chemical was harmful, the small amount added to a food was harmless. This may be so, but at that time there was little evidence to prove it. Furthermore, if a potentially harmful additive were permitted in foods even in small amounts, the consumer might get a harmful amount by eating several such foods at one meal. The harmlessness of such substances cannot be proved for it is a well-known principle of logic that one cannot prove a negative proposition. The Poison Squad and its successor, the Referee Board, tested the preservatives on "strong young men" who would most likely be the hardest fraction of the population to damage. How about weak old women, or children, or consumptives, or diabetics or any other special group? And what about the time effect? If the chemical does no harm in a year, does it mean that it is safe to eat regularly for 20 years? What about the effect of the various natural components of the food, do they make the additive more harmful or less so? Harmlessness can never be proved for there is no end to the questions that can be asked.

ACCOMPLISHMENTS AND WEAKNESSES

Those who argued for rigid enforcement pointed out that the law said nothing about how much of a preservative is safe, but simply stated that any substance which can be shown to be harmful in any amount cannot be added to food at all. In this they were correct.

Many provisions of the law were not controversial and were enforced as fully as possible. Nobody objected to the seizure and destruction of food that was spoiled, nor to the requirement that the weight of the food in a package must be as much as the label claimed. People paid a good price for luxuries like maple syrup and olive oil because of their flavor, and did not care to pay the same price for maple syrup that was half cane sugar or olive oil that was mixed with the cheaper and tasteless cottonseed oil. Consequently, many violations were prevented or punished, and the honesty and wholesomeness of the food supply were immensely improved. The law, like all other laws, suffered from the inability of the inspectors to catch all the violators—even a large and efficient city police force cannot catch all the thieves or all the speed violators.

Wiley retired as Chief of the Bureau of Chemistry on March 15, 1912, which raised a storm in the public press. The Bureau passed into other hands and in 1927 it was abolished; some of its research duties were transferred to the new Bureau of Chemistry and Soils. The Food and Drug Administration was created as the agency for the enforcement of the food laws.

The law was amended a few times and some of these amendments weakened it. One in particular provided that a drug is misbranded if the label contains any statement regarding its curative effects which is "false and fraudulent." This seems like a strong statement, but the courts ruled that the word "fraudulent" used in legal language means "willful misrepresentation." As a result of this decision the government not only had to prove that a claim on a label was false, but also that the offender knew that it was false, which was a practical impossibility.

Despite the weaknesses of the law and the mildness of its enforcement, hundreds of lots of food and drugs were found to be adulterated or misbranded and were seized and destroyed; also many cases went through the criminal courts. Some of these cases reached the Supreme Court, and the decisions often revealed weaknesses in the law. But with all its defects the law was much better than none and continued in force with varying effectiveness by various Secretaries until 1939.

Aside from the Pure Food Law's effectiveness, it served to furnish experience with the difficulties encountered in passing and enforcing even the most needed law.

CHAPTER 8

Still Another Law

Several hundred laws and local ordinances in the United States regulate food. To discuss all of them or even mention them individually is impossible. Therefore, I shall confine this chapter largely to some of the features of the food portion of the Federal Food, Drug and Cosmetic Act of 1938 and some of its ammendments.

ADVERTISING

By the year 1930 the quality of the food and drugs sold to the public had improved considerably because of the Pure Food Law. But the law was not the only cause of improvement in the quality of the food and the safety and effectiveness of drugs in the first three decades of this century. In spite of the bitter blows advertising now gets, and often deserves, it made a considerable improvement in the quality of food.

The advertising was not written to sell food directly, but to establish the name of a particular brand in the minds of the consumer. Once the name of the product became firmly established, the quality was guaranteed, for if a package was found to be adulterated or otherwise defective, the customer knew which brand to avoid. An established brand is often no better than many of its competitors, but it is a reliable product. To have a shipment seized by the FDA is a thought too horrible for contemplation by the sales manager of any famous brand of food. With so many brands of everything from caviar to cat food, the shopper is free to make her selections with the welfare of her family and her purse in mind.

A NEW FOOD BILL

With all the improvement in the quality of food and the safety of drugs there were still violations of both law and ethics—some of them were accidental, but others, alas, were deliberate, and in some cases the law was powerless to punish them.

It is an odd coincidence of history that another Roosevelt was in the White House when the second attempt to improve the quality of food and drugs became necessary. Social legislation in the early days of 1933 carried with it the Tugwell Bill for stricter regulation of food and drugs. Tugwell was an Assistant Secretary of Agriculture, and the Bill he drafted was so drastic that it brought opposition from nearly everybody in the food or drug business and from many members of Congress. It included three new features: the control of cosmetics, medical appliances, and advertising, none of which had been in the 1906 law.

The situation promised to be 1906 all over again with variations. The Bill was presented to the Senate June 6, 1933 and was referred to the Commerce Committee. The Committee held hearings on December 7 and 8, 1933, and the crowd that appeared—reinforced by magazine and newspaper publishers, cosmetic manufacturers, and advertising men—taxed the facilities of the Committee room. There was so much criticism of the Bill that it never got out of committee, but it was rewritten and presented again on January 4, 1934. Hearings began again on February 27 and lasted five days. As a result of these hearings the Bill was again rewritten and submitted on March 15, 1934.

Two years elapsed and still no new law was passed, but the hearings had attracted a great deal of interest by both the general public and members of Congress. Several Bills were presented to one House or the other, and finally Senator Copeland became interested. He rewrote the Bill that had failed to pass in 1934 and presented it to the Senate of the new Congress on January 3, 1935. A subcommittee was assigned and held hearings on March 2, 8, and 9, 1935. The testimony offered filled 372 printed pages, but again all efforts were futile for the 74th Congress sailed through its two sessions and adjourned without passing it. But Senator Copeland persisted and presented it to the 75th Congress on January 6, 1937. This time the Bill made it, but not until the third session of that body. The President signed the Bill on June 25, 1938. It is called the Federal Food, Drug and Cosmetic Act and five years were required for its passage.

Several lines of influence finally brought about the passage of the Bill. First, several States got tired of waiting and began to pass bills of their own. It suddenly began to dawn on manufacturers of foods and drugs that they would soon have 49 different laws to comply with. Hope of getting sone uniformity of regulation weakened their opposition to the Bill. In fact, at the final hearing some companies and trade associations actually came out in favor of the Bill.

The advertising provision was another cause of the delay. The Chairman of the Interstate Commerce Commission made a strong plea to have the advertising placed under the control of his Commission. The FDA and most of their supporters argued that the ICC had no laboratories in which to determine whether an ad was true or false and that an advertisement was really just an extension of the label. The controversy came to an abrupt end on March 21, 1938, when the President signed an amendment to the Trade Commission Act that gave control of advertising to the ICC.

With the opposition to the Bill weakened by these events, action was further spurred by a sensation greater than that of *The Jungle* a generation earlier. In September and October 1937 there were several deaths in the south central States that were traced to an elixir of sulfanilamide sold to the public. Inspectors from the FDA went into the territory and found that at least 100 people had died from the use of the drug. The inspectors collected several bottles containing medicine used by deceased persons during their last illness. An analysis showed that the medicine was sulfanilamide dissolved in diethylene glycol. It was this solvent that was poisonous and not the drug. Much to the amazement of everybody except the FDA officials, it was discovered that the old law had no provision against selling poisonous drugs—poisonous foods, yes, but poisonous drugs, no. Consequently, when the cases came to trial the charge was misbranding, and the maximum penalty was a fine of $500 or a year in prison or both. The misbranding charge came from the definition of an elixir as a solution of a drug in alcohol. This drug was labeled "Elixir of Sulfanilamide" but the solvent was diethylene glycol and not alcohol. The Federal Attorneys got around the mild penalty by seizing several lots of the medicine and treating each seizure as a separate offense, which, of course, it was. A United States District Court in Tennessee fined the company $16,800 and a similar court in Missouri imposed a fine of $9,800. The chemist for the company committed suicide.

The Elixir of Sulfanilamide disaster was a result of neglect rather than intent. Alcohol was heavily taxed and therefore very expensive. Tax-free alcohol was available to drug manufacturers, but getting it required considerable red tape. Diethylene glycol was much cheaper, and the drug company claimed that its manufacturer had assured them that it was not toxic; but neither company had made any thorough toxicity test.

THE FOOD, DRUG AND COSMETIC ACT

The new law contains several provisions that were not in the old one. It includes both cosmetics and medical devices, and its regulation of food and drugs is much more strict than the old law.

Drugs supplied the impulse that pushed the passage of the Bill through. But we are concerned here with food, and so we shall follow the adventures of drugs, devices, and cosmetics no further.

The new law prohibits adulteration and misbranding, and it also contains a method for establishing standards for foods.

The jurisdiction of the law, like that of the old law, covers food in interstate commerce, imports and exports, foods manufactured or sold in Federal territory, and to meals served on trains, planes, buses, and ships of United States registry. The law also releases the Secretary of Agriculture and the Secretary of Commerce from their duties as enforcers of the food law. The Secretary of Health, Education, and Welfare now has that privilege, which he exercises through the Food and Drug Administration (FDA). The Secretary of the Treasury is also relieved of most of his food law duties except that he must supply the Secretary of Health, Education, and Welfare with samples of imported items.

ADULTERATION

The law is filled with the usual ifs, ands, and provisos that lawyers delight in, but, in general, adulteration is defined in five categories:

(1) The food must not contain any poisonous or deleterious substance. It is also considered adulterated if it is putrid or decomposed, if it is packed under unsanitary conditions, if it is part of a diseased animal or one that has died otherwise than by slaughter, or if the container consists of or contains anything deleterious.

(2) If any valuable constituent has been removed or omitted, if anything has been substituted, if damage or inferiority has been concealed or if any substance has been added to increase the bulk or weight or make the food appear better than it is.

(3) If it contains any coal-tar color that has not been certified by the FDA.

(4) If it is confectionery and contains any alcohol or nonnutritive substance.

(5) If it is butter or margarine and any of the raw material used to make it was filthy or decomposed.

The last clause of Provision 1 is new and may seem strange. However, I once helped solve a problem for a cheese manufacturer that illustrates the need for such a provision. He packaged a process cheese in wooden pails for sale to institutional kitchens. The cheese developed an "off" flavor. Investigation disclosed that the cheese had dissolved creosote from the wood. The manufacturer of the pails had used creosote to preserve the wood and had neglected to inform the cheese manufacturer. Luckily, the latter discovered the trouble before the FDA did, and then the two manufacturers had a serious chat about who was to pay for the chemical analysis and the loss of several pails of the cheese.

There are three ways to color processed foods. If sherbert is made with orange juice, raspberries, or red cherries the product is naturally colored by one of the ingredients. In such cases the FDA considers the coloring process natural and does not regulate it.

The second method is the use of a vegetable dye as coloring. Among the natural dyes are annatto, dehydrated beets, caramel, carotene, carrot oil, paprika, saffron, riboflavin, and turmeric. In all these cases the FDA defines the color but does not regulate its use. These colors are mainly extracts of the flowers or leaves of plants, although synthetic carotene is permitted along with the natural product, and caramel is manufactured from sugar.

Coal tar dyes constitute the third group of colors and these are the subject of the color section of the law. Many dyes, or the substances from which they are made, are toxic, and so for many years the dye manufacturers and the FDA have carried on a continuous investigation of the safety of the proposed dyes, consequently the list of approved dyes is constantly changing as the animal feeding experiments furnish more information on toxicity.

As of December 1968, 8 dyes are approved for use in foods in general, and a few others are permitted for some special use. For example, Citrus Red No. 2 may be used to color the skins of oranges, but may not exceed 2 parts per million of the weight of the fruit, that is, 2 lb of the dye to 1 million lb of oranges.

The 1968 list of food dyes consists of Green No. 3, Yellow No. 5, Yellow No. 6, Red No. 2 (not Citrus Red No. 2), Red No. 3, Blue No. 1, Blue No. 2, and Violet No. 1. On June 10, 1971, after six years of testing, a new dye, Allura Red AC, was added to the list. The FDA sets specifications of purity for each of these permitted dyes. The dyes are made in batches, and each batch is analyzed and certified before it can be sold for use in foods and that certification is a demanding process.

The names of the dyes that may be certified are names assigned by the FDA or the manufacturer. The reason for this is obvious when we learn that the chemical name of Yellow No. 5 is trisodium-3-carboxy-5-hydroxy-1-p-sulfophenyl-4-p-sulfophenylazo-pyrazole.

In some cases the amount of a dye that may be used is specified, but no processor is likely to use more than is actually necessary for the dyes cost from $2 to $40 per lb.

A survey showed that the United States produces over 20 billion lb of artificially colored food annually, or 104 lb per person. Most colored food is a beverage or a confection although a wide variety of foods have color added. The cola drinks are colored with caramel and of the dyes in the above list, Red No. 2 leads, closely followed by Yellow No. 5, and then by Yellow No. 6. These three dyes constitute over 90% of the certified colors used. Blue, green, and violet are not in great demand.

Provision 4 eliminates metallic toys from boxes of popcorn and the pennies from pieces of candy so common many years ago. A large peppermint patty sold for a cent. Since one or two in every box contained a cent wrapped in waxed paper, whoever bought that piece got his money back. It was a good sales scheme, but children broke their teeth on the coins or sometimes swallowed them.

MISBRANDING

Although there are only 5 ways to adulterate food, there are 10 ways to misbrand it. Any food is misbranded:

(1) If the label is false or misleading in any particular.

(2) If it is offered for sale under the name of another food. For example, margarine is not butter and canned veal is not chicken.

(3) If it is an imitation of another food, unless the label bears, in type of uniform size and prominence, the word imitation, and immediately thereafter, the name of the food imitated.

(4) If its container is made, shaped, formed, or filled as to be misleading.

(5) The package must contain the name and place of business of the manufacturer, packer or distributor, and an accurate statement of the quantity of contents in terms of weight, measure or numerical count.

(6) Any information that is required on the label must be conspicuous and . . . in such terms as to render it likely to be read and understood by the ordinary individual under customary conditions of purchase and use.

(7) If there is a standard set for a food and the label bears the name of the food, then the food in the package must conform to the standard.

(8) If there is no standard for a food, the ingredients must be named on the label.

(9) Special dietary foods must state vitamin, mineral, and other dietary properties on the label.

(10) If it contains artificial coloring, artificial flavoring, or chemical preservative the label must say so.

Provision 1 omits the word "fraudulent," which had required the FDA under the old law to prove that the violator knew that his claims were false. It would seem to most of us that the above provision would cover the entire subject of misbranding, but Congress had other ideas.

The food industry usually solves the imitation problem by the use of a trademark; they do not care for the word "imitation." A cane sugar syrup with a maple flavor could be called imitation maple syrup, but it sounds better to call it Joe Doakes Table Syrup.

Provision 5 has a lot of explanation and qualification. For example, packages of less than $\frac{1}{2}$ oz are exempt, and the producer may give the address of the home office which might be in Chicago although the food was packed in California.

PENALTIES

The penalties are just the same for adulteration and misbranding. For a first offense the maximum fine is $1,000 or a year in prison or both. However, certain violations, particularly deliberate ones, may draw $10,000 and three years. After one conviction any additional ones come at the higher price.

STANDARDS

If there is a standard for a food, the ingredients need not be stated on the label unless some of them are optional. This is unfortunate for the names of the ingredients would be a great help to the allergy sufferer. If one is allergic to eggs, for example, he does not eat food that contains them. The theory, apparently, is that anyone who wants to know what a standardized food contains can get a copy of the standard and read it. But how many shoppers know how to get a copy of a food standard or even know that one exists? They do not know that they can write to the Food and Drug Administration, Washington, D.C., and ask for the standard. At present these standards are free. There are now standards for the following foods and any one of them can be obtained separately:

Part 14. Chocolate and Cocoa Products
Part 15. Cereal Flours and Related Products
Part 16. Macaroni and Noodle Products
Part 17. Bakery Products
Part 18. Milk and Cream
Part 19. Cheese and Cheese Products
Part 20. Frozen Desserts
Part 22. Food Flavorings
Part 27. Canned Fruit and Canned Fruit Juices
Part 29. Fruit Butters—Jellies, Preserves
Part 36. Shell Fish
Part 37. Canned Tuna
Part 45. Oleomargarine—Margarine

These standards cover over 200 individual foods. Other standards are under consideration, but the establishment of a standard is a long and tedious process—much the same as the passage of a food law. An established standard is part of the law.

The language of these standards is detailed, and most of them are long, for both definition and standard are included. One example, selected for its brevity, is that for sap sago cheese:

Sap sago cheese; identity. (a) Sap sago cheese is the food prepared from the skim milk of cows and other ingredients specified in this section by the procedure set forth in paragraph (b) of this section. It has a pale green color, and is made in the shape of a truncated cone. It contains not more than 38% moisture, as determined by the method prescribed in 19,500 (c).
(b)   The milk is allowed to become sour, and is heated to boiling temperature, with stirring. Cold buttermilk may be added. Sufficient sour whey is added to precipitate the casein. The curd is removed, spread out in boxes, and pressed, and while under pressure it is allowed to drain and ferment. It is ripened for not less than 5 weeks. The ripened curd is dried and ground, salt and clover of the species *Melilotus coreaulea* are added. The mixture is shaped into truncated cones. It is then cured for not less than 5 months.

A few other requirements gleaned here and there from the Federal Food Standards answer some questions that might come to mind. Ice cream in interstate commerce and in most states must contain 10% fat. However, Nevada requires 14%; Hawaii and Iowa 12%; and Texas, West Virginia, and the District of Columbia 8%. Nearly all standards require a gallon of ice cream to weigh 4.5 lb although Pennsylvania requires 4.75 lb, and a few states will settle for 4.25 lb.

The standards for ice milk are more variable than those for ice cream; milk fat varies from 2% to 10% and the weight of a gallon from 4.2 to 5 lb.

The common American cheese is limited to 39% water and when the water is removed the remaining solids must be 50% fat. Brick cheese can have 44% moisture, but the solids must also be 50% fat. Parmesan cheese, the hard grating kind, is limited to 32% moisture, but the solids need only be 32% milk fat.

Canned peaches and canned apricots are allowed one pit to each 8 oz, but canned cherries are limited to one pit in 20 oz.

TOLERANCES

Although the food standards specify exact limits for many of the ingredients, the FDA often sets tolerances to allow for possible variations in analysis or in processing procedure. An official would probably not bother to condemn a shipment of cheese if the chemist reported 49.8% fat, but the FDA would probably set a tolerance so all deficiencies of fat in cheese would be treated alike. The FDA does not publish these tolerances because it does not want the food processors to skimp on any of the legal requirements.

Tolerances are also set for filth and spoilage types of adulteration. It is not likely that anyone would condemn a barrel of apples because one fruit had begun to rot nor a carload of flour for a weevil or two. But the FDA must decide whether to tolerate two, three, or a dozen rotten apples to a barrel and then apply the tolerance to all lots of apples inspected.

The tolerance provision is one that often permits reconditioning of the food. There are many regulations that apply to reconditioning, such as release under bond, reinspection, and others. A few years ago a large shipment of lobster tails came in from South Africa, and the FDA found the number that had spoiled exceeded the tolerance. What to do? Here was an expensive cargo that had also accumulated freight charges—even disposing of so many spoiled lobsters was a problem. Consequently, the shipment was released under bond for reconditioning by an FDA-approved laboratory. A chemist and a carpenter spent several days on the job. The carpenter opened the boxes, the chemist inspected the lobsters and removed the bad ones, repacked the good ones, and the carpenter nailed up the boxes again. The lobsters passed the second inspection by the FDA and the owner got his lobsters at the additional cost of the chemist, the carpenter, and the loss of the spoiled lobsters. I might add that the chemist did not care for lobster for some time after he finished the job.

ADMINISTRATIVE CHANGES

Some provisions of the Law became effective when the President signed it on June 25, 1938, others a year later. As that date approached, it became obvious that so many changes, especially in label requirements, could not be complied with by the food and drug companies in so short a time. Congress solved the problem by extending the deadline date to July 1, 1940.

Another change in the affairs of the FDA also occurred. From the passage of the Law in 1906 to July 1, 1940, the FDA and its predecessor had been in the Department of Agriculture. However, in 1940 it was transferred to the Federal Security Agency, which became the Department of Health, Education, and Welfare in 1953. Thereafter, when the word "Secretary" appeared in FDA literature it referred to the Head of HEW and not USDA.

ADDITIVES

In the days of Wiley and the Poison Squad, the chemicals of doubtful safety added to food consisted mainly of seven preservatives, one sweetener, and a few coal tar dyes. Nobody paid any attention to the addition of spices, vinegar, and natural or artificial flavor unless they were used to conceal spoiled or inferior food. But as the years passed, chemists began to find other substances to add to food for some purpose that they considered desirable, although the public and the officials might have other ideas.

With the increase in commercial activity after the second world war, the FDA soon became swamped with additives. It was up to the Administration to prove the added chemical was harmful. Furthermore, not all additives were colors, flavors, or preservatives. Analytical methods had to be invented to detect the presence of substances nobody had ever had to look for in food.

Toxicological tests are animal experiments of long duration. A chemist has no way to determine whether a certain substance is harmful except to turn toxicologist, get some animals, and start feeding the stuff in question. The nature of these tests is well illustrated by those the FDA suggested in 1960:

(1) Acute oral toxicity tests with two species of animals; that is, does a dose make the animals violently ill or kill them.

(2) Chronic oral toxicity tests with dogs for two years.

(3) Chronic oral toxicity tests with one strain of rats for two years.

(4) Subcutaneous injections in rats at one level for two years.

After these results are obtained, if there is still any doubt about the safety of the substance then:

(1) Chronic oral toxicity tests with an additional strain of rats.

(2) Chronic oral toxicity tests with two strains of mice.

(3) Skin painting of mice at one level.

(4) Longer chronic toxicity testing with dogs.

What brought about these suggestions was a change in the law. The 1938 law said that a food is adulterated: "If it bears or contains any poisonous or deleterious substance . . . ." The FDA interpreted this to mean that if a substance is harmful in any amount, it cannot be used in food at all, and the Supreme Court agreed. This meant the coal tar colors and several other additives that had been used for years had to be prohibited. To relieve this impasse Congress passed an amendment to the law that became effective March 6, 1960.

The poison in any amount, or poison *per se* doctrine seems like a good one. However, many substances that are very poisonous in even a moderate dose are quite harmless in very small amounts. Also, many foods contain traces of copper, fluorine, manganese, and other elements that are actually required by the human body, but are poisonous in large doses.

The Amendment of 1960 gave the Secretary (in practice the FDA) the privilege of permitting the use of an additive if it is safe in the amount and under the conditions in which it appears in the food. It also transfers the proof of safety of the additive from the FDA to the one who wants to add it. This provision brought a flood of inquiries from manufacturing chemists and food processors asking for guidelines and tests to determine safe amounts of additives. It was in answer to these inquiries that the FDA recommended the tests just mentioned. These tests are not made on only one or two rats, mice, or dogs. In the case of rats, for example, the number may be as great as 200—150 for the test and 50 for a control group which has the food without the chemical. The idea of the control group is to find out whether whatever happens to the rats is actually caused by the chemical, or by the food itself, the weather, old age, or something else. The average life span of the white rat used in these tests is about 2 years.

The director of one well-established testing laboratory says a 2-year test really takes 3 years, because after the rats are fed for 2 years autopsies must be performed to learn of any damage that has occurred. With 200 rats that could take a year. If the second round of tests is required the total time to test one chemical may easily take 5 years. All this work may cost $100,000 or more to test a single chemical.

During the consideration of the amendment Representative Delaney of New York insisted that no known carcinogen could be used in any amount whatever, and his insistence prevailed. This means that when carcinogenic tests are required the costs go up another $100,000 or more.

The results of the tests of a chemical are presented to the FDA. If that Agency is satisfied, the Secretary issues a permit to the manufacturer to sell the chemical for use in food. In some cases the chemical is permitted up to some specified amount, perhaps 0.1%. In this case the chemists have a problem: how to determine the presence of such a small amount accurately. The search for a suitable analytical method may take several months.

Food additives have been a serious problem ever since the days of Wiley's Poison Squad, perhaps as far back as the beginning of history. After the agitation that brought about the passage of the Food, Drug and Cosmetic Act, certain events caused the public to

wonder about the safety of their food supply. For example, mono-
chloroacetic acid was often used to preserve wines, soft drinks, and
salad dressings. Several people became violently ill from drinking
a soft drink that contained it. After an investigation in 1940, the
FDA banned its use. Also, nitrogen trichloride, which had been used
to condition flour for 25 years, was found by a research chemist in
England to cause fits in dogs fed large amounts of it. Someone else
found it caused convulsions in cats, rabbits, and minks. The FDA
did not wait for a human to have convulsions. In 1949 they banned
its use.

The public concern for the safety of food was so great that President Eisenhower requested the Department of Agriculture, the
Department of Health, Education, and Welfare, and the President's
Science Advisory Committee to make a study of food additives.
These groups selected a panel of experts consisting of professors of
medicine, toxicologists, physiologists, directors of cancer research
laboratories, and some other scientists. The panel reported to the
President on May 14, 1960, that chemicals known to cause cancer
in experimental animals may also cause human cancer. Then, in
judicial language, they advised the FDA to continue accumulating
evidence on carcinogens and to give special concern to the enforcement of the carcinogen clause of the law. This stopped, at least
temporarily, the growing agitation among manufacturers for the
repeal of the Delaney amendment. Although the burden of testing
was shifted to the chemical manufacturers, the FDA still maintains
an elaborate testing program of its own.

Several hundred additives were in use when the additive amendment was before Congress in 1958. Some of them had been in use
long before there was a United States Congress. What to do about
these veterans was a problem. Unless they were specifically mentioned, the amendment would eliminate all of them. The food processors would not be able to smoke meat, pickle cucumbers, or add
oil of peppermint to candy. It would take years to test all of these
substances.

Congress solved the old soldier dilemma by including a special
provision—a grandfather clause—to the general effect that a substance could be used without testing if it had been in general use
before January 1, 1958, and was considered safe by experts qualified
by training and experience to evaluate its safety. The provision
created a problem for both the food processer and the FDA. How
does one go about finding a qualified expert and how many must
one have an opinion from? The law says "experts" and so obviously,
one would not do. The FDA solved the problem by selecting several

scientific societies and asking their presidents to nominate members they considered expert in the field of food safety. There were bacteriologists, chemists, physiologists, doctors of medicine, and others nominated; altogether the FDA gathered 800 experts.

The FDA drew up its own list of substances for omission from testing and sent it to their experts as quickly as possible. The experts eliminated only six substances from the FDA list; these six would have to be tested. The approved list contained 182 substances and came out November 20, 1959. Other lists followed, and by March 1961, the list of substances generally recognized as safe, abbreviated to GRAS, had grown to 768, classified in 13 groups.

The first group is called *anticaking agents* and consists of six items. All inert substances that do not absorb water, they are put into such products as salt and baking powder.

The second group consists of 32 *preservatives*. Sodium benzoate of Wiley fame is on the list, but it is limited to 0.1%. Not all these preservatives are for general use; calcium proprionate is used only to keep bread from molding. Several are used only to slow down the development of rancidity in fats.

Group 3 consists of 9 *emulsifying agents*. Five of these are restricted to use in dried eggs, the other four are for general use, such as to keep the oil and vinegar in a salad dressing from separating.

The fourth group is the *sweetners*. Sugars are foods and not additives. Cyclamates were in this list, but have been withdrawn and the food that contained them removed from the grocery trade (which cost one food company $11 million). This development leaves four varieties of saccharin as the only members of the group. The use of saccharin continues to be as controversial ever since the days of the Poison Squad.

The fifth class consists of 81 *nutrients*, or dietary supplements—the vitamins, calcium, iron, magnesium and other mineral salts, and some amino acids. Many of these items are foods and will be discussed in a later chapter.

Group 6 contains 28 *sequestrants*. There are several functions of these substances in the food industry. For example, iron in the water may combine with some substance in the flavoring of a soft drink to form an insoluble compound and cause cloudiness or even a precipitate in the bottom of the bottle. The sequestrant combines with the iron to form a soluble compound, and although the iron remains in the bottle, it does not form a cloud. Most of these sequestrants are salts of citric acid, the acid of oranges, or tartaric acid, the acid of grapes.

Group 7 is the *stabilizers*. These are gums and there are 12 of them. In ice cream, for example, the stabilizer helps to produce a fine even texture and keep it that way; ice cream has a strong tendency to grow large ice crystals and become grainy.

The eighth group consists of 79 substances for a variety of purposes, among them: Citric, tartaric, or other acids used to make candy or soft drinks sour; caramel to color soft drinks or other foods; calcium salts to make canned tomatoes firmer; papain to tenderize meat; and carbon dioxide to produce the bite and bubbles in soft drinks.

Group 9 consists of 46 *salts* used to add trace minerals to animal feeds. Among them are salts of cobalt, copper, iodine, and iron. Their importance will be discussed in a later chapter.

Group 10 is a list of 90 common *spices* and natural flavorings—everything from allspice to vanilla; if you can name it, it is probably on the list.

The eleventh group is closely related to the tenth. It is the *essential oils* and related natural flavorings and there are 173 of them. To illustrate the relationship of these two groups, group 10 contains cloves and group eleven, oil of cloves.

Group twelve contains 27 *artificial flavors*. These all come from the chemical factory and the only one that is likely to be familiar is vanillin, which is a byproduct of the paper industry and is much cheaper than the extract from vanilla beans.

Group thirteen contains 187 substances used in the manufacture of *packaging materials*. A great variety of chemicals are used to coat paper for food containers. In recent years, polyethylene, cellophane, and other plastic materials have come into use. Some of these substances are soluble in the fat or the moisture in foods and as the package stands on the shelf the substance slowly migrates from the wrapper into the food.

The actual amount of any one additive used in food is very small. In very few cases does it reach 1%; much less is more common, but the total amount of these additives used in 1965 reached the staggering total of 650 million lb. These figures are a large part of the cause for concern about additives that has disturbed the food industry and the FDA over the past two decades. Three pounds of additives per person each year—somebody had better have a good look at them.

Food processors are generally more interested in what an additive does to the food than they are in what it does to the consumer. If there is something the baker can add to bread to keep it from becoming stale, he does not have to pick up so much stale bread when he makes the next delivery. If a chemical will prevent rancidity in lard, the supplier does not have to collect so much lard and ship it to the soap factory. If butter, margarine, or oranges sell better when they have a bright color then dye them. Besides, candy and soft drinks would be rather monotonous if they were all colorless.

ACTIVITIES OF THE FDA

With all the spoilage, insect infestation, additives, adulteration, and misbranding, the FDA has its hands full. A standard of purity for the additive itself is necessary, for it may contain some of the chemicals from which it was made. While the additive may be safe, the raw materials may not be.

In addition to all the problems under the Food, Drug and Cosmetic Act and its amendments, the FDA is required to enforce several other laws. By 1962 the FDA had grown to over 2400 employees of whom over 600 were inspectors and about as many were chemists scattered throughout the country; some are in Washington, the others in the 18 districts into which the country is divided. Also bacteriologists, toxicologists, pharmacologists, medical doctors, and other scientists safeguard drugs and cosmetics as well as foods. Nearly half the personnel perform administrative duties—hold hearings, write letters, hire help, and do all the other things that administrators have to do. Unfortunately, Congress does not always provide for extra help when it assigns additional duties. However, by October 1966, the FDA had grown to 4,650 employees, and now it exceeds 6,000 to regulate foods, drugs, devices, and cosmetics that are imported, shipped in interstate commerce, or made and sold in Federal territory.

The FDA is concerned also with 100,000 dealers in foods, drugs, and cosmetics—56,000 retail drug stores, 5,000 places that handle hazardous household chemicals, and 318,000 public eating places including trains, planes, and United States ships. The scientists must devise and use methods to detect insects (dead or alive) and insect fragments or rat hairs. Also methods for bacteria, yeasts and molds, and pesticides used by the farmer to kill insects or other plant pests. Some of the scientists must know how to detect cancer in experimental animals. A recent amendment requires the FDA to judge the effectiveness of drugs as well as their purity and safety. If necessary, these scientists may also have to spend several days testifying in court.

STATE REGULATION

In addition to Federal regulation, each State has its own laws. Some of them have special provisions to regulate fresh eggs and dairy products that are not covered by Federal law or are processed and sold within the State. In addition to these laws, the State may have a separate board of health, just as every city has one. Usually, these boards are primarily concerned with matters of sanitation. They inspect food stores, markets and, restaurants and are also concerned with the health of the food handlers, for several diseases may be spread by foods.

Perhaps the best way to end this chapter is to recommend supplementary reading. I highly recommend reading the labels in the grocery store, preferably a supermarket, for a big library is always better than a little one. It will be an enlightening experience, and if you meet with such a word as nordihydroguairetic acid, think of your conversational advantage over your nonreading friends.

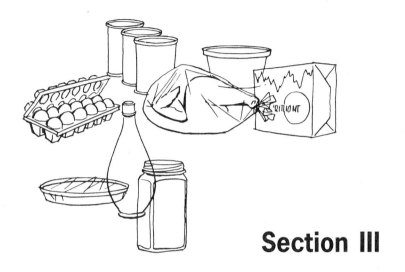

Section III

The Nature of Food
and Digestion

CHAPTER 9

Why Do We Eat?

No record exists to tell us who first began to think about why we eat or the various effects of foods, but we know that the ancient Greek philosophers and doctors commented along these lines. Socrates (470–399 B.C.) said the purpose of food is to replace the water lost through the skin and the loss of heat from the body.

Doctors have always observed the effects of food, but mainly the ease or difficulty with which it is digested. Hippocrates (460–364 B.C.), the "father of medicine," noticed that peas, beans, and lentils produce gas in the intestines. He also thought that growing bodies have more heat than those of older people and so require more food, and that neither overeating nor fasting is a good idea.

Obesity has apparently been a problem ever since man settled down to the comparative ease of domestic life. Hippocrates noticed that fat people are inclined to die early and recommended they labor much, drink little, and subsist on well-fed pork boiled in vinegar. This last recommendation is a little difficult to understand, for pork is not a food that tends to cause loss in weight. Perhaps people did not like pork boiled in vinegar and so would not eat much of it. The old Greek doctor had many other ideas about food; some proved to be correct, some doubtful, and some wrong. For example, the notion that certain foods must not be eaten together is pure fiction. However, the ideas of the ancient Greeks were passed along from generation to generation for over 2,000 years and were as reliable as anything that can be learned by simple observation.

People eat mostly for one of two reasons: hunger or appetite. Hunger and appetite are very different. Hunger produces gnawing pains, drowsiness, faintness, and headache. It is caused by the contraction of the muscles of the empty stomach and intestines. Appetite is largely psychological and has nothing to do with the need for food; it is the result of a number of things such as the odor of food or an attractive picture of food. Attractive food and surroundings may stimulate the appetite beyond reason, while a quarrel, bad news, or the appearance of a cockroach on a dinner plate may quench it entirely. Hunger can be suppressed only by eating, exhaustion, or disease.

Neither hunger nor appetite has ever been a proper guide to eating. Anyone with good digestion and good food may become hungry when he has no need for food at all. Almost anyone can eat candy, nuts, or a good dessert when he knows he has eaten too much already.

Leonardo da Vinci (1452–1519), the great Italian artist, inventor, and scientist, thought the body used up its food and if it were not replaced the body died. This conclusion was correct but he was wrong on one point for he said, "...nourishment can only enter into places where past nourishment has expired..." If this were true the waistline problem would not be with us.

About the year 1600 Professor Sanctorius, of the University of Padua, made some experiments. He weighed himself, all the food and drink he consumed, and all the urine and feces he passed. He even tried to measure the water in his breath by blowing against a mirror. Sanctorius published the results of his experiments in 1614 and reported the body loses a lot of weight through perspiration. How much was lost through the skin and how much by the breath he did not manage to determine, and so he reported both as "insensible perspiration."

CARBON DIOXIDE

A Belgian contemporary of Sanctorius made a discovery that had nothing to do with nutrition at the time, but became most important as the mysteries of that subject began to unfold. His discovery was the gas, carbon dioxide. The discoverer was Jean Baptista van Helmont (1577–1604). Of the Belgian nobility, he attended the University of Louvain and there was granted the M.D. degree in 1609. He introduced the word "gas" into the language and showed that there are different kinds of gases—both a new word and a new idea to the chemists of the day. Among his gases was carbon dioxide, which he galled *gas sylvestris* (that is, a gas from wood), for he learned that the gas was produced when wood charcoal burned. He also found it given off by fermenting grape juice and that it occurred in mineral waters and in caves. These discoveries interested chemists, and carbon dioxide became a popular subject for research. But the part the gas plays in nutrition was not explained for over a century.

Today, every schoolboy knows that all green plants grow by the combination of carbon dioxide and water under the influence of the green chlorophyll and the energy of the sun. This small bit of information is the result of over 300 years of research by hundreds of chemists and biologists. This reaction is the primary source of all our food except water and a few salts.

THE RISE OF CHEMISTRY

Chemistry became a science in the latter part of the 18th century and resulted in much new information. Henry Cavendish discovered hydrogen in 1766. Joseph Priestley and Carl Wilhelm Scheele discovered oxygen in 1774. Daniel Rutherford discovered nitrogen in 1772.

Priestley performed an exciting and important experiment, but he could not explain the results. He put a burning candle into a vessel in which air was confined. After a time it went out, which was no great surprise, but he put a sprig of growing mint into the vessel and left it for several days. Then he tried the candle again in the same vessel and found that it burned as well as it did in the first place. Nobody could explain this strange result, for neither chemistry nor biology was far enough advanced.

After many years and many experiments it became clear that Priestley had discovered what scientists call the "carbon cycle." The half of the cycle performed by the mint is photosynthesis and may be expressed by the equation:

$$6CO_2 + 6H_2O + \text{chlorophyll} + \text{sunlight} = C_6H_{12}O_6 + 6O_2$$

Here light supplies the energy and chlorophyll acts as a catalyst, causing the carbon dioxide and water to combine to form organic compounds and set oxygen free. The organic compound indicated in the equation is glucose, which is one of the simpler ones.

I don't know what Priestley's candle was made of, but since all natural organic substances are the result of the above reaction, we might use glucose instead, for it will burn either in a fire or in the body. The equation for the combustion is:

$$C_6H_{12}O_6 + 6O_2 = 6CO_2 + 6H_2O + \text{energy}$$

Burning the candle produces energy in the form of heat and light, while digestion of glucose produces body heat and mechanical energy for our everyday activities. The numbers are to balance the equations. If you count the number of letters C, H, and O, you will find the same number on each side of the equals sign—that is one of the things that is equal.

Antoine Laurent Lavoisier (1743–1794), a wealthy Parisian, began to put chemical facts in order and also to find some new ones by a series of brilliant experiments he made around 1775 and explained with keen logic. He is commonly called "the father of chemistry" for he deliberately set out to establish a new system of chemistry. This system has not changed since, although other chemists have expanded it considerably in the past two centuries.

Lavoisier began by heating several metals in sealed glass retorts. He heated each one on a charcoal grill for several weeks and weighed the retorts both before and after heating them—the two weights were the same in all cases. He next cracked the seal on the retorts and heard a hissing sound. Not to miss a trick he weighed each retort again and found them heavier. What he heard, of course, was air entering the retorts for the original air had combined with the metal. He also weighed the ash from the metal and found that its increase over the weight of the metal was the same as the weight of air that entered the retort after it was opened.

In October 1774, Priestley came over to Paris, visited Lavoisier, and, like all good chemists, they talked shop. Priestley told Lavoisier about the new gas he had gotten by heating red oxide of mercury, and that mice lived longer in it than they did in the same amount of air. He himself had inhaled a large amount of the gas and found his breathing felt particularly light for some time afterwards.

Priestley went back to England to continue experiments on his gas. Lavoisier was so impressed by Priestley's story that he got some oxide of mercury, heated it, and did several experiments with the gas it gave off. By 1783 he had reached some startling conclusions. The Priestley gas he named *oxygen*. Cavendish had already shown that air contains 21% oxygen and that oxygen combines with hydrogen to form water. With these facts and the results of all his own combustion experiments, Lavoisier could announce that when anything burns it combines with the oxygen in air.

Lavoisier also resurrected an idea that the English chemist, Robert Boyle, had advanced a century earlier: there are a few substances that are elements—all other substances are made up of different combinations of these few. Furthermore, different combinations of the same elements have different properties. For example, sugar and the acid of vinegar are each composed of carbon, hydrogen, and oxygen; but they have almost no properties in common.

One of the difficulties with the Lavoisier and Boyle theory of elements was how to tell which substances are elements. Water was not one; it was known to be made of oxygen and hydrogen. Lavoisier decided to consider a substance an element until someone showed that it could be decomposed. It was 50 years before chemists had any other means of distinguishing between elements and compounds. We now know there are 88 natural elements that combine to form several million compounds.

Lavoisier also established the first and most fundamental law of chemistry—the Law of the Conservation of Matter. We often hear this law stated, "matter can neither be created nor destroyed." This is not exactly so, and Lavoisier was much more modest in his statement. He simply said that the weight of the substances that go into a reaction is the same as that of the products formed. He confirmed his law a few years later by more experiments, and countless other chemists have since performed experiments that verify it.

RESPIRATION

There were few professional chemists before 1800. Cavendish was an English gentleman of great wealth. Scheele was a druggist. Priestley was a preacher, and several others were doctors. The Reverend Stephen Hales is more famous for his work in biology and chemistry than for his theology. After discovering that plants absorb air through their leaves and convert it into wood and other material, in 1727 Hale announced: "A part of the inspired air is lost in the blood, but it is as yet entirely dark what its use may be." And a secret it remained until Lavoisier launched his system of chemistry more than 50 years later.

The first chemist to throw any light on Hales' mystery was Adair Crawford (1748–1795), who invented an apparatus called a *calorimeter*, which is an instrument used to measure heat. There are now many types of calorimeter, but Crawford's consisted of a glass vessel immersed in water contained in a larger vessel. He operated it by sealing a substance and oxygen in the glass vessel, igniting it with a burning lens and measuring the rise in temperature of the water with a Fahrenheit thermometer. The water was weighed and the heat required to raise 1 lb of it 1 degree was his heat unit.

He put 100 oz of oxygen into the vessel with more charcoal than it would burn and then put 31 lb of water in his calorimeter. The burning charcoal raised the temperature of the water 1.93°. Next he tried a wax candle and got an increase of 2.1°. A live guinea pig was then put into the calorimeter with 100 oz of oxygen and it increased the temperature of the water 1.73°. This last experiment was the first ever made to show that the oxygen absorbed by the blood contributes to the heat of the body. From his experiments he came to the conclusion that the production of animal heat is much like that of burning.

Crawford was not the only one studying respiration in the 1770s. Priestley and Scheele both tried their hands at it. Priestley used mice, and Scheele made his experiments with bees. They proved that these living creatures converted oxygen into carbon dioxide, as did Lavoisier who proved the same thing with a sparrow in 1777.

In 1782 Lavoisier joined forces with the physicist Pierre Simon de la Place to study the production of heat by chemical action. They invented an ice calorimeter, which was similar to Crawford's except they used ice to surround the inner vessel and then weighed the water from the ice that melted.

They measured a large number of heat effects, but only two of them interest us here. They burned carbon in oxygen and measured both the heat produced and the amount of carbon dioxide formed. Then they placed a guinea pig and oxygen in the apparatus and again measured the heat and gas formed. For the same amount of gas produced, the guinea pig melted 13 oz of ice and the burning carbon, 10.5 oz.

While this work was in progress several chemists, including Lavoisier, were working on the composition of water, and by 1784 it became certain that hydrogen burns in oxygen to produce heat and form water. Lavoisier then saw why the guinea pig produced more heat than the carbon for the same amount of carbon dioxide; the animal's food contained hydrogen as well as carbon and the extra heat came from the burning of that.

After the work with La Place was finished, Lavoisier acquired a student, Armand Seguin, who served as both assistant and guinea pig. They first studied the respiration of a real guinea pig in an artificial atmosphere made by mixing oxygen and hydrogen. The animal did just as well as it did in normal air, which proved that the nitrogen in normal air plays no part in respiration.

The next step was the study of human respiration and Seguin, himself, was the subject. They were trying to learn what things affect respiration, and to do so they measured the rate at which oxygen was consumed. This took some inventing, for they had to have an apparatus to measure it. That problem solved, they found that when the room temperature was 26°C, he consumed 24 l of oxygen per hour, but if the temperature dropped to 12°, the oxygen consumption increased to 27 l. If he ate some food just before the measurement, the oxygen rate increased to 38 l. Work on an empty stomach required 65 l, but after a meal the same work required 91 l. These were the first experiments ever made to show the effect of external temperature, food, and work on the rate of respiration.

The first principles of modern chemistry were less than 22 years old when Lavoisier and Seguin applied them to the study of human physiology, and thus began the science of physiological chemistry, now called *biochemistry*. Lavoisier said he thought it might be

possible to measure the respiratory effect of, ". . . the philosopher
who thinks, the man of letters who writes, the musician who com-
poses." He also planned the study of digestion and of the blood,
with the hope of learning the cause and cure of disease, but, alas,
the experiments on respiration were the last he ever made.

Lavoisier's personal life was too complicated for more than
brief mention here. He owned a farm and carried on experiments in
agriculture. He was in charge of the government arsenal. He served
on a vast number of committees of the Academy of Sciences, which
was constantly called upon to advise the government on matters of
public concern. He had an active social life; he and Benjamin
Franklin lived near each other in Paris and were frequent dinner
companions. Unfortunately, both he and his father-in-law were
tax collectors and neither they nor the intelligencia were popular
with the French revolutionists. In November 1793, he was arrested
on several trumped-up charges, and on May 8, 1794, he and 27
others went to the guillotine. At the age of 51 the career of the
greatest chemist of all time was ended.

Lavoisier had thought the combustion that produces body heat
occurs in the lungs, but over the next half century several chemists
showed that the oxygen combines with the red corpuscles of the
blood and is carried to the tissues in all parts of the body to supply
energy where it is needed.

Respiration became a popular subject of research, and the
French Academy of Sciences offered a prize for the best thesis on
the subject. At least two competed for the prize. Each of them
studied the oxygen used, the carbon dioxide formed, and the heat
produced by a long list of animals. Cesar Mansuite Desprets (1792–
1863), Professor of Physics at the University of Paris, studied
ducks, chickens, pigeons, gulls, buzzards, owls, magpies, dogs, cats,
rabbits, and guinea pigs. Pierre Louis Dulong (1785–1838), Professor of Physics at the Polytechnical School in Paris, experimented
with cats, dogs, kestrels, water hogs, rabbits, and pigeons. In 1823
Desprets won the prize. Although neither of them reported anything new, they did extend the work of Lavoisier and Seguin to more
species of animals.

Twenty-five years later, Professor Henri Victor Regnault (1810–
1878) of Paris and a student assistant gave the subject of respiration
a thorough going over. They devised a better apparatus than their
predecessors had used and experimented on dogs, rabbits, chickens,
sparrows, marmots, reptiles, frogs, beetles, silk worms, and earth-
worms. They omitted fish because they knew that another chemist
was working on them, and they also regretted that they could not

study man as they had planned to do because they did not have enough money to construct the necessary apparatus.

These Frenchmen and many other chemists who did similar work work on a smaller scale must have convinced everyone that respiration is a function of all animal life. However, Regnault did add one new idea. He found that the oxygen consumed per unit of body weight was 10 times as much in a sparrow as it was in a chicken and gave the correct explanation; heat is lost from the surface of an animal, and a small animal has a much greater surface per unit of weight than a large one. If this fact is not clear, suppose that 1 cu. in. of a substance weighs 1 oz, then a 2-in. cube would weigh 8 oz. The small cube has a surface of 6 sq. in. per oz, but the larger cube has a surface of 24 sq. in. and therefore a surface of 3 sq. in. per oz.

DEVELOPMENTS IN CHEMISTRY

In science, one discovery often has to wait for another or for an invention. Understanding of the composition of foods and what happens to them after they are eaten had to wait for several discoveries in chemistry. The studies in respiration I have just described could not possibly have been made before oxygen was discovered, the composition of water was established, a calorimeter was invented, and analytical methods devised for the determination of oxygen and carbon dioxide. Likewise, what happens to food, from the time it is eaten until it is oxidized to produce heat and mechanical energy, could not be learned until the chemical nature of foods was discovered. And as it turned out, the foods are very complex organic substances. Sugar in a bowl looks like salt in its cellar, but no chemist is ever deceived by such a simple resemblance.

The chemistry of sugar and all the other carbon compounds is now called *organic* chemistry. The name comes from the fact that animals and plants are called organisms; therefore, any compound either of them makes is called an organic compound. Even in the days of Lavoisier chemists knew that plants produce sugars, alcohol, acetic acid, citric acid, and many drugs and poisons. By the year 1800, hundreds of organic substances were known, but chemists did not know very much about them except that they contained carbon and were very complex.

However, as analytical chemistry improved, some bold experimenters did begin to investigate the composition of the organic compounds and found they all contain carbon and hydrogen. Most of them contain oxygen, and some of them contain nitrogen, sulfur, or phosphorus.

In 1828 a German chemist, Friederich Wöhler discovered he had made urea, a substance a French chemist had found in urine 50 years before. Wöhler was trying to make something else, but instead of the expected substance he got urea. This result was sensational, for it was the first time a chemist had ever made a substance that was also produced by living organisms.

When a chemist wishes to make some natural organic compound, he first gets a pure sample from the natural source, analyzes it to see what elements it contains and how much of each. Suppose a chemist collects a lot of urine and separates the urea from the salt, water, and other substances that urine contains, no easy job. But after a few weeks, the chemist might have several ounces of the pure, white urea, which looks much like salt, sugar, or any other white, crystalline substance. He analyzes it and finds: carbon 20.00%, nitrogen 50.68%, hydrogen 6.60%, and oxygen 26.72%.

Our chemist now knows which elements make up urea and how much of each, but that doesn't give him any clue as to how to go about hitching these elements together to make the compound. This would be the end of the line with the knowledge chemists had in the year 1800. Then came some theories.

John Dalton (1766–1844), an English school teacher who worked at chemistry in his spare time, came to the conclusion in 1803 that elements are composed of small particles, which he called *atoms*. The smallest particle of carbon is an atom of carbon and any one of them weighs the same as any other. Likewise, hydrogen, nitrogen, and oxygen are made up of atoms; all the atoms of one element are alike and weigh the same, but the atoms of one element differ from those of another in weight and other characteristics.

Other chemists soon began to work with Dalton's idea, and their first big problem was to determine the weights of the atoms of the various elements. They finally decided to give the hydrogen atom the weight of 1, because it seemed to be the lightest element and that assumption turned out to be correct; hydrogen is the lightest element. Then numerous experiments and much reasoning showed that the carbon atom is 12 times as heavy as the hydrogen atom, and so they simply said that the atomic weight of carbon is 12, which is just a shorter way of saying the same thing. Likewise the weight of oxygen is 16, nitrogen 14, and so on with the other elements. All these determinations took a lot of work. It was nearly 70 years after Dalton announced his theory before chemists had a clear idea as to how many elements there are and what their atoms weigh.

Dalton had some ideas about his atoms besides their weight. He said that these atoms combine with each other to form compound substances and that all chemical changes consist of combination, separation, or interchange of atoms. He called the combinations, "compound atoms," but an Italian physics professor by name of Amadeo Avogadro named them *molecules* in 1811, and the name is still with us. An atom is still the smallest portion of an element, and a molecule is the smallest portion of a compound of two or more atoms, such as water, carbon dioxide, or urea.

Back in 1814 a Swedish chemist, Jons Jacob Berzelius (1779–1848), published a paper in which he recommended the first letter of the name of an element as a symbol for the atom; O for oxygen, H for hydrogen, and so on. However, there were several elements whose names began with C. He solved this problem by using a second letter from the name and so we have: carbon C, calcium Ca, chlorine Cl, chromium Cr, and so on. Some elements were metals and had been known by their Latin names for years, which accounts for such symbols as: copper Cu, iron Fe, gold Au, and silver Ag.

Berzelius analyzed over 2,000 substances for the percentage of the elements they contain, and I guess he got tired of writing the names of the elements, for he proposed the symbols as a kind of shorthand. Other chemists were slow to adopt Berzelius' symbols and they did not come into general use for over 40 years—scientists are slightly on the conservative side—but now no chemist could get along without them.

In addition to being a shorthand understood by chemists all over the world, symbols are combined into formulas for compounds, which tell a chemist more about the substance than the name does. For example, H_2O tells us that a molecule of water contains 2 atoms of hydrogen and 1 of oxygen. Since these atoms have the weights of 1 and 16, respectively, then the molecule of water weighs 18, and it is $2/18$ or 11.11% hydrogen and $16/18$ or 88.89% oxygen–all this information from the formula H_2O. Chemists have used these symbols in their notebooks, their published articles, and their books for the past 100 years.

The formulas of 1860, such as H_2O and CO_2 are what the chemist calls *empirical* formulas; all they show is the composition of the substance they represent. Since one molecule of water is 11.11% hydrogen, all water has that composition, for a drop or an oceanfull is simply a collection of a huge number of molecules.

In 1857 two chemists came up with an idea that soon enabled them to write *structural* formulas, which show how the atoms are attached to each other. By 1860 the news had gotten around, and

the organic chemists began determining the structural formulas
for their compounds, because to the initiated the structural formula
tells something about the properties of the substance and also gives
some clues as to how to go about making it. Here are three examples
of structural formulas:

$$
\begin{array}{ccc}
\underset{\text{Urea}}{
\begin{array}{c}
\ \ \ \text{H}\ \ \ \text{O}\ \ \ \text{H}\\
\ \ \ |\ \ \ \ \|\ \ \ \ |\\
\text{H---N---C---N---H}
\end{array}}
&
\underset{\text{Alcohol}}{
\begin{array}{c}
\text{H}\ \ \ \text{H}\\
|\ \ \ \ |\\
\text{H---C---C---O---H}\\
|\ \ \ \ |\\
\text{H}\ \ \ \text{H}
\end{array}}
&
\underset{\text{Acetic Acid}}{
\begin{array}{c}
\text{H}\ \ \ \text{O}\\
|\ \ \ \ \|\\
\text{H---C---C---O---H}\\
|\\
\text{H}
\end{array}}
\end{array}
$$

The lines, bonds, indicate which atoms are attached to which and
by how many bonds.

Foods are composed of organic substances far too complex to be
understood with the state of chemistry as it was in 1800 or even in
1840 when Renault published his paper on respiration. Not until
after 1870 was it possible to understand fully the changes that occur
when foods are digested and metabolized. Consequently, modern
work on digestion and nutrition began about a century ago.

Although Italian and French scientists had attempted to learn
why we eat, they learned very little. We might sum up their ac-
complishments by saying they learned that all animals inhale
oxygen, combine it with the food to produce carbon dioxide, heat,
and the energy with which they move about. The chemistry of the
day was not equal to telling anything more.

CHAPTER 10

How Much Should We Eat?

Chemistry developed slowly in America, and from 1870 to 1900 Americans went to Germany for advanced study of the subject. William Olin Atwater (1844–1907) was one of them. He returned to this country in 1892 full of ideas for research in food and nutrition. He went to Wesleyan University in Connecticut as a professor of chemistry. Soon afterwards, the USDA established an Experiment Station at Middletown and made Atwater its Director. He assembled a staff of assistants and began a thorough analysis of the common American foods. He published his first results in 1895.

But Atwater was not satisfied to do food analysis and began to pester his administrative superiors for money to build a big respiration calorimeter such as Regnault would have loved to have. Soon the money was forthcoming, and he and Edward Bennett Rose (1861–1921), Professor of Physics at Wesleyan, built the coveted apparatus (Fig. 10.1). It was 7 ft long, 4 ft wide, and $6\frac{1}{2}$ ft high, so that a man had plenty of room to sit, stand, or lie in it. It was insulated to prevent the escape of heat through the walls and had arrangements for admitting oxygen and collecting and analyzing the expired air, as well as an arrangement by which food could be handed in and excreta passed out without the loss of heat The heat was collected by water circulating through copper coils inside the apparatus; the temperature of the water was taken as it entered and again as it left the calorimeter; its volume was measured and the amount of heat calculated from this information.

In 1897 Atwater and Francis G. Benedict (1870–1957), another Professor of Chemistry at Wesleyan, began the study of human respiration with their new calorimeter. Later the Carnegie Institution of Washington established a nutrition laboratory in Boston and Benedict was made director of that. These two laboratories and two others in New York were all busy studying nutrition in the early years of the present century.

ENERGY AND WORK

When the nutritionist uses the word "energy," he means the capacity to do work and is not concerned with laziness or eagerness. Also, to him "work" is movement against a force; the simplest kind

Courtesy of USDA

FIG. 10.1. THE ORIGINAL ATWATER-ROSE-BENEDICT RESPIRATION CALORIMETER

of work is lifting a weight against the force of gravity. It takes a definite amount of work to lift a 1-lb weight 1 ft high; it takes just twice as much to lift a 2-lb weight 1 foot high or a 1-lb weight 2 ft high.

There are many kinds of energy. For example, a weight can be lifted by electricity, magnetism, heat, or human energy. Any one kind of energy can be transformed into another kind either directly or indirectly. Combustion produces chemical energy that reaches the air as heat, light, mechanical energy, and sometimes sound as in the case of the roaring bonfire.

Combustion in the body produces chemical energy by the combination of oxygen in the air with carbon and hydrogen of the food. Such combustion is a slow oxidation and produces neither sound nor light except in special cases. In the case of fireflies, over 90% of the energy emerges as light. Energy can also emerge as sound when the cat decides to yowl, the dog to bark, or the man to snore, talk, sing, or play the trumpet. Sound requires work and therefore takes energy, because to produce sound something must vibrate (that is, move back and forth against tension), such as the vocal cords, the violin strings, or the brass of the trumpet. These vibrating media do not move very far and so they take very little energy, and yet you may notice a trumpet player or a singer take a deep breath as the opportunity offers in order to have plenty of oxygen on hand for the necessary combustion. When we are silent the energy produced in the body becomes heat and mechanical energy—the energy of motion. When one is shut inside a closed room such as the Atwater calorimeter, all the energy finally appears as heat. Since heat is one of the easiest forms of energy to measure, the energy content of foods and the requirements of our bodies are always reported as heat units.

To measure heat, like anything else, we must devise a unit. All units of measure are arbitrary; there is nothing fundamental about a yard, a degree, a pound, or a dollar. Each is just a unit for the measurement of something.

The unit used to measure heat is the *calorie*. It is defined from the common method used for measurement, which is to warm water and then measure the rise in temperature and the amount of water heated. Of course we can measure water in several units and temperature in at least three, and so if we are to have a heat unit we must decide on which of these units to use. Consequently, the calorie is the amount of heat required to raise the temperature of 1 gm of water 1 °C. This is not very much heat for 1 gm of water is only about 1/28 oz or 1/5 of a teaspoonful. It takes 80 of these calories to melt 1 gm of ice and about 585 to evaporate 1 gm of water at room temperature. Therefore, measuring the heat of the human body in these calories would be something like measuring the distance from New York to San Francisco with a yardstick. The nutritionist solves this dilemma by using the *kilocalorie*, which is the heat required to heat 1 kg of water 1 °C. Since the kg is 1000 gm, the kilocalorie is 1000 calories. The small calorie is abbreviated to *cal*, and the kilocalorie to kcal or *Cal*. Many writers distinguish between the two calories by always writing the kilocalorie with a capital letter, Calorie. However you may write it, the calories you count at the table are the big ones.

HUMAN ENERGY

The energy requirement of the human body is easy to understand, although a few points are not exactly obvious. I have pointed out that all work requires energy and that work involves motion; therefore, the more a person moves about, the more energy he requires. But suppose a man is asleep and lying still, which is as motionless as a man can be. He is still partly in motion because his heart, lungs, and most of the other organs are going; if they were not he would not be alive long.

TABLE 10.1

DESIRABLE WEIGHTS

Height in In.	Men			Women		
	Low	Median	High	Low	Median	High
60	112	125	137	104	116	128
62	117	130	143	109	121	133
64	121	135	149	115	128	141
66	128	142	156	121	136	149
68	135	150	165	128	142	156
70	142	158	178	135	150	165
72	150	167	184	142	158	174

The amount of energy one uses at "complete rest" is called the *basal metabolism*. There is no such thing as complete rest, of course, but the nutritionists use the term to mean as complete as possible in both mind and body. Basal metabolism is usually measured in the morning before breakfast, 14 hr after the last meal, and at a comfortable room temperature. Any bed will do if it is comfortable. The subject breathes through a tube attached to a face mask or similar arrangement and exhales through another tube. The first tube comes from a tank of oxygen, which is measured on the way, and the second goes to an apparatus which measures the amount of carbon dioxide exhaled. From these two measurements the energy produced can be calculated. The whole apparatus is so mounted that it can be moved from bed to bed in a hospital or a laboratory. Nutritionists have measured the basal metabolism of thousands of people with this portable apparatus, which is much cheaper and more convenient than an Atwater-Rose calorimeter.

The actual amount of food oxidized by a person depends mainly on size, amount of activity, the atmospheric temperature, age, health, and how long it has been since the last meal. Race and sex make no appreciable difference except in so far as they affect the size and the activity. This at once raises the question of what the size of a person should be. It depends on height and weight. The height of any one adult does not change appreciably, but the weight does. What one should weigh varies a little with heredity and the build of the person and so it is impossible to give an exact weight for a given height. Several height-weight tables have been published, and Table 10.1 will probably include everybody:

The weights in Table 10.1 include light clothing and are for men and women from 25 to 30 years old, but the maximum should not be exceeded at any age.

The word *metabolism* covers two processes: the oxidation of the food to produce energy, and the formation of body tissues from the food as in the growth of young people. So many basal metabolism values have been determined by the nutritionists with different types of apparatus, all of which give nearly the same result with the same person, that we now know approximately what it should be for a healthy person of a given size, and also the factors that affect it.

Basal metabolism decreases with increasing age and is slightly lower for women than for men at all ages. The maximum metabolism is about 55 Cal per sq meter of body surface at the age of 2 years and then falls gradually to about 32 Cal at 90. The energy consumption during sleep is about 10% less than the basal. Climate makes a little difference but scarcely enough to measure. Starvation may reduce the basal metabolism to half its normal value, and some diseases lower it; but fevers and one type of goiter increase it. Doctors often find a basal metabolism determination very useful in diagnosis.

In addition to the energy used to operate body functions and to keep warm, considerable energy is used in voluntary activities. For persons of moderate activity, about 70% of the energy generated in the body is basal and the other 30% is used for all the things we do during the day. However, in case of extreme physical exertion, such as rowing in a boat race or digging a ditch, the muscular effort may use more energy than the basal.

In stating the energy required for the various activities, the nutritionists express it in Calories per kilogram of body weight. A kilogram is 2.2 lb, and so if you weigh 154 lb, you weigh 70 kg. By adding the basal to energy requirements of the various activities, experimenters have found the following values expressed in Calories per kilogram of body weight per hour: sleeping 0.93, lying awake 1.10, sitting 1.43, reading aloud 1.50, standing 1.50, hand sewing 1.59, dressing 1.69, typewriting 2.00, ironing 2.06, dishwashing 2.06, walking fast 4.28, swimming 7.14, running 8.14, and walking upstairs 15.80. These figures are very useful in estimating one's energy requirements, but they must be applied with some judgment. A typist, for example, may think she spends an 8-hr day typing, but she may spend most of the time reading copy, answering the telephone, or drinking coffee. Try the calculation. Divide your weight in pounds by 2.2. Then estimate the time you spend in these activities or similar ones. Multiply the hours of each activity by the appropriate number and add the results. Multiply by your weight. The total may surprise you.

The above estimates are average values, and there are individual differences in each activity. Any expert performs a given task with less energy than an amateur, whether the task is running, skating, dancing, singing, playing the piano, or washing dishes. People even differ in the amount of energy they spend in sitting; some sit without moving as much as an eyelid, others squirm, move their hands, tap on the arm of the chair, and are seldom still for 10 sec at a time. Thinking, however hard, does not increase the energy requirement enough to measure.

Although the mathematical expression of the energy requirement cannot be very precise for any one person, it is a good indicator of the amount of energy he needs. The results can always be verified by frequent weighing. If one is gaining weight he is consuming too much food for the amount of mechanical work he is doing, for the body stores food as fat when the intake exceeds the energy requirement. On the other hand, if too little food is supplied, the body oxidizes the fat it has stored until that is all gone and then starts on the other tissues of the body. A weight that does not change is in no way related to the proper weight because the person may have been too fat or too lean when the weight became constant.

STANDARD ALLOWANCES

In 1863 Congress chartered the National Academy of Sciences (NAS) to advise the government in scientific matters. It is a private organization with about 700 members chosen for their achievements in the various sciences. In 1916, under the stress of impending war, the Academy established the National Research Council (NRC) Then in 1940, when war clouds gathered again, a Food and Nutrition Board (FNB) was established as a division of the NRC, to recommend the proper food allowances for the population, because a scarcity of food threatened and there were the army, navy, and air force to feed as well as the civilian population. The Board consists of outstanding specialists in the field of nutrition. They issued their first report in 1941, but they have continued to study the subject and have issued several revisions. Table 10.2 shows their recommendations.

The Board estimates that the standard allowance for the decade between 65 and 75 should be reduced by 5% of the allowance at 65, and for the ages beyond 75 the allowance be reduced by 7% of that at 75.

Proper allowances for children and adolescents are harder to predict because they vary so much in activity—far more than adults do. In general, children under 10 require about 36 Cal a day

TABLE 10.2

RECOMMENDED DAILY CALORIES (1968)

	Weight	Age		
		22	45	65
Men	121	2350	2150	1950
	132	2500	2300	2100
	143	2650	2400	2200
	154	2800	2600	2400
	165	2950	2700	2500
	176	3050	2800	2600
	187	3200	2950	2700
	198	3350	3100	2800
	209	3500	3200	2900
	220	3700	3400	3100
Women	88	1550	1450	1300
	99	1700	1550	1450
	110	1800	1650	1500
	121	1950	1800	1650
	128	2000	1850	1700
	132	2050	1900	1700
	143	2200	2000	1850
	154	2300	2100	1950

for each pound of body weight; boys 10 to 22 require 23 Cal and girls in this age group, 16.

At all ages the recommendations are for the body weight the person should have and not what he does have. A bathroom scale used one or twice a week before breakfast will serve to check the accuracy of the estimates for any one person—you, for example.

Committees similar to our Board have recommended allowances in many countries: India in 1944, Holland 1947, Norway 1951, Australia 1954, Japan 1954, and South Africa 1956. Governments are taking the nutrition of their citizens seriously.

CONTROL OF BODY TEMPERATURE

Since the oxidation of food in the blood and tissues goes on all the time, why doesn't the temperature of the body continue to rise? The answer is that the body has the best thermostat on record; it keeps the temperature around 98.6°F (37°C), unless it gets out of order because of disease, and then the temperature may rise as much as 7°F or it may drop a degree or two. In health the body loses heat as fast as it is generated.

The heat is lost in four ways. About 65% of it is lost by radiation and conduction to the air in contact with the body—we cool off like a hot iron. This 65% assumes average temperature for the air. If the temperature of the air is above that of the body, there is no loss by conduction because heat does not pass from an object to a warmer one. Conversely, if the body is exposed to a low temperature or immersed in cold water, the heat loss by conduction is much greater than 65%. The 65% estimate is for a person in a temperate climate and with clothing adjusted to severe changes in weather and to air conditioning.

Under normal living conditions 30% of the heat loss is caused by the evaporation of water from the skin and lungs. A gram of water evaporated at body temperature absorbs 0.6 Cal of heat. As the air temperature increases, the evaporation of water becomes more and more important. At 98.6°F evaporation does nearly all the cooling. In hot weather or in case of much physical activity, the body perspires, providing plenty of water on the skin for cooling. Of course, it must evaporate to do any cooling; the drops that run off do not cool at all after the air temperature exceeds 98.6°F. Water evaporates faster in a breeze, and so a fan helps. It also evaporates faster in dry air. The discomfort in a crowded room or at high humidity is caused by slower evaporation and therefore less cooling.

The air we breathe, the food we eat, and the liquids we drink are usually well below the temperature of the body, but they are soon raised to body temperature and thus cause a little cooling. The cooling from this source is usually about 3% of the total. Then the urine, feces, and sweat carry out some 2% of the heat.

When we are exposed to very low temperature we require more Calories to heat the body. In return, the body takes some measures to stop the loss. Blood leaves the skin for the warmer internal regions, and sweat glands contract to stop the loss of water. We shiver, and as Mark Twain put it, "shivering was invented by the Almighty to enable us to take exercise without exertion." Cats and dogs curl up to reduce the area of skin exposed and men put their hands in their pockets, don an overcoat, or in extreme cases, take voluntary exercise.

OBESITY

The importance of regulating the amount of food consumed to correspond to the energy requirement of the body can hardly be overemphasized; too little will lead to lowered vitality and less activity, and too much to unpleasant or serious consequences. The amount of food consumed, of course, must be measured in Calories and not by either bulk or weight. A few almonds furnish as much energy as a whole head of lettuce, and a little chocolate candy will exceed a head of cabbage.

I have already pointed out that the young require more food per pound of body weight than an adult. They are not only more active, but the food must also supply material for the growth of the bones, muscles, nerves, and all the other body tissues. Around the age of 22 this type of growth stops, and any further increase in weight is due to the accumulation of fat.

When an excess of food over the energy requirement is eaten, the excess at any age is deposited as fat. An excess of 3,500 Cal produces 1 lb of fat, and so an extra 1,000 Cal a day would add 2 lb of fat a week. If this is continued, obesity soon arrives. Some fat, of course, is advantageous; fat under the skin insulates the body against cold, and internal fat supports the vital organs in cases of violent physical shock.

A publication of the HEW has this to say about obesity:

> Obesity is one of the most prevalent health problems in the United States today and it is regarded as abnormal by most physicians and laymen. Although the nature of the relationship between obesity and certain diseases is not clear, the higher mortality experience of obese persons and the additional hazard that obesity imposes in certain conditions make it a major health problem.

One of the effects of obesity is difficulty in breathing. This limits the oxygen supply, places a burden on the lungs and heart and increases the blood pressure. Obesity also diminishes the ability of the body to oxidize sugar and may lead to diabetes.

The various ill effects of obesity are hard to determine for there is no way to determine exactly how much fat a body contains except to analyze a cadaver, and that method does not have much personal appeal. However, statistics do show that the obese die younger, usually, but not always, of a heart ailment.

There are no national statistics on the prevalence of obesity. Several studies of special groups have been made, but they cannot be combined because the standards that were used were not the same in all cases. The height-weight tables are generally used, but they all allow a margin above and below the average. Is one obese when he exceeds the average for his height or the maximum? One study group showed that 15% of the girls of age 9 and 45% of those 16 were obese by one standard, and then a more liberal standard reduced these percentages to 2 and 15% respectively. It seems that about 10% of school children in general are overweight. One survey of college freshmen classified 29% of the men and 36% of the women as overweight. A life insurance company found that by the age of 50, 63% of the men and 67% of the women are overweight.

The individual is probably more concerned with his own condition than he is with statistics. How can he (or she) tell whether or not he is too fat? Excess fat is first deposited just under the skin and so a look in the mirror will help. Then, if you are past the age of 22 and your clothes begin to feel too tight, compare your weight with a height-weight table. If you exceed the maximum, it is time for action; if you exceed the average, consult the mirror again—your proper weight may be the minimum. In any event the chest measurement should exceed the waistline.

Prevention of overweight is easier, safer, and more fun than curing it, but if your weight has gotten out of hand, action may be necessary, or at least desirable. When this happens there is one thing to keep in mind, don't blame your glands, you cannot get fat on the food you do not eat. The excess fat comes from the excess food, and so the loss of weight means eating less food.

Starvation would seem to be the fastest method of losing weight and it is, but the body requires other things besides energy and to omit them is dangerous. In no case should the daily diet fall below 1,200 Cal and these should come from natural foods. There may be health conditions that require starvation, but it should never be undertaken without the *constant supervision of a physician.* Furthermore, in cases of ill health or excessive obesity of long standing, no weight reduction should be undertaken without medical advice. The prevention of obesity is a dietary matter; a cure may be complicated. Never take any drug to reduce unless a physician prescribes it. Even then the physician must keep track of the results, for serious consequences have followed the use of drugs without adequate medical supervision.

SPECIAL DIETS

Never use a special reducing diet. The obese must remember that to reduce the body weight is not enough, he must stay reduced, and a lifetime diet limited to buttermilk, grapefruit, skim milk, and bananas or other such diet is sure to become monotonous.

I suppose there has always been someone who advocated living on a monodiet. These advocates always insist that all of us should live on a single food. I can recall bread, meat, buttermilk, and grapefruit among the proposals for monodiets that have appeared within the present century. These fanatics, confident of the merits of their favorite food, are generally totally ignorant of the requirements of nutrition and equally unaware of the sad results of the experiments of the young English doctor, William Stark.

In Dr. Stark's report he mentions five bits of information that induced him to make the experiments: (1) Benjamin Franklin told him that he himself had lived for two weeks on bread and water only, and found himself stout and hearty on the diet. (2) A Doctor Mackenzie said that poor people in northern Scotland never ate animal foods; neither meat, milk, cheese, butter, nor eggs. (3) A Mr. Hawson remarked that a ship's crew ran out of provisions and some of them ate tobacco while others ate sugar. The latter died of scurvy, but the tobacco eaters survived. (4) An Italian physician, Dr. Cirelli, informed him that Neapolitan doctors frequently starved their patients as long as 40 days. (5) A Mr. Slingsby had lived for years on bread, vegetables, and milk with no other animal food and no wine and had been free from gout ever since he began the diet.

These widely scattered bits of information intrigued Dr. Stark, and he decided to see what he could learn about the essential nature of various foods. He selected himself as the subject of his experiments and described himself as, "a healthy man, about twenty-nine years of age, six feet high, stoutly made, but not corpulent, of a florid complexion with red hair."

Stark began his experiments with bread and water—20 oz of bread a day. In 2 weeks he lost 8 lb. Then he increased the bread to 30 oz a day and in the next 3 weeks lost only 2 lb. Finally, in a week on 38 oz of bread daily he gained 2 lb and at the end of the 6 weeks on bread and water alone, he felt well. For the next 4 weeks he lived on bread, water, and sugar and before the end of the stretch he developed ulcers in his mouth and his gums were sore and swollen; but after a few meals of meat, fruit, and wine, he recovered.

Stark was not through yet. For three weeks he went on a diet of bread, water, and olive oil. The mouth condition returned, but on four days of a general diet it disappeared. Two weeks on bread, water, and roast goose were satisfactory. Then followed for various short periods diets of meat only; bread, water, and beef; beef and suet; bread, flour, and honey; bread and cheese; flour pudding and suet. At the end of these experiments he developed scurvy. The experiments began early in June 1769 and on February 23, 1770, Dr. Stark died. And thus, two centuries ago several restricted diets were proved totally unsatisfactory by the tragic results of the experiments of a young English doctor.

REDUCING PROBLEMS

Some people reduce to normal weight and then go back to the old eating habits and are soon overweight again. According to mortality statistics that procedure is worse than remaining over-weight.

From the list of foods at the end of this chapter a diet can be selected that is low in Calories and still contains a variety of foods. To control its effectiveness weigh yourself daily and do not forget that a meal or a glass of water will cause a temporary increase and so try to weigh under the same conditions each time; probably the best time is just before sitting down to breakfast. The results may be slow at first because of the retention of water, but if there is no loss by the end of a week the Calories need to be further reduced.

Obesity is something that sneaks up on one like laziness and old age. People are poor judges of how much they eat. One hears a fat person say that he eats almost nothing and a lean one avers that he eats a lot. They are sincere, but they are generally both wrong. The fat one eats too much, or he would not be fat. Some thin persons do eat a lot but have poor digestion or poor metabolism. However, these last are not many; the usual thin person eats too little from habit, laziness, poverty, or misinformation.

Another factor in weight control also leads to obesity: lack of exercise. The physical activity of a boy of 10 would completely exhaust an adult, even a college athlete, in less than half a day. Besides the natural activity of youth, the schools manage to inflict exercise on the students, who need it much less than the teachers or administrators who prescribe it. Students in school and college play games, skate, ski, swim, dance, run upstairs or from class to class, and sometimes walk to and from school. Ten years after his last graduation the average man rides to work in a car, takes the elevator to his office, sits at a desk all day, and spends the evening sitting before a television set. He hires someone to mow the lawn, and his wife hires someone to do the cleaning, washing, and ironing. Tennis is soon abandoned, and only golf has a chance of remaining, especially if he can ride around the course in a golf cart. Survey your physical activities; how much have they declined since your last school days?

Although physical activities decline, eating habits do not, and the fat soon begins to accumulate. You might decide that an increase in activity would be an easier way to lose weight than dieting. Also remember two things about the energy value of foods. First, natural foods, such as fresh fruits and vegetables and even fresh meats, contain a high percentage of water. Since water does not burn, these foods have a low caloric value. On the other hand, dry foods such as nuts, candy, and cookies are all high energy foods because of the lack of water in their composition. The second point is that fat supplies more than twice as many calories per unit weight as either carbohydrates or proteins; therefore, fat meat, nuts, cheese, butter and fried foods are all rich sources of energy. It is the irony of fate that ice cream, cookies, pastry, candy, nuts—all the party refreshments—are high-calorie foods.

Dishes of the best cuisine are all highly flavored, which encourages overeating. To cut down the use of our two favorite flavors, salt and sugar, may ease the discomfort of a reducing diet.

The following list of foods will be a help in the selection of a diet for gaining weight or reducing, according to individual requirements. A portion of 100 gm has been selected for reporting the caloric content—it is about 10% less than 4 oz.

ENERGY VALUES OF FOODS

Less than 50 Cal/100 Gm

Beverages.—Beer, buttermilk, colas, sodas, vinegar.

Fresh Fruits.—Cantaloupes, cranberries, grapefruit, lemons, limes, oranges, papayas, peaches, strawberries, tangerines, watermelon.

Fresh Vegetables.—Cabbage, carrots, celery, cucumbers, lettuce, onions, sweet peppers, radishes, tomatoes, asparagus, snap beans, beets, broccoli, Brussels sprouts, cauliflower, collards, eggplant, kale, mushrooms, mustard greens, okra, rutabagas, spinach, squash, turnip greens.

From 50 to 100 Cal/100 Gm

Beverages.—Milk, table wines.

Fresh Fruits.—Apples, apricots, bananas, blackberries, blueberries, cherries, grapes, figs, pineapples, plums.

Vegetables.—Sweetcorn, green peas, potatoes.

Other Foods.—Clams, cooked breakfast cereals, finnan haddie, gelatin dessert, lentils, oysters, shrimp, condensed soups made with milk, yogurt.

From 100 to 300 Cal/100 Gm

Dried fruit, avocados, Canadian bacon, cooked dried beans, lean meats, breads and cakes, fish, chestnuts, chicken, duck and turkey, low-fat cocoa, light cream, eggs, fish, distilled liquors, ice cream and ice milk, jellies, liver, boiled macaroni, molasses, olives, pancakes, fried potatoes, boiled rice, fried scallops, scrapple, syrups, soybeans, sweet potatoes, tapioca pudding, veal, waffles, sweet wines.

Above 300 Cal/100 Gm

Raw bacon, fat beef, baking-powder biscuits, butter, some cakes (chocolate, cupcakes, fruit cake, gingerbread, pound cake), candy, cheese except cottage, ready-to-eat breakfast cereals, coconut, heavy cream, doughnuts, cooking fats, goose, nuts, salad dressings, frankfurters, liverwurst, salami, sugar, sweetbreads, wheat flour.

In planning a diet, the size of the serving must be taken into account. Four ounces of beer or soda pop may contain only 40 Cal, but a pint supplies 160.

Fried foods absorb fat and are much higher in energy value than the same food raw or boiled. A cooked cereal, such as farina or oatmeal, contains a high percentage of water and is therefore low in calories. Frozen fruits and vegetables and canned vegetables have about the same energy value as the fresh product, but canned fruits usually have a sugar syrup added and may therefore be in a higher energy class. Foods such as lettuce and asparagus are very low in energy, but the addition of a rich sauce such as Hollandaise or mayonnaise will raise them to one of the higher classes.

The manner of cooking is also important. For example, a 100-gm serving of boiled potatoes supplies 78 Cal; baked potatoes lose water and so 100 gm contains 93 Cal; but fried potatoes lose water and absorb fat, which brings them up to 274 Cal/100 gm.

The above list of foods should be adequate for the selection of all ordinary diets, but for those who want to calculate the energy of a diet more precisely, Agricultural Handbook No. 8 gives the average value of all the foods in the above list and many more.

Happy eating—and remember, we can live a few minutes without oxygen, a few days without water, and a few weeks without food.

CHAPTER 11

What is Food?

In Chap. 10 I have discussed the energy that enables an animal to live and carry on its numerous projects—the man to earn his living or play golf, the dog to chase a car or bury a bone, and the cat to leap upon his sunny shelf or fight his adversary. Such energy is produced by the oxidation of food in the blood or other tissues of the body. Now let us consider the nature of the food to be oxidized.

Even the most casual consideration tells us that the fat and lean of meat are different substances. A thorough examination by a chemist discloses that most natural foods contain many substances; some of them, however, in very small amount. The essential oil that supplies the characteristic flavor of an orange is only a tiny fraction of the weight of the orange, but it is a mixture of at least 20 different substances.

Natural foods are mostly water—70 to 95%. The energy comes from the dry portion, which chemists have found to consist mainly of three classes of compounds: carbohydrates, fats, and proteins. The energy from such substances as the citric acid in grapefruit, the tartaric acid in grapes, and the acetic acid in vinegar is so little as to be of no importance.

CARBOHYDRATES

The carbohydrates are the starches and sugars. There are several sugars, and the common one, which comes from the sugar cane or sugar beet, is called *sucrose*. It was a curiosity in Europe during the middle ages, and, according to the practice of the times, it was used as a medicine. It did not become common enough for use as a food until the settlement of the West Indies, about 1500.

I have mentioned the manufacture of starch from corn in Chap. 2. The separation of starch from wheat flour is an experiment well known to thousands of chemistry students. They make a stiff dough of flour and water, put it into a thin cloth bag, and knead it under water. Starch grains pass through the cloth and sink to the bottom of the vessel. After a few minutes, no more starch clouds the water and the bag contains a glue-like mass, which is called *gluten* because of that characteristic.

Grape sugar, *glucose*, is another natural substance that has been known for a long time, but Joseph Louis Proust (1754–1826), a Frenchman who taught chemistry in Madrid and did his research there until war ran him out, was the first to prepare a pure sample of it. During the Napoleonic wars France was cut off from the West Indies and her sugar supply, whereupon Napoleon offered Proust 100,000 francs to start a factory to make glucose from grape juice. Proust declined, probably because it was Napoleon's army that chased him from Spain. However, by 1812 Gottlieb Sigismund Kirchoff in Russia had made glucose by boiling starch with dilute sulfuric acid.

Sucrose, lactose, and glucose are the common sugars. *Lactose* is the source of the sweetness in milk; sucrose and glucose account for the sweetness of fruits and such vegetables as carrots, beets, and onions. Sucrose is now manufactured in huge tonnage from the sugar cane and sugar beet, and glucose from starch.

There are two other sugars that we meet now and then. The natural one is *fructose*. It is the sweetest of all the sugars and accounts for the unusual sweetness of honey. The other somewhat common sugar is *maltose*, which does not occur naturally, but is made by the action of malt on starch in the manufacture of beer and whiskey. About the only place maltose is ever encountered is in malted milk.

A peculiarity of starch and all the sugars is that the hydrogen and oxygen are always in the ratio of $1:8$ by weight, which is the ratio of these 2 elements in water. Since the atomic weight of hydrogen is 1 and that of oxygen 16, there must be 2 atoms of hydrogen to each one of oxygen. This gives the formula of H_2O for water; starch is $C_6H_{10}O_5$; glucose and fructose are $C_6H_{12}O_6$; sucrose, lactose, and maltose are all $C_{12}H_{22}O_{11}$. These misleading formulas imply that the substances consist of carbon combined with water. The formula for glucose could be written $C_6(H_2O)_6$—and other formulas similarly. This led, in 1844, Professor Carl Schmidt of the University of Dorpat to suggest the name *carbohydrate*, which still applies to the starches, sugars, and some related substances.

The chemical nature of the sugars was not cleared up until the German professor, Emil Fischer (1852–1919), did so in about 1890. He discovered the H_2O in the formulas is just a coincidence. The following structural formulas that Fischer found for glucose and fructose show they are not simply carbon and water.

```
        H                         H
        |                         |
   H—C=O                     H—C=O—H
        |                         |
   H—C—OH                      C=O
        |                         |
H—O—C—H                  H—O—C—H
        |                         |
   H—C—O—H                   H—C—O—H
        |                         |
   H—C—O—H                   H—C—O—H
        |                         |
   H—C—O—H                   H—C—O—H
        |                         |
        H                         H
```

   Glucose   Fructose

There are many kinds of carbohydrates in nature; most abundant of all is cellulose, which forms the structural tissues of all plants. Absorbent cotton and tissue paper are nearly pure cellulose. Cellulose is not digested by homo sapiens, and when a nutritionist refers to carbohydrates in the diet, he means starch and the sugars, for they are the important carbohydrates in foods. Nutritionists consider cellulose as roughage, not because it is rough, but because we eat it in all vegetables that are leaves or stalks and it is not digested but is eliminated unchanged in the feces. It just furnishes bulk to the intestinal contents.

FATS

The fats and oils were very common substances long before the carbohydrates were noticed. In meats, fats occur in layers such as the suet of beef. Olives and many seeds contain oil. Ancient China, India, Sumer, and Egypt all had vegetable oil industries.

Fats and oils are the same in their chemical nature; the difference is in the melting point. If the substance is a solid at room temperature, it is a fat—butter, lard, tallow. If it is a liquid at room temperature, it is an oil—olive oil, peanut oil, corn oil.

In 1823 Michel Eugene Chevreul (1786–1889), published the results of his 10 years work on the chemical nature of the fats. He was Professor of Natural History in the Museum of the Jardin Des Plantes, which was one of the most important research institutions in Paris. After publishing his book on the fats, he turned his attention to dyes. However, he is best remembered for two things: his book on the fats and the fact that he lived to the age of 103. His 100th birthday was celebrated in 1886 by many scientific societies.

At one of these celebrations there were said to be 2000 scientists. Even the city of Paris celebrated.

We do not need to follow the course of Chevreul's research on the fats, but it is interesting to know that it was so well done that only details have been added since. He studied several different fats including human fat, and practically all fats have been investigated either by Chevreul or some of the many chemists who have followed him.

The simplest chemical property of the fats is their saponification, that is, their conversion into soap,

$$\text{Fat} + \text{lye} = \text{glycerol} + \text{soap}$$

Glycerol is an alcohol with the formula,

$$
\begin{array}{c}
\text{H} \\
| \\
\text{H--C--O--H} \\
| \\
\text{H--C--O--H} \\
| \\
\text{H--C--O--H} \\
| \\
\text{H}
\end{array}
$$

Lye is sodium hydroxide, NaOH, and the soaps are mixtures of the sodium salts of several different acids. How many acids and which ones depend on the fat used. The acids are called *aliphatic*, or fatty acids. The simplest one is butyric acid, which is obtained from butter: the second in size and complexity is caproic. The formulas for these two acids are,

Butyric Acid   Caproic Acid

All the aliphatic acids have the carbon atoms in a straight chain, but differ in the length of the chain. Curiously, they always increase by two carbon atoms from one to the next, and they all have an even number of carbon atoms. The most common acids in the composition of fats are shown in Table 11.1. The formulas have been condensed to save space, but up to and including arachidic, each acid differs from the preceding one by two CH_2 groups just as caproic differs from butyric. The last four acids in the table are unsaturated be-

TABLE 11.1
THE COMMON FATTY ACIDS

C_3H_7COOH	Butyric	$C_{17}H_{35}COOH$	Stearic
$C_5H_{11}COOH$	Caproic	$C_{19}H_{39}COOH$	Arachidic
$C_7H_{15}COOH$	Caprylic	$C_{17}H_{33}COOH$	Oleic
$C_9H_{19}COOH$	Capric	$C_{17}H_{31}COOH$	Linoleic
$C_{11}H_{23}COOH$	Lauric	$C_{17}H_{29}COOH$	Linolenic
$C_{13}H_{27}COOH$	Myristic	$C_{19}H_{33}COOH$	Arachidonic
$C_{15}H_{31}COOH$	Palmitic		

cause they do not contain as much hydrogen as they could. Under the proper conditions oleic acid will add 2 hydrogen atoms, linoleic will add 4, and linolenic will add 6; in each case the product will be stearic acid. The chemist indicates unsaturation in his formulas by using two bonds to connect two adjacent carbon atoms. This leaves these two carbon atoms with only one hydrogen atom each. Thus,

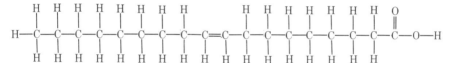

Oleic Acid

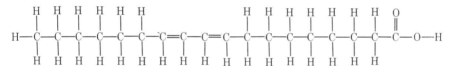

Linoleic Acid

The unsaturation in a given acid is always at a definite position in the carbon chain. If we count the carbon atoms beginning with that of the COOH group as 1, oleic acid is unsaturated in the 9-10 position; linoleic at 9-10 and 12-13; and linolenic at 9-10, 12-13, and 15-16. These 3 acids and stearic, the saturated one, all have 18 carbon atoms in the chain. Each differs from the others in many properties—the addition of hydrogen is only one example.

The names of the fatty acids are derived from the name of the fat from which they were first obtained. The first four acids in Table 11.1 are obtained mainly from milk fat. The second, third and fourth, Chevreul found in goat's butter, which accounts for the names derived from the Latin *capra*, a goat. All the first four acids are liquids and have the strong odor of rancid butter, a goat, or certain kinds of cheese for which they furnish the characteristic flavor; but when they are attached to glycerine they have very little odor of any kind.

The exact composition of fat from milk varies somewhat with the animal's feed, but if the acids in butterfat are separated from the glycerine they are in about the following proportions: butyric 3–4%, caproic 1.5–2%, caprylic 0.8–2%, capric 2–3%, lauric 3–5%, myristic 8.5–10%, palmitic 22–30%, stearic 7–12%, oleic 31–41%, linoleic 3–4.5%. Palmitic and oleic acids together make up about 60–70% of the total, and, in fact, these 2 acids are the principal ones in all the food fats.

The milk fats of most mammals contain several of the acids from butyric to lauric, that is, acids with 4 to 12 carbon atoms. The body fats of animals, on the other hand, and also the fats from botanical sources, seldom contain any of these low-carbon acids. Coconut oil is an exception to this last statement; it may yield: 8–9% caprylic, 4–7% capric, and 46–51% lauric. Some other seeds of the less common palm trees yield fats that contain these low-carbon acids. The vegetable fats of the temperate zone that appear in the food stores seldom contain any acid of lower molecular weight than palmitic. Oleic, linoleic, linolenic, and arachidonic acids are liquids while palmitic, stearic, and arachidic are solids—some stearic acid is used to make candles. In general, the glycerides of the liquid acids are liquids and those of the solid acids are solids. Consequently, the vegetable oils have a higher content of the unsaturated acids. Table 11.2 shows the approximate acid content of some of the food fats:

The difference in the acid composition of the fats affects their uses, their keeping quality, their behavior when heated, and several other physical and chemical properties. The composition makes little difference to the person who eats them, although some of the unsaturated acids have been found to be essential in the diet. These will be discussed in a later chapter.

In the fat, these acids are attached to glycerol and the compounds are called *glycerides*. If we were to make a glyceride in the laboratory, we would add a fatty acid to some glycerol, add a catalyst and heat the mixture. The equation would be basically this:

Glycerol   Butyric Acid   Glyceride   Water

TABLE 11.2

PRINCIPAL ACIDS OF SOME FATS AND OILS

	Myristic	Palmitic	Stearic	Oleic	Linoleic
Fats					
Beef fat	2.0	32.5	14.5	48.0	3.0
Butter	12.0	28.0	13.0	28.5	1.0
Chicken fat	7.0	25.0	6.0	36.0	14.0
Pork fat	1.7	25.5	13.7	50.2	8.9
Oils					
Corn	—	7.8	3.5	46.3	41.8
Cottonseed	—	20.2	2.0	35.2	41.7
Olive	0.5	9.5	7.5	82.3	5.5
Peanut	—	11.5	3.0	55.0	26.0
Safflower seed	—	4.2	2.0	26.3	67.4
Soybean	—	11.5	4.0	24.5	33.0

I have shown in the equation only one of the three hydroxyl groups of the glycerol; this would make a *monoglyceride*. Another acid molecule would make a *diglyceride* and still another would make a trilgyceride. Mono- and diglycerides are used as emulsifiers (see Chap. 8) but those of the natural fats are the triglycerides. If we used only one kind of acid in our laboratory experiment, the product would be a *simple* glyceride; but if we used two or three kinds of acid the glycerides would be *mixed*. Nature uses a mixture and so the natural fats are mixtures of mixed glycerides.

Some glycerides are solids and some are liquids at room temperature, and that is why solid fats soften when warmed and do not melt sharply like ice. As the fat is warmed one glyceride after another melts as its melting point is reached until the last one is melted, and the fat becomes a liquid.

All the glycerides are digestible and all furnish the same amount of energy, 9 Cal/gm.

PROTEINS

The chemists of the 17th century had one procedure they never failed to apply to a natural product, destructive *distillation*. They put the product into a metal or an earthenware retort, sealed it, heated it gradually, and collected any liquid that came out of a tube attached to the retort. They hoped to find a valuable drug among the products. They always obtained water, sometimes an oily liquid, and always a gas, usually methane CH_4, ammonia NH_3, or some sulfur compound. They seldom collected the gases and all they learned about them was their odor. All the natural substances left a residue of charcoal, and so it became general knowledge that all animals and plants contain carbon—that is, after it was discovered that charcoal is carbon.

Animal and plant products give a different odor when they burn; the difference is easier to demonstrate than describe. Burn a piece of paper or a splint of wood and note the odor. Then do the same with a feather, a hair, or a bit of wool. The difference will be remembered without the benefit of any notes. The animal odor is that of the blacksmith shop so familiar to earlier generations.

Back in the 18th century the difference in odor came to be a test for a plant and animal substances. Then somebody happened to test beans and got the animal odor, and so it became common to say that beans, peas, and some other seeds contain animal substances.

In his *Natural History*, Pliny (23–79) calls the white of egg, *albumen* from the Latin word for white. Egg white is an animal substance, and so those substances that gave the animal odor came to be known as *albuminous* substances. The term is a description rather than a name, but it was not until 1838 that these substances got a real name. Gerardus Johannes Mulder (1802–1888), Professor of Chemistry at the University of Rotterdam, analyzed several albuminous substances and coined the word *protein* for them; proteins they have been ever since.

The first protein to be prepared in rather pure form was gelatin, which was made by boiling bones or meat in water. Chemist after chemist continued to explore the plants and animals for proteins well into the 19th century and finally concluded that there is no living matter that does not contain protein.

While chemists were searching plants and animals for proteins, a few of them became curious about their chemical nature. The first to report the outcome of such curiosity was one of the most famous chemists of his day and a friend of Napoleon, Claude Louis Berthollet (1748–1822), who made a thorough study of ammonia gas, shown by Scheele to be a compound of nitrogen and hydrogen.

In 1811 Berthollet heated a weighed sample of dried meat in a retort and collected the ammonia and measured it. Then he repeated the experiment with dried cheese and found that the same weight of the cheese gave more ammonia than the meat did. This work settled two questions: proteins contain nitrogen, and not all proteins are alike. His experiment was used by him and others for many years to show that proteins from different sources are different.

The next clue to the structure of the proteins came in 1820 when Henri Braconnet (1781–1855) began to examine them. He had previously discovered that when sawdust, straw, and some other plant materials are boiled with dilute sulfuric acid they are converted into glucose. He tried the method on the proteins by dissolving some gelatin in dilute acid and boiling the solution for 20 hr. He then removed the acid and evaporated the solution. White crystals separated out as the water evaporated. He collected and examined them. They tasted sweet, and so he naturally called them "sugar of gelatin." But he himself soon exploded this idea for he tried to ferment a solution of them with yeast and they did not ferment. When he burned them they gave the animal odor and when he rubbed them with a strong alkali they gave off the odor of ammonia. They were obviously not crystals of sugar, and so the name was changed to *glycine*, derived from a Greek word that means "sweet."

Braconnet next tried boiling wool in dilute acid and got some crystals, which gave the burning test for protein but were not sweet. He named the substance *leucine* from the Greek word for "white."

No further information was forthcoming as to the nature of proteins until 1846 when the German chemist, Liebig, boiled cheese curds with acid and got some crystals. They were different from those Braconnet had gotten from either gelatin or from wool, and he named them *tyrosine* from the Greek word for cheese.

Glycine from gelatin, leucine from wool, and tyrosine from cheese indicated that the proteins differ from each other and appear to be complicated substances. Some had been known to contain sulfur ever since Scheele had found it in milk and egg protein back in the 18th century. He identified the sulfur by the fact that it tarnished silver—every housewife knows these proteins are good at that.

Progress in learning the chemical nature of the proteins was slow, but in the latter half of the 19th century they received a lot of attention. First, the chemists tried to purify the proteins they got from seeds or other sources. They found that some were soluble in water, some did not dissolve in water but did dissolve in dilute acids, some dissolved in alcohol and some in salt solutions. These differences in solubility helped in the separation of proteins from starch and from each other. Wheat, milk, eggs, blood, and some other natural products were found to contain two or more proteins.

In 1883 Johan G. T. C. Kjeldahl (1849-1900), a Danish chemist, was employed by a brewer to study the carbohydrates and proteins in the grains used to make beer. He found the method used for the determination of nitrogen at that time too slow for his purpose and invented a better one. He did so well that the Kjeldahl method, with a few changes in detail, is still used by chemists everywhere to find the amount of nitrogen in foods.

The analysis of proteins for nitrogen revealed a variation from about 15 to 18% with an average value of 16%. Although the nitrogen determination showed that proteins are different, it was no help in discovering why or how they differ. So the chemists turned their attention to the glycine, leucine, and tyrosine, obtained by earlier chemists from different proteins. Every few years chemists found other substances similar to those 3, until by 1935 the number had grown to 22.

While the list of these compounds from different proteins was growing, chemists were busy examining the nature of the individual substances. They all turned out to be amino acids. Glycine, the first one to be discovered, is the simplest of the lot; but it was not until 1846 that the German chemist, Emil Fischer, determined its structure. The structure of the others soon followed. The two discovered first have the following structures:

Glycine

Leucine

Organic chemists call any compound with a COOH group an acid and any with an NH_2 group an amine because of the similarity of the group to ammonia, NH_3. Consequently, any compound with one or more of each of these groups is an *amino acid*.

To determine the structure of these 22 amino acids was a big job, but chemists now have formulas for each of them. They all have one acid and one amino group, and some of them are very complicated in structure.

After the general nature of the amino acids was settled, the next problem to be solved was the manner in which they are joined together in the natural proteins. Shortly after 1900, Emil Fischer, who was working on the structure of the amino acids, began to find the answer to the question. An enormous amount of work by Fischer and others showed that the usual protein from any food contains at least 18 different acids.

It soon became clear that there are many proteins. Fischer devised methods for the determination of the several amino acids and with these it was soon found that the acids occur in different proportions even when the same ones are present. For example, suppose you had chain links of 22 different colors and an unlimited number of each color; the number of different chains you could make would be countless. You could make straight chains or branched chains; you could omit one or more colors; you could vary the number of each color used; you could put the colors together in an infinite number of different orders. The proteins are the chains, and the links are the amino acids.

How do the links join together? The amino acids join in different ways, but the principle union is formed by the elimination of water between the NH_2 group of one molecule and the COOH group of another. Take two molecules, for example:

$$H-N-C-C-O-H + H-N-C-C-O-H =$$

$$H-N-C-C-N-C-C-OH + H_2O$$

| Glycine | Glycine | Glycylglycine |

The OH and H inside the square drop out and combine to form water. A O H union is formed, which is called an amide group.

$$-C-N-$$

The new compound still has an NH_2 group at one end and a COOH group at the other, so the chain can go on and on indefinitely in either direction by the addition of more glycine units or any or all of the other 21 acids. Some of the acids, such as cystine, have two or more of one or both functional groups, and when one of these acids is included in the chain, a branch can form.

Plants are excellent chemists. They are able to use any compound that contains nitrogen and that will dissolve in water so the plant can absorb it. Farmers help their crops by supplying sodium nitrate, $NaNO_3$, urea, $CO(NH_2)_2$, ammonium sulfate, $(NH_4)_2SO_4$, or some other simple compound of nitrogen; the plant does the rest. In three months a bean vine absorbs water, a nitrogen compound from the soil, and carbon dioxide from the air and makes several ounces of first class protein, although the air contains only 0.04% carbon dioxide. Give the world's best chemist all the carbon dioxide, water, and sodium nitrate he wants, and he can make a little protein of a sort, but it would take him years to do it. Some of the plants pick up a bit of sulfur or phosphorus or both from the soil to make the kind of protein they fancy. The leaves, roots, fruits, and seeds of a plant all contain a different kind of protein. Likewise the nerves, muscles, skin, and milk of the mammals all contain a different protein, or several different ones. In fact, it seems no two people have the same tissue proteins except identical twins.

No animal does as well as the plants—none can use water, carbon dioxide, and salts of nitrogen to make proteins. Animals must have amino acids to start with or proteins that they can digest to amino acids, which are absorbed into the blood stream as such. Each tissue, then, takes whatever acids it needs to form its own particular protein, and if any are left over they are oxidized to supply energy. A young growing body needs a lot of these acids for construction purposes, and an adult also needs some for repairs, because tissues wear out. If the acids left over are more than enough to supply the energy needed, the excess is converted into fat and stored for future energy needs. This is another process that a chemist can carry out within his body but not outside it—*in vivo* but not *in vitro* as the scientists put it. To convert amino acids into fat *in vitro* should win a Nobel prize for anybody.

As you can see, we animals are absolutely dependent on plants for all our food except salt, water, and a few other mineral substances of which we need very little.

CHAPTER 12

Digestion

Very little natural food can serve as nourishment just as it is; glucose is about the only natural substance that can. While the chemists were trying to find what foods are made of, the physiologists were trying to learn just what food must be to be used as nourishment. The wood of a tree, the straw of wheat, the stringy fibers of celery are all useless in their original farm, as the physiologists soon found. But the chemists learned that the hard and stiff parts of plants are cellulose, or some similar substance. In 1819 Professor Braconnet discovered these substances became glucose if boiled with dilute sulfuric acid. Up to now, we have not had to resort to sugar from straw or sawdust, but the time may come.

The physiologists ignored cellulose as food and spent their efforts on what happens to starch, fats, and proteins after they are eaten. The chemists had learned that sugar from the cane and beet is different from that of the grape or milk, but any of them would serve as food. They also learned that apparently all plant proteins are foodstuffs, but the same cannot be said for the animal proteins. Hair, wool, silk, fur, hooves, horns, skin, cartilage, and fingernails are all proteins but not foodstuffs, although one often sees someone nibbling at the last item on the list.

It soon became evident to the physiologists that foodstuffs must undergo enormous changes in the human body, because the body tissues are profoundly different from the foodstuffs that nourish them. There is very little carbohydrate in the animal body, and human fat is not much like either the vegetable fats or milkfat. Certainly the hair, skin, and muscles bear little resemblance to the proteins of eggs, milk, or wheat.

The word food is used loosely to designate anything edible whether it is a natural product such as wheat, fish, or potatoes; a partially processed product such as flour; or viands for the table such as an apple pie. If it is edible it is food regardless of what must be done to it before it is eaten. Because of this uncertainty of meaning, the nutritionists use the word *foodstuffs* for those portions of the foods the body can use, mainly the carbohydrates, fats, and proteins.

Claudius Galen (A.D. 130–200), a famous Greek physician, wondered what happens to food in the body and made some experiments with hogs to find out. He concluded that the stomach makes the food into particles small enough to pass through the walls of the intestines into the blood stream. He was not far wrong, but it was 15 centuries before anybody got further with the explanation.

A Frenchman with the elaborate name of René Antoine Ferchault de Réaumur (1683–1757), like most scientists of his day, was interested in a great variety of subjects. In 1751 he published a paper on digestion in birds. Some kinds of birds swallow berries, or even mice and other small animals, and after digestion throw up the seeds, bones, or other indigestible matter. This gave Réaumur an idea. He captured a kite, which is a large bird of the hawk family. He put meat and bones into short tubes closed at the ends with wire screens and fed them to the kite. After a period of time, the kite dutifully returned the tubes, and Réaumur found that part of the meat and some of the bones had been dissolved. He then put pieces of sponge into the tubes to absorb the digestive juice and succeeded in getting 4 cc (less than a teaspoonful) of the digestive fluid. A cloudy liquid that was acid, it tasted salty and bitter. He put a piece of meat into it and found that the meat was digested, but the liquid had no effect on starch.

About 25 years after Réaumur published the results of his experiments, a Scottish doctor published similar results from a study of human digestion. He found a showman who made his living swallowing pebbles, and had him swallow silver balls that were perforated and contained meats, cheese, vegetables, or cereal grains. When the balls had passed through the digestive tract and were recovered, he found that the meat, cheese, and most of the vegetables had been digested, but the whole grain cereals had not been affected.

An Indian by the name of Alexis St. Martin in northern New York state was wounded by a gunshot, and as a result he had a permanent opening in his stomach. His physician, William Beaumont, took advantage of this misfortune to study the digestive process for several years. Beaumont published the results in 1833, and although he had not learned much that was new, his unique opportunity of studying human digestion made a strong impression on the physiologists of this country and Europe.

In nearly a century after Réaumur had begun his study of digestion, physiologists had established the fact that meat and some vegetable material are digested in the stomach. It was not much information for so much work, but it was all they could learn until chemistry caught up with them. The English chemist, William Prout (1785–1850), had shown that the gastric juice contains hydrochloric acid, HCl. But what else there is in it and what happens to the food during digestion were still complete mysteries.

Anselm Payen (1805–1881) was a French chemist who manufactured inorganic chemicals and was the first to use bone-black in sugar refining. By 1835 he apparently tired of chemical industry and became Professor of Industrial and Agricultural chemistry at the School of Arts and Crafts in Paris. He was very active in research and published over one hundred papers; the most important ones were biochemical. He gave cellulose its name, and also discovered that cellulose and starch have the same empirical formula, $C_6H_{10}O_5$. He found that starches from different sources, such as wheat and potatoes, have the same chemical formula although the grains are of different sizes and shape. Probably, his most important work in biochemistry was reported in 1883 in a paper published jointly with Professor Persoz of the Strasbourg School of Pharmacy. They had added alcohol to a solution of malt extract and got a precipitate. They separated this precipitate from the solution, added some of it to a solution of boiled starch, and found it converted the starch to sugar. They proceeded to purify their precipitate until they got a product that would convert 2000 times its own weight of starch into sugar.

Biochemists were well aware that many chemical changes are caused by living organisms. Malt, for example, which changes starch to sugar, is sprouting barley. Then, after Payen and Persoz isolated their substance from malt, it became clear that such changes were not always caused by the life processes. To distinguish between the two processes, the living organisms were called *organized ferments* and the separate extracts *unorganized ferments*. These names soon became confusing because there were many instances in which nobody could be certain whether the vital process was necessary or not. Consequently, in 1878 the German physiologist, Willy Kuhne, coined the name *enzyme* for the active catalyst of these chemical changes.

Physiologists now tried to see how many enzymes they could separate from living matter that had already been found to cause chemical changes. Sprouting seeds, yeast, ripening fruits, the animal stomach, the pancreas, the small intestine, and many other plant and animal sources were searched for enzymes.

The biochemists were more concerned with the number and properties of the enzymes than they were with where they came from. Many years of research revealed the fact that they are catalysts made by plant or animal tissues to speed up whatever chemical processes that tissue has to perform. A simple illustration of this function is the activity of the enzymes in malt. The natural function of the barley seed is to produce a new barley plant. The seed contains the embryo of the new plant along with a lot of starch and protein to feed it. The starch and protein are insoluble in water so they will keep, but when the seed becomes moist it produces an enzyme to change these substances to something soluble. One enzyme changes the starch to sugar and another changes the proteins to amino acids. The embryo can now absorb these soluble materials and grows into a sprout, which begins to produce chlorophyll and leaves as soon as it reaches the light. The enzymes of the seed have now performed their function, and the chlorophyll takes over and catalyzes the combination of water and carbon dioxide to form the tissues of the growing plant.

Enzymes are specific; one that will convert starch to sugar will not affect protein at all, and vice versa. Each enzyme requires certain conditions, such as the presence of water, and some also require the presence of acid while others demand the absence of it. Each one has a favorite temperature at which it is most effective. A higher or lower temperature reduces its efficiency, and if the temperature is high enough it inactivates the enzyme entirely. The enzyme is simply cooked; that is, it is coagulated like the white of a boiled egg. This happens when food is blanched or cooked.

When chemists first began to recognize enzymes, they gave them arbitrary names, such as the *pepsin* of the gastric juice, the *ptyalin* of the saliva, and the *rennin* from the calves stomach. But chemists like to have the names of substances tell them something about the substance. For example, "salt" tells us nothing about that substance, but "sodium chloride" tells us what elements compose the substance and how much of each. For this reason the biochemists adopted a systematic nomenclature for the enzymes, and these names tell us as much as we can expect from one word. The names all end in *ase* and the stem of the word tells us the kind of reaction the enzyme catalyzes; the *amylases* catalyze the change of starch to sugar (Latin, *amylum*, starch), the *proteases* work on proteins, the *lipases* split fats and *sucrase* changes sucrose to simpler sugars. The enzymes frequently have a first name that tells where they come from, such as salivary amylase from the saliva or pancreatic amylase from the pancreas.

THE DIGESTIVE PROCESS

During the research on enzymes done by biochemists in the past 100 years, the human digestive tract naturally received its share of attention. As a result, we now have a clear picture of what happens to food after it enters the mouth.

It is common knowledge that if a solid is to react with a liquid in a reasonable length of time it must be mashed up or finely ground, because the action can take place only at the surface of the solid, and as I have pointed out (see Chap. 9), the smaller the particle the greater the surface. If anyone cares to demonstrate this idea all he needs to do is to put a chunk of rock candy into water and some fine sugar into the same amount of water at the same temperature; stir both of them and notice which dissolves the faster. This basic idea explains the first purpose of chewing. To swallow large chunks of fruit, meat or other solid food puts the stomach in the position of the water with the rock candy in it. In fact, I once knew a young woman who had an acute attack of indigestion. The doctor believed in heroic treatment and used a stomach pump. He brought up whole grapes she had swallowed the week before—she apparently ate like a duck.

When food approaches the mouth, or even when we wish it would, the salivary glands go into action—the mouth waters. The saliva contains an amylase, and the second reason for chewing is to mix the saliva with the starch of the food. Starch held in the mouth for several seconds begins to taste sweet, because the amylase changes it to the sugar, *maltose*. Nothing happens to the fats and proteins chemically in the mouth. All the food passes along to the stomach where the solid food is stored near the entrance while the amylase completes its job.

The mechanical action of the stomach moves the food forward where it meets the strongly acid gastric juice. The acidity stops the action of the amylase in case some is left that has not finished its task, and the pepsin of the stomach begins to digest the protein. As the protein digestion proceeds, the stomach contents become less acid, and by the time they are passed into the small intestine they are slightly alkaline.

In the small intestine, the food meets several enzymes, some from the pancreas and some from the walls of the intestine. Among them they complete the digestive process, for some are proteases, some lipases, and some amylases.

Each protein is different from all the others, and so we cannot write a formula. We might express their digestion by the following crude equation:

Protein + water + protease = 18 to 22 amino acids

Although the simplest formula for starch is $C_6H_{10}O_5$, the real formula is a large unknown multiple of this and is usually written $(C_6H_{10}O_5)_x$. When acids or enzymes act on a suspension of starch in water, the starch splits into several components of decreasing molecular weight of which the smallest is glucose. A few of these changes are shown by the following equation:

$$\underset{\text{Starch}}{(C_6H_{10}O_5)_x} + \underset{\text{Water}}{H_2O} = \underset{\text{Dextrin}}{(C_6H_{10}O_5)_y} + H_2O =$$

$$\underset{\text{Maltose}}{C_{12}H_{22}O_{11}} + H_2O = \underset{\text{Glucose}}{C_6H_{12}O_6}$$

Maltose is called a *disaccharide* because its molecule reacts with water to form two molecules of a simpler sugar, a *monosaccharide*. Sucrose and lactose are also disaccharides and in water that contains an acid or one of certain enzymes, their molecules split into two:

$$\underset{\text{Sucrose}}{C_{12}H_{22}O_{11}} + \underset{\text{Water}}{H_2O} = \underset{\text{Glucose}}{C_6H_{12}O_6} + \underset{\text{Fructose}}{C_6H_{12}O_6}$$

The equation for the digestion of lactose would be the same as that for sucrose, but the monosaccharides produced would be glucose and galactose. In summary then, the complete digestion of carbohydrates produces one or more of the monosaccharides: glucose, fructose, or galactose.

During digestion, the fats are split into glycerol and fatty acids, which vary with the fat digested. The following equation will serve as an example:

$$\underset{\substack{\text{Mixed}\\\text{Glyceride}}}{\begin{array}{l} CH_2OCOC_{15}H_{31} \\ | \\ CHOCOC_{17}H_{33} \\ | \\ CH_2OCOC_{17}H_{33} \end{array}} + \underset{\text{Water}}{3H_2O} = \underset{\text{Glycerol}}{\begin{array}{l} CH_2OH \\ | \\ CHOH \\ | \\ CH_2OH \end{array}} + \underset{\substack{\text{Palmitic}\\\text{Acid}}}{C_{15}H_{31}COOH} + \underset{\text{Oleic Acid}}{2C_{17}H_{33}COOH}$$

Notice that all digestion is a reaction of the foodstuff with water, or what the chemist calls a *hydrolysis*. As the digested food passes along the intestines it consists of 3 sugars, mostly glucose, about 20 amino acids, glycerol, and several fatty acids. Also present are salts and some other substances that were in the food, such as acids, chlorophyll, cholesterol, and vitamins. Such is the food as it passes through the intestinal wall into the blood stream to be distributed to the various tissues for growth, repair, or the production of energy.

Section IV

The Essentials of Nutrition

CHAPTER 13

What Must We Eat?

By the end of the 19th century the chemists had identified the carbohydrates, fats, and proteins as the main nutritive components of the natural foods, and had determined their chemical nature. Also research with both men and experimental animals had explained the digestive processes. The nutritional requirements had not fared so well.

Early in the century Francois Magendie (1783–1855) discovered that the nitrogen, which is such an important part of animal tissue, comes from the protein of the food and not from the nitrogen of the air. This profound discovery singled out the proteins for special attention from physiologists and chemists.

The carbohydrates and fats were looked upon merely as sources of energy, but since the muscles and organs of the body consist largely of protein, obviously protein must be supplied by the food. The physiologists made some efforts to determine the adequacy of certain proteins and the amount of protein required in the diet, but these problems remained unsolved. Such was the knowledge of nutrition at the beginning of the 20th century.

THE GELATIN PROBLEM

Meat is the most obvious source of protein. During the Napoleonic wars, meat was scarce in France, and the Academy of Sciences appointed a committee with Magendie as chairman to study the possibility of using gelatin as a substitute. Gelatin was made by boiling bones in water and was cheap. Apparently, all the committee did was to think about the problem and read such literature as they could find on the subject, for they reported very promptly that everybody knew that gelatin is the chief nutrient in broth and that writers on the subject consider gelatin the most nutritious of all animal matter.

The Academy was not satisfied with this report and appointed another committee with Magendie again as chairman. This time the committee did some experiments and took their time, for they did not report until 1841—30 years after their appointment. Their report extended beyond the merits of gelatin.

The committee found that dogs could not live on either sugar, fats, gelatin or egg white alone. They got along very well on bones, but not on gelatin even when bread was eaten with it. That answered the original question; meat could not be replaced by gelatin. The committee had five reasonably pure proteins to work with: gelatin, egg albumen, fibrin from blood, gluten from wheat, and zein from corn. The dogs could not live on the fibrin any better than on the gelatin. The Magendie Committee also tried combining gelatin, albumen, and fibrin and found some improvement, but the dogs did not thrive long on the combination. There was obviously more to a satisfactory diet than a single protein or even a few proteins.

NUTRITIONAL RESEARCH IN AGRICULTURE

The members of the Magendie committee were by no means the only students of nutrition in the early 19th century. As far back as 1802 Albrecht Daniel Thaer, a Court physician in Hanover, Germany, began agricultural experiments on his farm. His contribution to nutrition consisted largely of his finding that common farm animals, cattle, horses, and sheep, get along very well on well-cured hay with no other feed. He tried feeding experiments to determine the relative value of various kinds of feeds and reported that 10 lb of good hay are equal in feed value to 45 lb of wheat straw, 20 lb of potatoes, 52 lb of turnips, or 6 lb of wheat.

A French chemist, Jean Baptiste Boussingault (1802–1887), after several years in South America returned and married a woman who owned an interest in a large farm in Alsace. There he settled down and began experiments in agriculture. He reported his results at intervals from 1836 on. In 1839 he was appointed Professor of Chemistry at the Conservatory of Arts and Crafts in Paris. Thereafter, he alternated between his academic duties and agricultural experiments, ultimately becoming one of the outstanding chemists of his day.

Among Boussingault's discoveries was the fact that alfalfa and red clover can make protein from the nitrogen of the air, but wheat and oats cannot. In the course of the next half century other investigators extended this finding of Boussingault's to include the other plants of the pulse family, such as lentils and the various kinds of peas and beans as protein makers.

Boussingault also discovered that iodine is a cure for one type of goiter, but his greatest contribution to our knowledge of human nutrition was the discovery that certain mineral substances are essential in the diet and that the failure of an animal to thrive on a single foodstuff, or even a single food, may be due to the animal's inability to eat enough of it to meet its energy requirements. These two ideas gave the experimenters something to consider when they planned their feeding experiments. It began to appear that learning the facts about nutrition is rather complicated.

Other contributors to our knowledge of nutrition were John Bennett Lawes (1814–1900) and Joseph Henry Gilbert (1817–1901) at the Rothamstead Experiment Station in England. For the first 10 or 15 years the Rothamstead scientists explored the subjects of fertilizers and plant growth. Then, about 1850 they began to publish the results of their animal feeding experiments. Their interest, of course, was in the farmer's problems: What is the best kind of feed for the animals? Would it be more profitable to eat or sell grains and certain vegetables, or should they be fed to the cattle, sheep, or hogs? Should these animals then be eaten or sold? Lawes and Gilbert used 349 sheep and 80 hogs for their experiments. Between 1850 and 1860 they reported that a sheep gained 8 or 9 lb for every 100 lb of mixed feed eaten and that hogs gained 17 lb for every 100 lb of feed eaten.

Since animals, at best, are poor converters of their feed to meat, only those countries with plenty of grazing land can afford the luxury of much meat. This fact is substantiated by the annual consumption of meat in various countries. In pounds per capita these are: New Zealand 222, Argentina and Australia 211, United States 182, Canada 156, Netherlands 107, Italy 72, Spain 65, and Japan 20.

Lawes and Gilbert made at least one direct contribution to human nutrition. They exploded the theory, widely believed at the time, that protein is the foodstuff required for muscular activity. They found that proteins are not even as good as the fats and carbohydrates.

Agricultural research has received a lot of attention through the years. The United States government now maintains several laboratories for the purpose and every State has at least one. Their combined contributions to our knowledge of food and nutrition have been enormous, for they soon began to apply research discoveries to man.

THE PROTEIN PROBLEM

About 1870, Carl Voit (1831–1908), Professor of Physiology at the University of Munich, attacked the protein problem. He fed proteins to dogs, but paid more attention to the other features of the diet than his predecessors had done, because he had the feeding experiments of Boussingault to guide him. He found that gelatin can replace part of the protein in the diet but not all of it. This still left an unanswered question: Why is gelatin an inadequate source of protein? Since Voit's time several investigators have wrestled with the problem; a German in 1884, another in 1885, an American in 1907, and finally an American research group in 1928. The best opinion now is that gelatin lacks certain amino acids and has a short supply of some others. These deficiencies keep gelatin out of the list of proteins that are nutritionally complete.

As the 19th century ended, biochemists were busy isolating pure proteins from natural sources. One of the most active of these investigators was Thomas Burr Osborne (1850–1920) of the Connecticut Experiment Station at New Haven. For 25 years, beginning about 1890, Dr. Osborne isolated proteins from cereals, beans, peas, nuts, and the seeds and leaves of many other plants; toward the end of his work he isolated several proteins from animal sources also.

Osborne purified the proteins as well as he could and analyzed them for the elements they contain, namely, carbon, hydrogen, nitrogen, sulfur, phosphorus, and iron. In a list of about a dozen proteins, the nitrogen varied from 15.5% in egg albumen to 18.0% in legumin from beans. Also, the sulfur varied from 0.4% in legumin to 1.7% in the lactalbumen of milk. Phosphorus constituted less than 1% of the ovovitellin of eggs. Only oxyhemoglobin of the blood contained iron, and that only 0.34%. These analyses showed beyond doubt that proteins differ in composition and indicated that there is an enormous number of them. They are different when they come from related sources such as wheat and barley; and even when they come from the same source, such as the two in a grain of wheat.

Analysis for the chemical elements did not throw much light on the chemical nature of the proteins except to show that in addition to the usual carbon, hydrogen, nitrogen, and oxygen, some of them also contain sulfur, phosphorus, or iron

Seventeen amino acids had been discovered by 1902, and Emil Fischer had devised methods for the determination of each of them in a protein. Osborne was quick to apply Fischer's analytical methods and to improve some of them. With this new tool he determined the amino acid content of his purified proteins, which indicated the differences between them much better than the analysis for the elements did.

It then seemed that the amino acid content of a protein must have something to do with its usefulness in nutrition, and so in 1909 Osborne joined forces with Professor Lafayette Mendel (1872–1935) of Yale to clear up the question of the importance of the amino acid content of the proteins by feeding them to rats. They published their results in 1911. The first problem had been finding a diet on which rats would grow and live normally. They succeeded only when they removed all the protein from milk and used the resulting whey as a source of the mineral elements. At this time no mixture of pure salts of calcium, iron, and the other minerals known to be essential had been satisfactory.

After a suitable diet had been found for the growth and general welfare of the rats, Osborne and Mendel began feeding the purified proteins, one at a time, to test their adequacy in nutrition. They found that casein or lactalbumen from milk, egg albumen, and edestin from hempseed were complete proteins; that is, the one protein supplied all the nitrogen requirement of the rats. On the other hand, zein from corn and gliadin from wheat were incomplete: the rats did not thrive on them alone. These incomplete proteins do not contain all the essential amino acids, and when lysine, histidine, and tryptophane were added, the protein content of the diet became satisfactory.

For the first 15 years of the present century, amino acids and incomplete proteins were the hottest topic of nutritional research. The most noteworthy experimenter in the field was Professor William Cumming Rose of the University of Illinois. Dr. Rose had done his graduate work at Yale and had his training in nutrition in Mendel's laboratory. He received the Ph.D. degree in 1911. After graduation he continued his research on amino acids and proteins. By 1935 he had solved the principal problems in protein nutrition.

Rose studied the need for the various amino acids in the diet by including the pure acids in diets that were otherwise adequate and studied the effects on both experimental animals and healthy young men. He and his associates discovered that the amino acid requirements are not the same for all species; rats, pigs, chickens, and men have somewhat different requirements.

By 1922 21 amino acids had been isolated from proteins, but Rose discovered that there was at least one more and that it was essential in nutrition. Not dismayed by this stumbling block, he isolated the new acid, purified it, and determined its formula by some of the most brilliant research in organic and biochemistry. He named the new acid *threonine*.

Professor Rose next determined which of the 22 amino acids are essential to the human diet. All of them are present in the body tissues, but the body can make some of them from others. However, Rose's work with young men showed that the following acids must be present in the food: leucine, isoleucine, lysine, methionine, phenylalanine, threonine, tryptophane, and valine. In addition to

TABLE 13.1
PROTEIN-INTAKE RECOMMENDATIONS OF THE
FOOD AND NUTRITION BOARD

	Age	Amt Daily, Gm
Children	1–3	25
	3–6	30
	6–8	35
	8–10	40
Males	10–14	45
	14–22	60
	22–75	65
Females[1]	10–14	50
	14–22	55
	22–75	55

[1] Pregnant women and nursing mothers need 10 to 20 gm more than indicated allowance.

these eight acids, histidine is required during the growing period by all the experimental animals studied.

The work of Rose and his associates cleared up the nature of the protein requirement and why proteins have different nutritional effects. Why proteins differ in nutritional value has been settled at last.

The amino acid requirements of women and infants have since been determined, and something has been learned of the amount of these acids required. Also the amino acid content of the proteins of several foods is known, but the Food and Nutrition Board (FNB) makes no recommendation of the quantity of any amino acid required. The solution of the dietary problem at present is to include a variety of foods in the diet. Milk and eggs are probably the most reliable sources of complete proteins.

Biochemists have been busy for over a century trying to determine how much protein must be included in the daily diet. Through the years the conclusions have varied from 40 to 200 gm a day. The early experimenters did not know that the proteins differed in nutritional value nor that the requirement varies with age, sex, whether the subject is fat or lean, the amount of fat and carbohydrate in the diet, and other factors. Despite all the difficulties, the FNB has reviewed the results of many experiments and makes recommendations for the daily diet, shown in Table 13.1.

It is almost impossible to get enough protein with a purely vegetarian diet; the chief characteristic of the following list of foods is that those high in protein are all from animal sources. The figures in the list are percentages, but if we consider the usual 100-gm portion, they become grams of protein.

High Protein—12 to 25%

Dried beans, macaroni, noodles, oatmeal (dry), cheese (blue, brick, camembert, cheddar, cottage), cocoa, eggs, fish, lentils, meats (except bacon), crabmeat, nuts, scallops, shrimp, spaghetti, turkey, wheat flour.

Medium Protein—6 to 12%

Green lima beans, breads, corn grits, rice, cream cheese, clams, bacon, pecans, oysters, pancakes, popcorn.

Low Protein—1 to 6%

Artichokes, asparagus, avocados, bananas, snap beans, beets, beet greens, broccoli, Brussels sprouts, buttermilk, cabbage, cauliflower, coconut, collards, sweet corn, cream, eggplant, figs, ice cream, kale, lettuce, milk, mushrooms, okra, olives, onions, oranges, parsnips, canned peas, potatoes, dried prunes, pumpkin, radishes, raisins, spinach, sweet potatoes, tomatoes, turnip greens, yogurt.

Very Low Protein—Under 1%

Apples, apricots, blackberries, blueberries, butter, cantaloupe, carrots, celery, cucumbers, grapefruit, honey, jellies, lemons, peaches, pears, pineapple, plums, strawberries, tangerines, watermelon.

NONPROTEIN FOODS

During the 19th century the carbohydrates and fats were studied for their energy value, but nobody seemed to worry about their importance in the diet for any other purpose. In fact such information accumulated gradually from the study of the proteins. Someone discovered that experimental animals do not thrive on a purely protein diet. Rats were found to have a shorter life on a diet that contained 26% protein than on one that contained only 10% protein.

The amount of carbohydrate and fat we eat is a matter of habit and varies widely from person to person. The average citizen of the temperate regions is likely to get 10% of his calories from protein, 24% from fat and 66% from carbohydrates. However, a survey made in the United States in 1955 revealed the astonishing fact that fats accounted for 44% of our caloric intake. Proteins are the most expensive and carbohydrates are the cheapest.

When a mixture of foods is eaten and digested, the intestines contain amino acids, fatty acids, glycerol and the sugars, glucose, fructose, and galactose. All these substances are carried to the liver by the portal vein. The liver changes some or all of them to glucose and to *glycogen*. Glycogen is the compound by which energy is stored temporarily. A white powder much like starch, it is stored in the liver and in the muscles.

The normal glucose content of the blood is 0.1%. As the glucose from a recent meal drops below this level, the glycogen splits into glucose, which enters the blood stream to maintain the supply of energy. When the glycogen is used up we are likely to feel weak or chilly because other fuel is supplied more slowly. As one of my students explained it, glycogen is to keep us from starving between meals.

Glucose is obviously the most important carbohydrate. In fact it appears to be indispensable, for when the diet does not supply it, the body makes it out of the digestive products of the fats, proteins, or other carbohydrates.

THE SPECIAL ROLES OF FAT

Hilaire Marie Rouelle (1718–1788) discovered that fats are soluble in chloroform, ether, and benzene, a discovery which resulted in an analytical method for the determination of the amount of fat in food. The method is very simple. A sample of the food is weighed, dried, and extracted with several portions of ether. The portions of ether are combined and filtered through a porous paper to remove any particles of the solid food that may be floating about in it. The filtrate is caught in a weighed dish and the ether allowed to evaporate, which it does very rapidly. When the ether has all escaped, the dish is weighed again. The gain in weight is the weight of the fat that was in the food sample, and since the weight of the sample is known, the percentage of fat is easily calculated.

In 1843 a controversy arose that is hard to understand in view of the ease with which fats could be determined. The French chemists held that cows get enough fat from their food to account for both the fat of the milk and their body fat. Liebig and his followers in Germany insisted that the animals made some of this fat from the carbohydrates in their feed. When it was so easy to determine how much fat there is in the feed, one wonders why the argument went on so long. Of course it would be difficult to determine how much body fat the animal stored, but a diet of hay or grain would not contain as much fat as there is in the milk alone. After the middle of the century, Boussingault, Lawes, and Gilbert, and several other chemists established beyond a doubt that farm animals produce both body fat and milk fat from the carbohydrates in the feed. Countless experiments in the last 100 years have shown that we of the human species do likewise.

After the "carbohydrate to fat" question was settled, the nutritionists turned their attention to the energy value of the foodstuffs. A gram of carbohydrate or protein was found to supply 4 Cal, but a gram of fat supplies 9. This is obviously why nature chose fat for the storage of energy in the body; it takes up only half as much room as either of the other foodstuffs.

The dietitions were interested in how much fat to include in the diet, which meant that all the common foods had to be analyzed for their fat content so that the dietition would know how much fat she was adding in a pint of cream, an egg, or a serving of beans. Pure fats rarely appear on the dinner table since the cruets of oil and vinegar for use on salads became less common. Butter and margarine are the most nearly pure fats, and they are only 80% fat. Since the body can make its own fat, the biochemists paid no attention to the question of whether or not one fat was as good as another in nutrition.

The nutritionist divides the fat of the diet into "visible" and "invisible" fat. In the first class are: butter, margarine, cooking oils, and shortening. The per capita consumption of these fats in the United States in 1970 was: butter 5.3 lb, margarine 11.0, lard 4.6, shortening 17.3, and salad and cooking oils 18.2 for a total of 53.2 lb of fat.

It is difficult to know how much invisible fat there is in the American diet, but it appears to equal the visible fat or even to exceed it. The invisible fat is that of the natural foods. Meat bought in the market contains considerable fat, although the cook may remove some of it or it may be left uneaten on the plate.

All fish contain fat although the cod and red snapper contain less than 1%. Mackerel contain 12%, pompano 9.5%, mullet 6.9%, canned salmon 6 to 12% according to variety, and canned tuna 3 to 4% unless it is canned in oil.

Foods of plant origin seldom contain as much as 1% fat, but there are 3 notable exceptions to this statement: avocados, nuts, and olives. Avocados contain from 11 to 16%. Nuts vary from one kind to another but most of them contain from 50 to 70% fat. Olives vary from 12% in the green variety to 35% in the ripe ones.

Such are the fats we eat. Why do we eat them? I suppose the chief reason is because we like them. Fried foods, in general, are more palatable than the same foods boiled. Shortening in cakes and pastry is a must, and butter, margarine, and olive oil are extensively used in cooking. Then there is the melted butter on sea food; Hollandaise and cream sauces garnish vegetables; salad dressings invariably contain a liberal supply of some vegetable oil.

Another reason for eating fats besides palatability is the feeling of comfort and satiety they provide. Fats are digested more slowly than the other foodstuffs, and therefore they delay hunger pangs longer.

IMPORTANCE OF UNSATURATED FATS

In 1929 Professor George Oswald Burr and his associates at the University of Minnesota published a paper that opened up a new line of thought on the subject of fats; it announced that fats are essential in the diet of the rat. Rats were fed a diet without any fat in it and they grew more slowly than those on a complete diet. Furthermore, they developed a severe skin disease and died. When a little lard was added to the diet, the rats started to grow immediately and recovered from the skin disease.

The discovery that fats are essential in the animal diet raised a number of questions and the Burr group undertook to answer them. By 1930 they were able to report that only the unsaturated fats promoted the growth of the rats and prevented or cured the skin disease.

Other information was immediately forthcoming from Minnesota and elsewhere. The experimenters soon found that linoleic and arachidonic acids were the effective ones. The body can make the saturated fatty acids and also oleic from carbohydrates, but cannot make linoleic. The really essential acid is the arachidonic, but the body can make it from linoleic if there is any of that acid in the diet. All this had been learned by 1938.

Oleic acid has the same carbon chain as stearic but it has one double bond in the formula, which means that it has two hydrogen atoms less than stearic; its formula is $C_{17}H_{33}COOH$. It is called *monounsaturated* because it has just one double bond. Linoleic acid $C_{17}H_{31}COOH$, has two double bonds along the chain and therefore lacks four hydrogen atoms of a full complement. Linolenic acid, $C_{17}H_{29}COOH$, has three double bonds. Arachidonic acid, $C_{19}H_{33}$-COOH, bears the same relation to arachidic that linolenic does to stearic because it lacks six hydrogen atoms. All these acids with more than one double bond are what the biochemists call *polyunsaturated* acids.

All the early research on the fatty acid requirements was done with rats or other small animals, but it was not long before the investigators began to wonder about the fat requirement of the human species. The proper diet for infants has always been a problem. Some fail to thrive on cow's milk and others cannot tolerate it at all; therefore goat's milk, soybean milk and skim milk have all been substituted with varying success. But Dr. Burr and his Minnesota group found that infants on a skim milk diet develop skin infections that can be cured by adding some polyunsaturated fats to the diet. The subject was followed up at the University of Minnesota and elsewhere and the necessity for these acids in the infant diet was fully established. This conclusion is supported by the fact that human milk fat contains arachidonic acid and seven times as much linoleic as cow's milk fat.

CHOLESTEROL

By 1950 some investigators found that the polyunsaturated acids influence the amount of cholesterol in the blood. Cholesterol is a white, solid alcohol with the empirical formula, $C_{27}H_{45}OH$, and its 27 carbon atoms are linked together in a very complicated pattern. It is insoluble in water and something like candle wax in consistency. In fact it melts at 300°F, which is a high temperature when we recall that body temperature is 98.6° and the boiling point of water is 212°F.

Cholesterol was discovered in gall stones back in the 18th century, and then in 1814 Chevreul found it in animal fats. Probably all animal fats contain some of it and the body makes it from the fatty acids.

Cholesterol is a normal constituent of the animal body. Infants have 50 to 100 mg in 100 cc of blood; children 3 to 14 have about 180 mg and adults somewhere around 240 mg, but the exact amount depends on age, diet, exercise, and some other factors. The function of cholesterol in the body is not known, but it is present in nerve tissue and so it is apparently essential.

About the year 1940 diseases of the heart and arteries became the subject of extensive research. Atherosclerosis is a disease which causes the inner walls of the arteries to thicken and harden because of cholesterol deposits. The past 25 years of intensive research have not answered all the questions about diseases of the circulatory system although some points have been established. Much of the research has been statistical in nature, for example, men with coronary artery heart disease have blood cholesterol 50 to 100 mg above normal. One research group found that populations with high rates of coronary heart disease also had abnormal amounts of cholesterol in the blood. Two other groups found a correlation between the amount of fat in the diet and disease of the arteries.

In 1950 a research report announced that the polyunsaturated fatty acids will lower the amount of cholesterol in the blood. This announcement created a great furor, because the public at once assumed a cure for diseased hearts and arteries had been discovered. But it has not been proved that high blood cholesterol causes these diseases or that lowering it will cure them. High blood cholesterol may cause these diseases, and then again, the diseases or something else may cause the high cholesterol. Statistical data are only circumstantial evidence.

The correlation between the amount of fat in the diet and atherosclerosis has not been definitely established, but all the evidence indicates that low fat content is desirable and that unsaturated fats are preferable to saturated ones. A recent investigator has pointed out that the deposits that clog the arteries are only half cholesterol; the other half is fat. Some English scientists have shown that stress, aggressiveness, and smoking cause increased pulse beat and increased blood pressure, as well as an increased secretion of adrenalin. Increased adrenalin in turn causes an increase of sugar and fat in the blood, and since these are not consumed as energy, they are deposited as fat and cholesterol. The fact that exercise seems to lower our chances of atherosclerosis indicates that the English scientist's theory may be correct.

The amount of cholesterol in the common foods is so small compared to the amount the body makes from fat that most scientists think it is of little importance. Physicians, however, are inclined to warn against it, just to be on the safe side. The amount of unsaturated fats is important although there is no occasion to panic over them. The exact amount of these acids needed is unknown, but it is apparently very small. They occur in practically all fats of plant origin and some of the animal fats. Beef fat and butter are the mostly highly saturated of the common food fats and anyone with a personal interest in the matter should go easy with them and keep the total amount of fat eaten well below the American average of 100 lb of fat a year.

The determination of which acids are present in a fat and how much of each is a long and difficult procedure. Furthermore, before the work of Burr became widely known, there was not much reason for making such an analysis. Consequently, the polyunsaturated acid content of very few of the hundreds of fats is known. The common salad oils on the market contain the following percentages of the polyunsaturated fatty acids: safflower 72, corn 53, soybean 52, cottonseed 50, sesame 42, peanut 29, and olive 7%.

CHAPTER 14

Essential Minerals

There are 88 chemical elements in the crust of the earth: in the atmosphere, the natural waters, and the solid earth to the depth that man has penetrated. Likewise, all the plant and animal life from the smallest bacterium to the elephant is composed of some of these elements. Table 14.1 shows the composition of the human body. In addition to the 12 elements shown in Table 14.1 there are slight traces of copper, iodine, cobalt, zinc, and fluorine.

The most abundant elements in the human body, carbon, hydrogen, oxygen, and nitrogen, are the same elements that are most abundant in all other plant and animal life. Since the word "organism" covers all plants and animals, chemists usually think of these as the organic elements. Their importance in nutrition has been discussed under their compounds: the carbohydrates, fats, and proteins.

Nutritionists usually call the other elements inorganic, and since they occur in nature as minerals, they are often called the "mineral elements."

Toward the end of the 18th century, a Swedish analytical chemist found that bones contain calcium phosphate, but the announcement did not bring forth any chemists or biologists to study the need for these elements in the diet.

In 1776 a French chemist reported that the blood contains sodium, potassium, and calcium. An English physician discovered in 1791 that birds must have calcium to make calcium carbonate for egg shells.

By the 1840s research on the mineral elements of the body was in full swing. In 1847 Boussingault had shown by experiment that oxen must have salt. Liebig was able to announce in 1850 that blood contains sodium phosphate, and that other body fluids contain potassium, iron, and magnesium phosphates. Also in 1850 Professor Heinrich Rose of the University of Berlin published the mineral content of blood, horse flesh, cows' milk, egg yolk, ox bile, and urine.

Although the 1840s saw much active research on the mineral content of the body tissues, it was another 30 years before chemists began to study the need for these elements in the diet. By 1879 one

164

TABLE 14.1
BODY COMPOSITION

Element	%	Element	%
Oxygen	65.0	Sulfur	0.25
Carbon	18.0	Sodium	0.20
Hydrogen	10.2	Chlorine	0.15
Nitrogen	3.0	Magnesium	0.05
Calcium	2.0	Iron	0.004
Phosphorus	1.0	Manganese	0.001

chemist had shown that calcium is required for the coagulation of blood, a discovery of the utmost importance in surgery ever since.

From the 1870s to the present, many chemists have contributed to our knowledge of the roles of the various mineral elements in nutrition. Space does not permit us to follow the individual discoveries, and so I shall just report the present state of our knowledge of the subject. In some cases this knowledge is the result of a total of many years of work by many chemists. The determination of the importance of an element in the diet is not an easy task.

CALCIUM

Calcium is the most abundant mineral in the body. The average man contains over 2.5 lb of it of which 99% is in the bones and teeth. These hard tissues are a kind of calcium phosphate called hydroxyapatite with the rather complex formula, $Ca_{10}(PO_4)_6(OH)_2$.

Bones are not dead matter like the bark of a tree, but contain some protein and continually exchange mineral matter with the blood from birth to death. That bones are active tissue is widely known—a broken bone soon heals. Changes in teeth take place much more slowly than in bones.

The amount of calcium in blood is about 10 mg in each 100 cc of blood when the adult human body is in calcium balance; that is, when the amount excreted is the same as that in the food eaten. This is only 1 part of calcium in 10,000 parts of blood, but it serves several purposes; it controls the texture of the cell membranes, affects the heartbeat and the nerve and muscle action, and regulates the activity of several enzymes.

In addition to the need for calcium by our physiological processes, more is required by pregnant women and growing children to furnish building material for growing bones and teeth.

Over 150 years ago, chemists discovered that a lack of sufficient calcium in the diets of children produced the disease called *rickets* in which the lack of bone development caused bow legs and other

TABLE 14.2
CALCIUM-INTAKE RECOMMENDATIONS OF THE
FOOD AND NUTRITION BOARD

Age	Amt Daily, Mg
Infant (under 1 yr)	500
1–8	800
.8–18	1300
18+	800

deformities of the skeleton. Nature tries to take care of the calcium supply of the young—calves grow much faster than children, and so cow's milk contains three times as much calcium, six times as much phosphorus, and six times as much vitamin D as human milk. All three of these substances are required for proper bone development.

It is very hard to determine just how much calcium is needed in the human diet because the bones act as a reserve supply. When the diet does not furnish enough to maintain the proper concentration in the blood, the bones make up the deficit. There are other difficulties; calcium is excreted in the sweat and urine, and the presence in the diet of phosphoric, oxalic, citric or, phytic acid in the foods interferes with the absorption of calcium from the intestines. In making its recommendations, the FNB assumes absorption of only 40% of the calcium in the diet.

These recommendations of the Board for both males and females from birth to beyond the 75th year are made in detail, but the figures can be applied only in a hospital or other institution that has continuous scientific control. For the guidance of diets in general the following daily allowances shown in Table 14.2 should be sufficient.

In order to be properly nourished it is extremely important to have an adequate supply of calcium in the diet—especially in the diet of the young. The development of the bones and teeth demands it. Fortunately, milk is the chief food of the very young, and it is the best source of calcium—a quart contains 2000 mg. The substitution of soft drinks for milk in the diet of children should be a criminal offense.

The following sources of calcium will serve as a dietary guide; the figures express the number of milligrams of the element in 100 gm of the food: milk 118, cheese 100–900, ice cream 140; collards 250, turnip greens 246, kale 240, mustard greens 183, broccoli 100; dried prunes 90, dried apricots 67, raisins 62, oranges 41; salmon 154, shrimp 115, oysters 90, scallops 25; dried beans 144, whole wheat bread 99, eggs 54.

Most other foods are lower in calcium than those listed above, but they are by no means negligible. With the exception of butter, the dairy products lead the list, then the leafy vegetables that are usually cooked. Fresh fruits are rich in calcium but their high water content results in low percentages. Meats are low in calcium and so are the cereals unless they are enriched with it.

PHOSPHORUS

The bones and teeth contain about half as much phosphorus as calcium, but the soft tissues contain more phosphorus than calcium. The adult man contains 670 gm of phosphorus or nearly $1\frac{1}{2}$ lb; the bones contain 80 to 90% of the total and the remainder is distributed through all the other tissues.

Phosphorus, like calcium, is not simply a structural element of the body but comes and goes as it takes part in metabolism. One experimenter fasted for 31 days and excreted both these elements every day of the fast. Near the beginning of the fast he excreted 0.274 gm of calcium and 1.27 gm of phosphorus daily, but the amount excreted decreased daily, and by the last day they had dropped to 0.138 and 0.58 gm respectively.

The blood contains 2 to 4.7 mg of phosphorus in each 100 cc. Besides the calcium phosphate formation in bones and teeth, phosphorus combines with the fats and the proteins to form compounds that are essential components of the heart, brain, and other vital organs.

The many functions of phosphorus in the body and its constant excretion has made it hard to determine exactly how much is required in the diet. Consequently, the amount recommended has varied widely through the years. The FNB now recommends that the amount should be about the same as that of calcium in the several age groups.

The best sources of phosphorus in the diet are milk, cheese, meat, eggs, seafoods, and the whole-grain cereals. Since these foods are usually abundant on most menus, phosphorus is much less likely to be deficient than calcium is.

IRON

Back in the 17th century a doctor, Thomas Sydenham, made a tonic by dissolving iron in wine, and used it for the treatment of anemia. It was a useful tonic, but it was a purely trial-and-error discovery because it was made long before it was known that there is iron in the blood. From this discovery to the present, the chemistry of blood and the function of the iron in it have been subjects of research. McCollum's *History of Nutrition* states that between 1871 and 1900 there were 260 papers published on the subject of iron in nutrition, and the subject still attracts research scientists.

With all the research that has been done on iron in nutrition it might seem that everything would be known about the subject by now. But, unfortunately, many complications make it hard to reach definite conclusions. To begin with there is less than 3 gm of iron in the adult human body. It is part of several tissues, although most of it is in the blood and nearly all of it is combined with protein. The iron in blood is part of the protein, hemoglobin, which makes up the greater portion of the red corpuscles. It is the iron in this protein that carries oxygen to all the tissues of the body; each molecule of hemoglobin can carry four molecules of oxygen. The total amount of hemoglobin in the adult body is around 800 gm and it contains 2.75 gm of iron. Since a red corpuscle wears out in four months or so, the diet must supply the iron to make new corpuscles.

The body loses 1 mg of iron or more a day. The loss in urine is well known, but iron is also lost in sweat and in cells that peel off the skin, or are removed by shaving, cutting hair, and paring nails. These latter are not all daily events and sweat is hard to collect; consequently, the amount of iron lost daily is an unsettled problem.

If there is not enough iron supplied to the blood, anemia results. Doctor Sydenham cured this kind of anemia with his iron tonic back in the 17th century, for salts of iron are absorbed as well as iron from food. Unfortunately, there are other causes of anemia besides a dietary deficiency of iron. Bacteria may destroy the corpuscles; there may be internal hemorrhage; or there may be poisons such as lead, arsenic, or hydrogen sulfide that interfere with the normal absorption and metabolism of the iron.

Even if anemia is caused by too little iron in the diet it is not a simple matter to correct it. A chemical analysis of foods tells us the iron content, but that is no guarantee that the blood will receive that much iron from the food because there are other components of the food that may interfere with the absorption of the iron into the blood stream. For example, iron phosphate is insoluble in water; consequently, if there is a large amount of phosphate in the food, it will form an insoluble compound with the iron which will pass along the intestines like so much sand and be excreted in the feces. Other substances that interfere with the absorption of iron are phytic acid in bran, oxalic acid in spinach, and some other leafy

TABLE 14.3
IRON-INTAKE RECOMMENDATIONS OF THE FOOD
AND NUTRITION BOARD

	Age	Amt Daily, Mg
Children	1–3	15
	3–10	10
Males	10–18	18
	18–75+	10
Females	10–55	18
	55+	10

vegetables. Only 4% of the iron in bran is absorbed, 13% from spinach, and 50% from beef.

How much iron, then, is required? The recommendations of the FNB are shown in Table 14.3. Beef liver seems to be the best source of iron for hemoglobin formation; the livers of other animals come next. Bread and milk are both low in iron. Since milk is so common in the diet, most States permit the sale of fortified milk, which may have iron added to it along with iodine and some vitamins. The practice differs from State to State, but 15 States permit the addition of 10 mg of iron to a quart of milk. Some States merely require the amount added to be stated on the label.

The lack of iron in the foods that make up the bulk of the American diet led to the proposal to add iron to some of them. The enrichment of white flour and other cereals was proposed by the FNB as early as 1936, but there was so much opposition to it that nothing was done until 1941. The enrichment standards finally adopted include three vitamins and iron. The present standards for the enrichment of cereals include the amounts of iron expressed as milligrams to be added to a pound of the food: white bread, rolls, and buns, 8 to 12.5; cornmeal and grits, 13 to 26; white flour, 13 to 16.5; macaroni products and noodles, 13 to 16.5; and white rice, 13 to 26.

In 1943, War Food Order No. 1 made the enrichment of flour mandatory. The order was withdrawn in 1946, but in the meantime, 19 states had passed laws requiring the enrichment of white flour and its products. At present (1971), 28 states have such laws. Consequently, 85% of the bread and rolls sold in the United States, and practically all the white flour sold in grocery stores, are enriched. Four ounces of enriched bread supply 20% of the daily iron requirement.

MAGNESIUM

In 1910 chemists of the USDA published a Bulletin entitled *Calcium, Magnesium and Phosphorus in Food and Nutrition.* The authors had found that magnesium is absorbed from the intestinal tract and becomes part of the bones and some of the other tissues. They did not show that it is a required nutrient or that it has a definite function in the body.

Some 15 years after the publication of this Bulletin, a French scientist showed that magnesium is essential for the growth of mice, but it was not until 1960 that scientists reached the definite conclusion that magnesium plays an essential part in human nutrition. Its importance in the nutrition of plants had been discovered several years earlier when the element was found to be part of the chlorophyll molecule.

The adult human body contains about an ounce of magnesium; half of it is in the bones and the remainder is in the blood and other soft tissues. It is part of several enzymes in the body.

The amount of magnesium required in the diet has not been definitely established. It varies with the amount of protein and also with some of the other mineral elements present in the diet. Serious magnesium deficiency is rare and, although minor deficiencies do not produce glaring symptoms, deficiencies do occur. Consequently the FNB has included the element in its 1968 recommendations as shown in Table 14.4.

Magnesium is present in most foods and no one class is outstanding in that respect. The following foods supply the indicated number of milligrams in 100 gm of the food: dried beans 170, oatmeal 144, rice 88, spinach 88, whole wheat bread 78, lentils 80, dried apricots 62, collards, 57, cornmeal 47, macaroni 48, dried prunes

TABLE 14.4
MAGNESIUM-INTAKE RECOMMENDATIONS OF THE
FOOD AND NUTRITION BOARD

	Age	Amt Daily, Mg
Children	Infant–1	40–70
	1–10	100–250
	10–12	300
Males	12–75+	350
Females	12–32	350
	22–75+	300

40, cheddar cheese 45, turnip greens 58, sweet corn 48, shrimp 42, okra 41, grapefruit 33, bananas 33, raisins 35, oysters 32, snap beans 32, kale 37, potatoes 34, and most other foods contain from 7 to 29 mg.

CHAPTER 15

Trace Elements

By the early years of the 20th century the dietary need for considerable amounts of calcium, phosphorus, and iron had been well established, but the nutritionists were soon to learn that there are other mineral elements that the body requires in very tiny amounts. Quantities so small that they are generally referred to as trace elements.

IODINE

The most intriguing of the trace elements is iodine; it has a long and checkered history. There is not very much of it in the world; it ranks 65th in abundance among the 88 chemical elements. The richest known deposit is that mixed with the sand of the Atacama desert in northern Chile, and this is the source of the iodine in the drug stores. Next to the Chilean desert, the best source of iodine is seaweed, which contains about 0.1% of it. Sea water contains about 0.03 mg to the liter and fresh water from none to 0.02 mg to the liter. Soils vary in iodine content from none to 10 mg in a kilogram of soil.

An adult man contains 25 mg of iodine and nearly all of that is in the thyroid gland. This is the iodine with which we are concerned here.

Goiter is a very common disease of the thyroid gland. Doctors estimate that even today there are 200 million cases of it in the world. Seaweed has been used as a remedy for 3000 years, and burnt sponge was used back in the 13th century. The modern treatment dates from shortly after the discovery of iodine in 1811.

By 1816 William Prout, an English doctor, was using a salt of iodine in the treatment of goiter, and in 1820, Jean Francois Coindet, a Swiss doctor, published a paper in which he advised the uses of small doses for the same purpose. Then in 1831 Alexander von Humboldt, the celebrated German statesman, naturalist, and traveler, described goiter in Colombia and said the Indians there knew of a salt deposit that would cure it, whereas salt from other sources would not. Von Humboldt got a sample of this salt, and also samples of salt from other sources in Colombia, and brought them to the French chemist, Boussingault, for analysis. The analyses

172

showed that the curative salt contained iodine and the other samples did not.

For three-quarters of a century the use of iodine in the treatment of goiter was controversial; some doctors said it did more harm than good. But the entire 25 mg of iodine in the body is less than 1/1000 oz—about as much as a half dozen crystals of granulated sugar. Consequently, the daily requirement would be an amount just about big enough to be seen. Many doctors did not understand this and gave doses that were far too big. In fact I know a doctor who did that very thing in rather recent years.

It has long been known that the number of cases of goiter was very different in different geographical areas. A French chemist published a paper in 1876 that showed a connection between the iodine content of the soil and the number of cases of goiter in a region. However, statistical data are always suspect and his paper just added to the controversy. Physicians gradually withdrew from these arguments, and for over 50 years they managed to forget the evidence that related the cause of goiter to the absence of iodine.

Three of the better known areas in which goiter flourished were the area around the Great Lakes in the United States and Canada, our Pacific-Northwestern States and Switzerland. In these and many other geographical areas, even the farm animals had goiter, and the cause was definitely traced to the lack of iodine in the soil and in the drinking water.

In 1895 the goiter problem came to life again when a German chemist discovered that the thyroid gland is rich in iodine. Then in 1914 the biochemist, E. C. Kendall of the Mayo Clinic in Rochester, Minn., isolated a chemical substance from thyroid glands, which he called *thyroxine*, and showed that it contained considerable iodine in its composition. Kendall's discovery definitely indicated that iodine was essential to the welfare of the thyroid gland, and it stimulated research on the subject of iodine and goiter.

Dr. David Marine, Professor of Internal Medicine at Western Reserve University, and some associates reasoned that if the lack of iodine is the cause of goiter in these goitrogenic areas, then administration of iodine to the population should prevent it. To test the idea they made arrangements with the school system in Akron, Ohio, for some experiments. They selected 2000 school children and gave them small doses of iodine twice a week for one month twice a year. The results were that 2 of the 2000 children had enlarged thyroid glands, whereas 500 of another 2000 children in the same school system, who had not been given iodine, had enlarged thyroids. This was the first controlled experiment on the correlation of iodine to the welfare of the thyroid gland. All previous information on the subject had been the result of clinical observation. After Dr. Marine got such remarkable results at Akron, other scientists made similar experiments both in this country and abroad, notably in Switzerland, Argentina, Guatemala, and Mexico.

The soil and water in Michigan contains little or no iodine, but the livestock had been taken care of accidentally several years before Marine's experiment. There are salt wells in the state, and around 1870 they began to be used as commercial sources of salt. In the process of purifying the salt there was an impure residue unfit for use as table salt, and so the manufacturers sold it to the farmers for their cattle. Since this crude salt contained iodine, goiter disappeared from the farm animals.

How to get iodine to the general population was a problem. There were three main proposals. Goiter attacks at an early age, and it was proposed to add iodine to candy. But the process was expensive, and it was found to be impossible to get all the children to eat this particular candy; it was tried in some schools but failed. The second method was to add iodine to the drinking water, but less than 1% of a city water supply is drunk by the populace, and besides, farmers and villagers have individual water supplies. The third and most successful proposal was the addition of iodine to table salt.

Salt was first iodized in this country in 1924 by adding 1 part of iodine in the form of potassium iodide to 5000 parts of salt, and its presence was stated on the label. One of the objections to adding iodine to drinking water was that the iodine might harm some people. However, this argument did not apply to the salt because it was labeled and anyone was free to buy it or not. Later the amount of iodine added was reduced to 1 part in 10,000, where it now stands, and about half the table salt sold in this country is iodized.

At least 11 countries now iodize their table salt, and the amount of iodine added varies from 1 part in 10,000 in the United States and Canada to 1 part in 200,000 in Poland. In at least two countries, Canada and Switzerland, all salt for home use must be iodized. In Switzerland this requirement has reduced the number of goiter cases by over 80%.

The amount of iodine required daily has never been determined, but surveys made in Finland, Holland, the Congo, Northern India, Venezuela, Chile, and the Argentine indicate that 0.05 to 0.075 mg a day is enough. Our FNB recommends the amounts shown in Table 15.1.

TABLE 15.1
IODINE-INTAKE RECOMMENDATIONS OF THE
FOOD AND NUTRITION BOARD

Age	Amt Daily (Mg)
Infant (under 1 yr)	0.025–0.045
1–10	0.060–0.110
10–35	0.100–0.150
35+	0.090–0.100

Where is one to get this iodine? In many parts of the country the fruits and vegetables contain it, but the only reliable sources are seafood and iodized salt, which contains 0.1 mg/1 gm of salt.

The manner in which the food industry has developed has considerably reduced the likelihood of an iodine deficiency in this country. Seafood is now available at every grocery store, and in the course of a day one may eat tomatoes from Mexico, Florida, California, or New Jersey; pineapples from Hawaii or Puerto Rico; potatoes from Virginia, Idaho, or Maine; and other foods from a variety of places. In the days when a family lived on the food from its farm or from the farms arounds its village, the danger of iodine deficiency was much greater, but it is still a real hazard.

COPPER

A French chemist reported the presence of copper in the human body in 1840 and others found it to be present in the ash of various plant and animal tissues in the middle of the 19th century. But they all considered it to be accidental and not essential to either the plant or the animal. It was the 1920s before chemists proved that copper is essential to plant growth.

The human body contains 100 to 150 mg of copper, approximately 60% of it in the muscles, 20% in the bones, 17% in the liver, 4% in the blood, and 1% in the brain. The copper in the blood is a catalyst in the formation of hemoglobin; that is, it aids in the formation of hemoglobin, but does not become part of it. Copper is also an essential part of several enzymes, one of which catalyzes the formation of the proteins: elastin and collagen. Elastin is the protein of the walls of the blood vessels, and collagen is the protein of the tendons and bones. Another of these enzymes that contain copper is involved in the production of energy. Still another aids the production of melanine, the dark pigment of suntan.

The daily copper requirement of an adult varies with the intake of iron. If the iron consumed is between 6 and 10 mg, then 1.5 mg of copper is enough. The FNB recommends 2 mg a day. The livers of animals are rich in copper and most meats and vegetables contain some of it. Cow's milk contains from 0.15 to 4.5 mg in a quart. A mixed diet of natural foods will probably supply the recommended 2 mg a day.

FLUORINE

In certain areas of the United States the natives have mottled teeth, which are of soft, chalky texture. However, they are not as liable to decay as normal teeth. Early in this century the Public Health Service made a survey of the country to locate the regions in which mottled teeth are common. They discovered several areas in Arkansas and Illinois where the defect was limited to those of the population who had lived there since childhood. Meanwhile, scientists were studying the effect of fluorine on experimental animals because analysis of the drinking water in the affected areas indicated that fluorine might be the cause of the trouble. The survey was confined largely to the cities where the schools provided plenty of children for examination and, of course, all such cities had water systems that supplied the whole population with drinking water. By 1931 the cause of mottled teeth was traced to water that contained from 4 to 7 mg of fluorine in a liter, that is, 4 to 7 parts per million (ppm).

A strange result of the investigation of mottled teeth appeared in 1938. The solution of the problem had led to the analysis of water supplies for their fluorine content, and a chemist found that in Galesburg, Ill., where the water contained 1.9 ppm of fluorine, 273 children native to the city had 236 tooth defects or less than 90 per 100 children, while at Quincy, Ill., where the water contained only 0.1 to 0.2 ppm fluorine, there were 700 tooth defects in 330 children of the same age group as those examined in Galesburg or 212 per 100 children. Many similar examinations were then made, and the conclusion was reached that 0.5 to 1 ppm of fluorine in water reduces tooth decay by about 65%. More than that has no greater effect, and over 4 ppm causes mottled teeth. Health studies made in several cities with different amounts of fluorine in the water indicate that fluorine has no deleterious effect on general health.

After consideration of hundreds of experiments and observations in the matter of fluorine in nutrition, the scientists have decided that children should have 1 to 2 mg of fluorine a day. The problem is how to provide it. For cities with a water system the fluorine can be added to the water. The element is not expensive, and so even though the great bulk of city water goes for sanitary or other non-nutritive purposes, the cost is still small. The amount added is usually 1 ppm.

In 1945 Grand Rapids, Mich., became the first city in the United States to add fluorine to the water supply. In 1951 the U.S. Public Health Service officially approved the practice, and by 1968 82 million Americans were drinking fluoridated water. Salts of fluorine are added or removed to bring the fluorine content to 0.6 to 1 ppm.

No satisfactory method has been found for supplying fluorine to those who live in the country or in small villages and have individual sources of drinking water. Fluorides have been added to tooth pastes and they are somewhat effective in preventing decay.

Some have feared that fluorine from other sources might result in too much fluorine if it is added to the water supply, but the only other source is food and the amount of fluorine in foods is too low to cause trouble.

MINOR ELEMENTS

Four other mineral elements have been found in the body and appear to have some function there, but they are present in such small amounts that their function in nutrition, if any, has not been determined. These elements are zinc, manganese, and selenium. Cobalt is the fourth and its role will be discussed in connection with the vitamin of which it is a part. Traces of still other elements have been reported, but their importance has not been established. Theoretically, ocean water contains traces of all the elements, and a popular newspaper columnist is now recommending its consumption to ensure getting traces of all the elements, apparently on the hypothesis that since some trace elements are important others may be also. Consequently, Pacific Ocean water is now sold in Florida for $1.75 a pint. However, the FDA points out that it has no demonstrated value whatever. Furthermore, ocean water contains 3.0% sodium chloride, and any intake of it would result in a very high salt diet.

CHAPTER 16

Salt and Water

The mineral substances that come and go in the body in greatest abundance are salt and water. The salt content of the body is about 100 gm, and water constitutes 65% of the total body weight.

As long ago as 1805 Dr. Samuel L. Mitchell, Professor of Chemistry at Columbia University, wrote a letter to a friend in England in which he expressed the opinion that salt is essential in the diet of herbivorous animals. As evidence in support of his opinion, he pointed out that domestic herbivora, such as horses, cattle and sheep, have a craving for salt, and that wild herbivora, deer and bear, for example, make long treks to "salt licks," that is, to places where salt or salt water appears around springs or in marshes.

Mitchell's opinion either did not become widely known at the time or made very little impression on his contemporaries, for nobody attempted to verify it by experiment for nearly 40 years. In 1847 Boussingault experimented with oxen and found they did not thrive unless they were given salt.

The need for salt in the herbivorous diet is now well established and salt troughs may be seen on cattle ranges, but, strange as it may seem, much less is known about the salt requirement of the human diet. The difficulties of the research discourage investigators. Grass and the other foods of the herbivora contain very little sodium, and so it is rather easy to plan a diet for them that is nearly free from salt, but men and rats are omniverous and their natural food is salty so that a salt-free diet is hard to plan. In spite of the difficulties, however, the scientists have accumulated considerable information.

A man of average size (154 lb) contains 4 oz of sodium and 9 oz of potassium. The potassium is mostly within the cells and the sodium mainly in the fluids that circulate outside the cells.

A deficiency of potassium retards the growth of the young and may cause the death of cells in the adult. The amount of salt also regulates the volume of fluids in the body.

The nutritional requirements of these elements must be considered together, for the relative proportions of them on opposite sides of the cell membranes, affects the nerve impulses and the contraction of the muscles including those of the heart.

It is difficult to estimate the daily requirement of these elements because they are both very soluble in water and are therefore readily excreted. Sweat contains from 0.5 to 1.25 gm of salt and a variable amount of potassium in a liter. Other body fluids contain both elements and so they are lost normally in sweat and urine and also by vomiting, bleeding, and diarrhea.

It is estimated that the American diet contains from 6 to 18 gm of salt and 1.4 to 6.5 gm of potassium daily. The requirement varies with the climate and activity, because of the loss in sweat. The FNB recommends from 2.7 to 8 gm of potassium daily.

Potassium occurs widely. Fresh fruits average 200 mg and the common vegetables 475 mg in 100 gm of food. Some other common foods contain: dried apricots 1260, dried prunes 940, raisins 763, rice 214, meats around 300, milk 145, eggs 130, and bread 85. But potassium compounds are very soluble and if vegetables are boiled and drained they may lose half the element or more.

The FNB recommends 1 gm of salt for each liter of water consumed, which should amount to 2 to 3 gm a day. But the actual amount required varies with the individual and his activities. A baker, a steel furnace operator, or even a golfer on a hot day sweats profusely and loses a lot of salt, whereas a sedentary worker in an air-conditioned room loses practically none by way of sweat. A lack of salt renders us more liable to heat stroke and an excess either leads to or aggravates high blood pressure, for which physicians frequently prescribe a low-salt diet.

For those who need a low-sodium diet, fruits of all kinds are recommended—few of them contain more than 1 mg salt in 100 gm of the fruit. Vegetables are somewhat higher in sodium than the fruits are, but they are still very low—few of them contain as much as 50 mg to 100 gm of food.

Foods of animal origin are higher in salt content than the vegetables are. Fresh meats contain 50 to 90 mg, milk 50 mg, and eggs 122 mg per 100 gm.

Some processed foods have a very high salt content; dried beef leads the list with 4300 mg/100 gm, which is 4.3%. Other salty foods are olives 2400, soda crackers 1100, bacon 1021, butter and margarine 987, 40% bran 925, American cheese 700, breads 590, salted peanuts 410, soups as eaten 400 mg.

WATER

Of all the substances the body requires, water is second only to oxygen. The body is 65% water; it occurs in all the tissues and performs some function in each of them. All chemical action in the body (whether digestion, the production of energy, growth or some other function) requires water. Lack of water first causes thirst, then fatigue followed by the inability to work, and finally exhaustion. It has been suggested that the consumption of water made the difference between failure and success in climbing Mt. Everest. The Swiss party, which failed, drank less than a pint of water a day, during the last three days of effort, while the British expedition, which succeeded, drank 5 to 7 pt daily.

Normally about half the water lost by the body is eliminated by the kidneys for the removal of waste substances. A diet high in protein or in salt or other minerals requires more water because the final products of protein metabolism are urea and other solid nitrogen compounds, which can be removed only in solution. The minerals are also solids and require water for their excretion. Consequently, an ample supply of water reduces the work of the kidneys.

The specific heat of water is higher than that of any other substance; that is, it takes more heat to raise its temperature a given number of degrees. For this reason, the high water content of the body helps to protect it from sudden changes in temperature. The normal body temperature is 98.6°F, and even when one dives into cold water, the body temperature does not drop suddenly to the temperature of the water, but changes only slightly and the body's thermostat soon brings it back to normal.

The other half of the water is eliminated by respiration and sweat. The evaporation of water from the skin and lungs is the chief cooling mechanism of the body, and above 98.6°F it is the only one. The heat loss is 580 Cal for each quart of water evaporated at body temperature. Under some conditions the loss of water by evaporation is much greater than the loss through the kidneys. Each breath exhaled is saturated with water vapor; in cold weather this vapor condenses and is visible as small drops of water—you can "see your breath."

The rate of evaporation of water from the skin is affected by several factors, such as the temperature and humidity of the surrounding atmosphere. A temperature of 120°F with dry air may be more comfortable than 90° with high humidity because the water evaporates more rapidly into dry air and thus cools more effectively. The loss of water from the skin has been found to vary from 0.8

l a day at 22.5 degrees below zero to 6.2 l in a desert atmosphere at 90.5°F.

The amount of water evaporated from the skin also increases with the physical efforts of the individual, because greater exercise generates more heat to be eliminated and the body tries to maintain its normal temperature. The water lost by an athlete may vary from 3 to 10 l a day; a football player or a baseball pitcher may lose as much as 15 lb or 7 l of water in a single game.

In 1968 the FNB recommended the intake of 1 ml of water for each Cal of food consumed. To the person who consumes 2500 Cal, this is 2.5 l a day. Any intake of water less than a third of a liter (less than 1 pt) of water a day is dangerous even at cool temperatures, a low Calorie diet, and little activity.

There are three sources of water in the diet; the water drunk as such or as milk, fruit juice, or other beverage; the water that is part of fruits, vegetables, and other foods; and that from the oxidation of foodstuffs in the body, especially the fats. Strange as it may seem, when fats are oxidized in the body they produce more than their own weight of water. For example, tripalmitin which is a component of several natural fats burns with the following results:

$$C_{51}H_{98}O_6 + 72.5\ O_2 = 51\ CO_2 + 49\ H_2O + heat$$

806 gm	2320 gm	2244 gm	882 gm	7657 Cal
Tripalmitin	Oxygen	Carbon Dioxide	Water	

The equation shows that 806 gm of this fat produces 882 gm of water. Carbohydrates produce less water than the fats when they are oxidized, but the amount is considerable. The equation for the oxidation of granulated sugar shows that 342 gm of the sugar produce 198 gm of water. Proteins also yield water on oxidation, but less than the carbohydrates.

The water that we get from food is an easier source to understand. Most foods have been analyzed many times and their water content is recorded in government bulletins and elsewhere. In general, beverages are about 90% water. Fruits vary from 76% in bananas to 93% in watermelon. Sweet potatoes are 70% water and white potatoes 80%, but most vegetables contain more than 90%. Cheese contains from 30 to 50% water, eggs 75%, country ham 42%, ice cream 62%, fresh meats including poultry and sea food 60 to 80%, and bakery products 25 to 45%.

Although water ranks high among the dietary requirements, it is one of the most neglected. If you spend a 24-hr day at home, try the following experiment: Fill a gallon jug or four quart bottles with water and drink only from that supply during your day. If you drink a cup of coffee or a glass of milk or other beverage, fill the empty cup or glass from the jug and throw the water away. If you are a big eater with little or no soup, fresh fruit or fresh vegetables, the jug should be empty at the end of the 24-hr day. There are few cases in which more than a quart should remain. You will now have a good idea of the amount of water you consume.

Section V

The Vitamins

CHAPTER 17

Discovery of the Vitamins

In the 19th century nutritional research centered around the dietary needs for the carbohydrates, the fats, the proteins, and the three minerals—calcium, phosphorus, and iron. By the late years of the century, some chemists felt the problems of nutrition had been solved. That there might be essential organic substances that are required in very small amounts, like some of the minerals, seems not to have occurred to them, although plenty of evidence is scattered throughout the literature of the past three centuries.

The oldest disease known to be of nutritional origin is scurvy in which the gums become sore and spongy, bleed easily, and may become infected. The teeth loosen, the skin becomes thick and scaly, hemorrhages of the small blood vessels cause spots on the skin, wounds do not heal, and death follows.

Scurvy was a serious disease of the northern cities from the earliest historical times. The disease was described in the *Ebers Papyrus* which was written about 1500 B.C. Hippocrates, the famous Greek physician, described the disease before 370 B.C. and Pliny reported that it was troublesome in the Roman army in the first century A.D. Before the discovery of America, sea voyages had been short; but after 1500, ships made long voyages from Europe to the new world and to the Orient, and scurvy became a problem at sea.

As early at 1564, a Dutch physician recommended oranges for sailors to prevent or cure scurvy. However, his remedy did not seem to catch on, probably because oranges were both scarce and seasonal. James Woodall, an English doctor, announced 75 years later that lemon juice is a good remedy for scurvy. How these early physicians discovered the effectiveness of the citrus fruits, we do not know; scurvy is a northern disease and the citrus fruits are subtropical.

Whatever the reason for the failure of the scurvy cure to become widely known, it was more than a century before we hear of it again. In 1753, Dr. James Lind published *A Treatise of the Scurvy*. In his book, Lind reported the result of an experiment he had performed when he was the doctor on the English ship, *Salisbury*.

There seems to have been many remedies for scurvy in use at the time, and Lind proposed to test them. He selected 12 sailors who had scurvy and housed them in the same room aboard ship. He fed all of them the usual ship's diet. Two were fed this diet only; 2 were each given a quart of cider a day; 2 received 25 drops of sulfuric acid in water 3 times a day; 2 received 2 spoonfuls of vinegar twice a day; 2 got ½ pt of seawater daily; and 2 had 2 oranges and 1 lemon each day until the supply ran out.

One of the men who ate the citrus fruit was able to go back to work after six days and the other shortly after. Those who drank the cider showed some improvement. The other six were no better than the two that had only the regular diet. Lind was a true scientist, and this is said to be the first controlled experiment in medicine that has been recorded.

It might seem that the publication of this book would mean the end of scurvy, in England at least, but it did not even eliminate it from the British navy, for lime or lemon juice was not added to the naval diet until 1795, over 40 years later. The American navy was 16 years behind the British in the addition of citrus juice to the ration.

Our army was still more conservative than the navy. During the Civil War scurvy was a problem, but nothing was done about it. It was also a problem in mining camps, prisons, as well as in armies and on naval and commercial ships that made long voyages. What did all these institutions have in common? The answer is food. In northern cities fresh foods were scarce and expensive, and in armies and on ships the food consisted of dried beef, dried beans, flour, salt pork, and similar foods that furnished plenty of energy, satisfied hunger, and kept well.

There were several known cures for scurvy besides citrus fruits. Any fresh fruit or vegetable, some grasses, and some tree leaves were effective; some more so than others, of course. Onions were effective, but they took up too much room for use on sailing ships. A pound of onions supplies only 157 Cal, while a pound of flour supplies 1520.

The scurvy problem was not the only nutritional disease of the 19th century. The Orient had a problem that the West did not hear much about until 1887.

Admiral Takaki, Director General of the Medical Service of the Japanese Navy, found that between 1878 and 1883 the average number of beriberi cases treated each year was 323.5 of each 1000 sailors—nearly a third of the crew had this paralyzing disease. Takaki was impressed by the better health of the British sailors and thought that the difference might be due to the difference in diet.

A Japanese training ship with a crew of 276 returned from a cruise of 272 days with 169 cases of beriberi, of which 25 were fatal. Dr. Takaki got permission from the naval authorities to repeat the cruise. He changed the diet by adding meat and milk and replacing part of the rice with barley. The ship returned from the cruise with only a few cases of beriberi and no deaths from the disease. An investigation revealed the fact that the men afflicted with the disease had refused to eat the new ration. Takaki reported the results of his experiment to the West in 1887 by an article in an English journal. He had shown that beriberi could be prevented by proper selection of the diet.

About the same time that Takaki was making his investigation of beriberi, the Dutch were having trouble with the disease in their East Indian colonies and their Oriental navy. Also soldiers in barracks and the inmates of prisons were dying of the disease after a few months residence.

In 1886 the Dutch government sent a Commission, consisting of a doctor and a bacteriologist, to investigate the health situation in the East. The Commission had an assistant who was a young army surgeon, Dr. Christian Eijkman. The bacteriologist thought he found a microbe that caused the disease and recommended disinfection of the prisons and the barracks. But the bacteriologist was not very sure of his conclusion and when the Commission returned, he urged the government to exempt young Eijkman from military duty to do research on the beriberi problem. He must have been a powerful persuader for the government complied with his request at once and even gave Eijkman a laboratory in the military hospital at Batavia (now Djakarta), the capital of the Dutch East Indies.

In his new laboratory Eijkman tried to confirm the Commission's microbe theory by inoculating chickens with fluids from the bodies of beriberi patients, but he was unsuccessful. Then for some reason he changed the feed of his chickens from crude rice to white rice from the hospital supply, and it wasn't very long until his chickens had severe cases of polyneuritis whether they had been inoculated or not. Further investigation showed that polyneuritis in chickens is the same disease as beriberi in man. It is primarily a disease of the nerves. The earliest symptoms are fatigue, mental depression, loss of appetite, and digestive disturbances. Then follows numbness in the legs, wasting away of muscles followed by swelling, paralysis, enlargement of the heart, and death.

It took the chickens about a month to contract polyneuritis, and then in about six months they all got well. This was a bit puzzling until Eijkman recalled that a new manager of the hospital had forbidden him to feed the chickens the expensive white rice, and he had gone back to the crude rice.

Dr. Eijkman does not seem to have been familiar with Takaki's experiment, but the diet of his chickens was the only thing that had been changed and he decided to investigate the matter of diet further. He selected two groups of chickens and fed one group white rice and the other group crude rice. Those fed the white rice developed the disease and those on the crude rice did not. He reported this result in a Dutch East Indian journal in 1890 and in a German journal in 1897.

All of Eijkman's work had been done with chickens, but he asked his friend, Dr. A. G. Vorderman, who was an inspector in the civilian medical service, to check the cases of beriberi in the jails. This he did and found that in the prisons in which the inmates milled the rice there was very little beriberi, but in those supplied with white rice there was plenty of it. Dr. Vorderman then undertook some experiments by supplying rice in various stages of milling and in 1897 reported that the white rice was surely the cause of beriberi and that if the disease were not too far advanced, the brown rice would cure it.

In 1896, after eight years in the tropics, Dr. Eijkman went back to Holland on leave, became Professor of Hygiene at the University Utrecht, and did not return to the East. But the Dutch were determined to see beriberi conquered and the government commissioned another young surgeon by name of Grijns to continue research in Batavia. Shortly after 1900 he reached the conclusion that some foods contain very small quantities of organic substances that are essential to health; he called them "protective substances."

By the opening of the 20th century evidence in the literature on nutrition showed that both scurvy and beriberi were caused by the lack of some organic nutrient in the diet, but the papers were in several different languages and widely scattered throughout the literature. Few biochemists read them. Professor F. Gowland Hopkins of Cambridge University did read them and began to search for these evasive nutrients in 1906. He announced his first results in a lecture in 1909, but because of his health he did not publish the paper until 1912.

In the opening sentences of his paper Professor Hopkins says:

> The experiments described in this paper confirm the work of others in showing that animals cannot grow when fed upon so-called synthetic diets consisting of mixtures of pure proteins, fats, carbohydrates and salts, but they grow very well if as little as 1% of milk is added to the purified diet. They show further that a substance or

substances present in normal foodstuffs (milk, for example) can when added to the dietary in astonishingly small amount, secure the utilization for growth of the protein and energy in such mixtures.

In his second paragraph Professor Hopkins points out that recent work on the cause of beriberi and scurvy lead to the same conclusion. With the prestige of Cambridge University and some of his earlier discoveries in nutrition behind him, Professor Hopkins' ideas became widely known and accepted. In 1929 he and Dr. Eijkman received the Nobel prize in medicine and physiology for their contributions to our knowledge of nutrition.

Another biochemist, who must have been well qualified to read the literature, was Casimir Funk, who was born in Warsaw, Poland, in 1884. Twenty years later earned the Ph.D. degree at the University of Berne in Switzerland and then held positions in Germany, England, France, Poland, and the United States.

Dr. Funk published a paper in English from his position at the Lister Institute in 1912 in which he reviewed the literature and emphasized the ideas that Hopkins published the same year. The references at the end of his paper indicate that Funk had covered the nutritional literature very thoroughly. He called his paper *The Etiology of the Deficiency Diseases* and listed beriberi, polyneuritis in birds, epidemic dropsy, scurvy, ship beriberi, and pellagra, and also suggested that rickets may belong in the list. In his opening paragraph Funk states that the research of the preceding 20 years had definitely established these diseases to be caused by something deficient in the diet, and "that there is now enough evidence to convince anybody who cares to consider it."

Several chemists, including Funk, were trying to extract from yeast, rice polishings, and other foods, the substance that prevents beriberi. Funk stated that by 1911 it was well known to be soluble in water and alcohol, of rather small molecular weight, destroyed by heating to 130°C, and neither a salt nor a protein. He thought he had obtained the pure material and found it to contain nitrogen; consequently, he proposed the name *vitamine* for this and any other substances that prevent a deficiency disease. He compounded the name from the Latin, *vita*, life, and *amine*, the name of a group of organic compounds that contain nitrogen. Literally, the name means "amines essential to life." The name was a better one than Grijn's "protective substances" and caught on at once with the biochemists.

We now come to the United States for the next discovery of vitamins. In 1907 Elmer V. McCollum completed his studies for the Ph.D. degree at Yale and found a job as Instructor in Agricultural Chemistry at the University of Wisconsin, which then and thereafter was one of the main locations for research in food and nutrition. He was hired for research on the nutrition of farm animals, which was directed by Professor Hart, Head of the Department. Some cows had been fed on wheat, some on corn, and some on oats, with very different results; the problem was to find out why.

McCollum began by reading all the literature he could find on animal nutrition. He covered all the pertinent papers published between 1870 and 1907, but didn't find anything that was directly helpful. He then discussed the problem with Professor Hart and they decided that McCollum should analyze the blood, milk, urine, and feces of the cows, but these analyses gave no clue to the cause of the differences in the effects of the three grains. In the course of his reading, McCollum had come upon 13 journal articles, scattered throughout the literature, that proved animals cannot live on diets of pure carbohydrates, fats, proteins, and minerals, and one investigator had found that mice could not live on such a diet, but got along very well on milk. This gave McCollum an idea. Very few of the natural foods had been tested for their individual adequacy in nutrition and he thought it was time somebody tried to discover what is lacking in purified diets that some natural foods possess. Of course, he knew that citrus fruits contain something that prevents scurvy and that yeast and rice bran contain something that prevents beriberi. But what were these elusive substances?

Experimentation in nutrition has used a variety of animals from cows to canaries. Cows are not ideal experimental animals; they are too big, too expensive, eat too much, and live too long. McCollum decided that rats would be a big improvement; they grow to maturity in a short time, cost little, eat little, and the entire life span can be studied in about two years. Consequently, McCollum was all for the use of rats and, with the audacity of youth, he went to Professor Hart and explained that the analyses were not showing anything, that cows were too big to work with, and that he wanted to conduct experiments with rats. But Professor Hart was proud of his cow experiment and astonished that McCollum wanted to abandon it so soon. In McCollum's own words, "The interview was brief and stormy" and the answer was "No."

Two days later the young chemist met Stephen M. Babcock on the campus. Babcock had retired as Professor of Agricultural Chemistry, a position that he had held for many years and in which he had done excellent work. In the course of the conversation McCollum mentioned his proposal to work with rats and found that Professor Babcock was very enthusiastic about it. He took McCollum to the Dean of the Agricultural College where he got another "No," with the explanation that the farmers of Wisconsin were trying to exterminate rats and were not willing to have tax money spent to feed them. But Babcock was a highly honored and influential person around the University and persuaded the Dean to allow McCollum to undertake the project. This was before the days of lush research grants by the Federal government and the various "Foundations," and the Dean did not set aside any money for the project.

Going over the head of the boss is usually a hazardous procedure, but Professor Hart apparently did not hold it against McCollum, for he was promoted from the rank of Instructor in 1907 to that of Professor in 1913, and any college teacher can tell you that to call that unusually rapid promotion is the understatement of the profession.

McCollum proceeded to make rat cages out of boxes he had salvaged. When he needed some wire netting for one side of the cages, he was refused a requisition for the necessary $2, and so bought it out of his salary of $1200 a year. He next caught some rats, but they were so wild and savage that he gave them up and bought a dozen white rats.

He prepared the rations for his rats while he was making the analyses for the cow experiment; analytical processes usually include rather long periods of waiting for something to heat, to react or to do something else that cannot be hurried. He took care of the the rats outside of his regular working hours.

Progress was naturally slow with only one person working part time, and with extra chores, such as making more cages to house his increasing rat colony. Fortunately, in July 1909 Miss Marguerite Davis, who had just graduated from the University of California, but who lived in Madison, asked McCollum to accept her as a graduate student in biochemistry. She soon learned, or developed, the technique of animal experimentation which increased the speed of the research considerably, but rat experiments were new and it took some time to work out methods of procedure.

The first important result was announced in a journal article published in 1913. It reported that when they added butter fat or the fat of egg yolk to a deficient diet, the rats grew and seemed to be in good health; but if lard or olive oil were the fat used, the rats failed to grow, acquired a bad eye disease, and finally became blind. The nutrient in butter and egg fat was absent from lard and olive oil. They named this nutrient *Fat Soluble A*.

In their experiments they used commercial milk sugar (lactose), and they later found that if they purified this sugar, the rats failed to thrive. Obviously, milk contained a water soluble substance that was also essential in nutrition and they called it *Water Soluble B*. These names bore eloquent testimony to the fact that they had no idea of the chemical nature of these substances except their solubility.

In 1917 Dr. McCollum transferred to the School of Hygiene of the Johns Hopkins University and took most of his rats along, but left about 100 behind for experimental use in his old department. Professor Hart was using rats by this time and was directing numerous experiments carried out by students, assistants, and other members of the Department. At Hopkins, McCollum continued his research in nutrition until his retirement nearly 30 years later.

The publications of Hopkins and Funk in England and of McCollum and Davis in this country touched off a flood of nutritional research throughout the world. A curious feature of this research is that, with few exceptions, all of it was done by chemists. The chemists did well when they were investigating energy, proteins, fats, carbohydrates, and minerals, but they sometimes had difficulty describing what happened to the animals when something else was missing from the diet. With experimental animals they usually depended on rate of growth, length of life, or other obvious effects, such as loss of hair, paralysis, or failure to bear young. But other defects began to appear and the chemist found it hard to describe them. Eventually the pathologists became interested and helped out with more precise descriptions of the diseased conditions that developed from the deficient diets.

One of the early difficulties in vitamin research was the confusion of names. In England and in Europe the chemists followed Funk's recommendation and used such terms as *antiscorbutic vitamine* and *antiberiberi vitamine*. In the United States they were more likely to talk about Fat Soluble A and Water Soluble B, or one of several other names that had been proposed. A reader of the literature could seldom be certain whether one man's vitamine was the same as another's, or a different one altogether. Furthermore, it was soon shown that some of these nutrients do not contain nitrogen and chemists began to object to the *amine* part of the name *vitamine*.

In a short journal article published in 1920, Sir Jack Drummond, Professor of Biochemistry in University College, London, settled the naming problem apparently satisfactorily, for it is still in use. He proposed to drop the last letter from the word "vitamine," which would give it an ending that chemists do not use for any class of compounds and would therefore not prejudge the chemical nature of those nutrients. He also proposed to drop McCollum's Fat

Soluble A and Water Soluble B and simply name the substances vitamin A and vitamin B. He suggested that these names would be satisfactory until the chemists discovered the chemical nature of the substances and then the chemical names could be used. The simplicity of the scheme was a powerful recommendation in its favor, and it has been used ever since.

By the year 1920 physiological experiments had shown that there are several vitamins, but almost nothing was known about the chemical nature of any of them. Even though nearly all the experimenters had been chemists, their experiments and observations had been physiological and not chemical. Animals had been fed diets of known composition, their rate of growth measured by daily weighings, and any health defects noted. Also, clinical effects of restricted diets (such as army, navy, and prison rations) were observed.

Agreement on the nomenclature of these nutrients as vitamin A, B, etc., and the record of their physiological effects were big steps forward. Now the investigators could single out a vitamin, describe all its physiological effects, and report which foods contained it. The decade of the 1920s was develoted largely to nutritional research of this kind.

One of the big problems of the early years of vitamin research was the determination of how much of the vitamin a food contains. Since the chemical nature of no vitamin was known, the only method of assay was a feeding experiment. For vitamin A, for example, a method proposed by Professor Drummond was further perfected and standardized by Professor Henry C. Sherman of Columbia University. The method was much more complicated than one might imagine. A rat colony had to be raised through several generations on one diet in order to overcome individual differences in the response of the rats to changes in diet. Rats from such a colony were selected when they were 3 or 4 weeks old and fed a diet without a vitamin until they ceased to grow. This took 4 or 5 weeks, then different rats were fed different amounts of the food under assay so as to determine how much it took to produce a growth rate of 3 gm a week. This required 5 to 8 weeks during which all the food, as well as the rats, was weighed daily. The more food it took, the less vitamin the food contained. If it did not contain any, no growth occurred regardless of the amount of food eaten.

Despite this long and tedious method of assay, many foods were tested by several different laboratories. A book on nutrition published in 1934 gave the vitamin A, B, C and G content of 179 foods. Even with all the work required for the analysis, the results were only comparative and were indicated by + signs:

+ + +   an excellent source
+ +   a good source
+   an appreciable source

Obviously, such a method was unsatisfactory, but it was the best that could be devised at the time.

By 1930 chemical investigation on the nature of vitamins was in full swing, and since then the vitamins have been isolated and identified chemically. Methods for their determination have been devised and most of them are now manufactured on a commercial scale. The physiologists can now use the pure vitamin to study the effect of too much or too little of the vitamin on the physical welfare of man or other animal. Although much has been learned, the search for further knowledge still goes on.

CHAPTER 18

Fat Soluble Vitamins

The Fat Soluble A discovered by McCollum and Davis turned out to be a mixture of two vitamins that are now called vitamins A and D. Later, scientists discovered two others that are also soluble in fat solvents and in fats. These are vitamins E and K.

VITAMIN A

Vitamin A is a complicated alcohol with the simple formula $C_{20}H_{29}OH$ and a chemical name so long and complicated that even the chemists call it Vitamin A. It is a pale yellow, crystalline solid that melts at 147°F. Chemical methods for the determination of vitamin A give fairly accurate results and the amount of it is usually reported in International Units (IU). One such unit is 0.3 microgram (mcg), and a microgram is 1 millionth of a gram.

The vitamin occurs only in animal tissues or products. Fish livers lead the list with cod liver oil at 1000 IU per gram of oil, and halibut and tuna liver oils at 50,000 to 100,000 IU per gram. The fish liver oils supplied the drug trade with vitamin A until 1941 when war orders banned the fishing vessels from the Pacific, and then the chemists proceeded to synthesize it for the drug trade.

A complication that caused the chemists many long hours of work and much argument was the fact that the body can make vitamin A from carotene, the yellow pigment so prominent in carrots. It also occurs in other foods, particularly in leaves where it is hidden by the green color of the chlorophyll. Vegetable foods, then, must be analyzed for carotene as well as for vitamin A. An International Unit of carotene is 0.6 mcg from which the body can make 1 IU of vitamin A. For reporting the vitamin content of a food, the two sources are combined as units of the vitamin.

A deficiency of vitamin A in the diet has a great variety of effects on health. The observation that led to its discovery was the failure of young rats to grow. Although no controlled experiments have been made with children to test this effect, the nutritional needs of the rat has been found to be so similar to man's that there is good reason to believe growing children need a good supply of this vitamin.

194

One sign of vitamin A deficiency in human adults is its effect on the mucous membranes of the body, which is first noticed in the eyes. The lids become swollen and then infected, which in severe cases leads to blindness. All other mucous membranes are affected, especially the respiratory and gastrointestinal passages. Vitamin A deficiency also causes "night blindness," which is failure of the eyes to respond to changes in the intensity of light. The vitamin affects general health, and it has even been shown that an adequate supply prolongs the life of rats beyond the normal span.

Experts agree that the requirement of vitamin A depends on the normal weight of the person, and that 20 IU for each kilogram of weight is a minimum requirement. This amounts to 1400 units a day for the average man, but because some people do not convert all the carotene in the diet to the vitamin, the FNB recommends: 1,500 IU for infants under 1 year, 2,000 to 4,500 IU for children 1 to 12, and 5,000 IU for all those over 12 years old.

An ordinary mixed diet of natural and fortified foods will probably supply the 5,000 IU recommended. But some individual nutritionists recommend 10,000 to 12,000 units. If foods are the only source of vitamin A, there is no danger of getting too much. The only natural sources that are extremely high in vitamin A content are the fish liver oils, and not many of us are likely to consume them if we can avoid it. Cod liver oil used to be common in the diets of infants, and I knew one father who acquired a taste for it because his young daugher would not take it unless he did.

The numbers of IU of Vitamin A in 100 gm of some foods are: beef liver 43,900; calf liver 22,500; dried apricots 14,100; carrots 11,000; sweet potatoes 8,800; spinach 8,100; turnip greens 7,600; mustard greens 7,000; margarine 4,800; cantaloupe 3,400; butter 3,300; broccoli 2,500; dried prunes 2,170; green onions 2,000; cream 1540; American cheese 1,200; eggs 1,180.

In general, liver, dairy products, and the green leafy vegetables are the best sources of vitamin A, it occurs widely in less amounts in other fruits and vegetables.

VITAMIN D

Now let's look at the other member of the Fat Soluble A mixture. Vitamin D is concerned with the bones and teeth. The problem of the proper development of these hard tissues has a long history. Herodotus, the Greek historian, visited a battlefield where the Persians had defeated the Egyptians in 526 B.C. He noticed that the skulls of the slain Persians were very fragile and those of the Egyptians were very strong. The Egyptians attributed the difference to the effects of sunlight; they went bareheaded from childhood, whereas the Persians wore turbans to protect them from the sun. Research that was done some 2500 years later supports the Egyptian explanation.

Rickets is a condition of poor bone formation, a disease of childhood. The most obvious symptoms are bow legs, knock knees, or other bone deformation. It undoubtedly has been common since man began to wear clothes and live in houses. Named and described in the medical literature as early as 1600, its cause was not known even as recently as 1917. The disease was most common in cities and in children born in the fall and winter.

The proof of the cause of rickets began with the experiments of Sir Edward Mellanby, Professor of Physiology at the University of London. Several drugs for the cure of rickets had been tried over the previous three centuries, and at the time of World War I, an emulsion of linseed oil was a remedy sold widely in England. Some doctors had had success with cod liver oil and had concluded that rickets is caused by a lack of fat in the diet. Professor Mellanby decided to investigate these remedies and used puppies for the purpose. He fed them a diet on which they developed rickets and then added various fats to see if they would cure the disease. He found that linseed oil was no good at all, and that cottonseed, olive and babassu oils, lard, and some other fats were no better. Therefore, lack of fat was not the cause of rickets.

Cod liver oil and butter fat did prevent the disease, and the cod liver oil was the better of the two since much less was needed. These two fats contained Fat Soluble A, and Mellanby decided rickets was definitely a deficiency disease and probably this vitamin cured it. He published these conclusions in a journal article of December 14, 1918, although he had announced some preliminary results in January of that year.

Professor McCollum and his colleagues at Johns Hopkins had noticed that rats acquired rickets on certain diets, but there was one thing in Mellanby's report that they did not understand. The London professor had found that meat was somewhat effective against rickets, and meat does not contain any vitamin A. Consequently, the American group began to look into the matter.

They heated cod liver oil and passed oxygen into it until all the vitamin A was destroyed, but the oil still prevented rickets. They also found that coconut oil, which contains no vitamin A, prevents rickets. They confirmed Mellanby's findings that most vegetable fats are worthless against rickets and added shark and burbot liver oils to the effective list. With all these results McCollum concluded:

"These experiments clearly demonstrate the existence of a fourth vitamin whose specific property, as far as we can tell at present, is to regulate the metabolism of the bones." The results were published June 20, 1922.

After 1922 several other investigators entered research on the antirachitic vitamin, but they encountered a complicating factor, the effect of sunlight. As early as 1913 an investigator had found that sunlight affected the severity of rickets in rats. Another investigator announced in 1920 that he had used ultraviolet light to cure rickets in children.

Before proceeding further with the effect of light on rickets it may be in order to review the subject of light itself. Light consists of energy waves of various lengths. These wavelengths are very short, and the physicists always express the length in units of the metric system. A meter is about a yard in length and a millimeter is $1/1000$ of a meter. The thickness of 2 or 3 sheets of the paper in this book would be about a millimeter. For distances measured with a microscope, there is the micron (μ), which is $1/1000$ of a millimeter. However, the wavelength of light is much shorter still and is measured in millimicrons $(m\mu)$—the millimicron of course, is $1/1000$ of a micron.

Light of different wavelengths has different properties, color, for example. Light in the range of 700 to 620 $(m\mu)$ is red, 620 to 590 is orange, 590 to 525 is yellow, 525 to 500 is green, 500 to 450 is blue and 450 to 400 is violet. The divisions between the colors are not sharp; one color shades gradually into its neighbors like the colors of the rainbow. Neither are the limits of vision sharp, some eyes can see longer red or shorter violet than others, but the limits of 400 to 700 $m\mu$ probably includes all the visible light. Wavelengths just above 700 in length are called *infrared* and those just below 400 are the *ultraviolet*. Ultraviolet is invisible, of course, but when it shines on certain substances it causes them to glow with one of the colors, a property used both for scientific purposes and for theatrical effects. The ultraviolet also affects a photographic plate and causes sunburn.

Visible light passes through glass, water, and several other substances, but the ultraviolet does not penetrate glass or even air very well, especially if the air contains dust or fog. The ultraviolet that prevents rickets is between 275 and 300 $m\mu$ in wavelength and the most effective region is around 280.

It took a lot of work to learn why ultraviolet can take the place of vitamin D in the diet. By 1924 the biochemists had found that milk, yeast, and some other foods contained the vitamin after they

had been exposed to the ultraviolet. Since the antirachitic vitamin
was the fourth discovered, it became "vitamin D." It was soon found
to belong to a group of complicated alcohols called *sterols* of which
cholesterol is the best known. The simplest formula for vitamin D is
$C_{28}H_{43}OH$. The chemists have learned how these 73 atoms are
attached to each other, but a diagram to show it is more picturesque
than informative and need not concern us here.

Several of these sterols have the formula $C_{28}H_{43}OH$, and one of
them is common in fungi, such as yeast. It is called *ergosterol*, and
when it is exposed to ultraviolet it becomes vitamin D. The vitamin
D sold in drug stores formerly came from fish liver oils, but is now
made by irradiating ergosterol isolated from yeast.

Not all sterols are turned into vitamin D by the action of the
ultraviolet, but the skin and its appendages, hair, wool, fur, and
feathers contains one called *7-dehydrocholesterol*, which does become
vitamin D when exposed to sunlight. The D vitamins from the
several sources are white, crystalline substances that melt between
239° and 244°F.

The discovery of vitamin D was one of the greatest medical
discoveries of all time. It has been estimated that in Europe in 1900,
90% of the young children had rickets and many of them died of
the disease.

All that had been written about the disease through the years
now became clear. It was more common among the poor because of
their diet. It was more common in the cities, especially the foggy
and smoky ones, for the lack of sunlight. It was more common in
children born in the fall and winter because of the shorter days,
weaker sunlight, and colder weather, which encouraged more time
in the house and more clothes when the children were taken out for
fresh air.

Since the mineral matter in the bones and teeth is calcium phosphate, the diet must contain an adequate supply of calcium and
phosphorus. However, without vitamin D most of these elements
are excreted and so do not enter into the bones and teeth.

The knowledge of vitamin D was put into service by both the
medical profession and the public almost at once, far quicker than
the three previous vitamins. There were two main reasons for this.
The work on the other three vitamins was done by chemists and
reported in the chemical literature, which doctors seldom read.
Moreover, physicians were loath to believe that anyone outside
the profession of medicine could make any contribution to it. In
the case of vitamin D, at least two of the investigators had medical

connections, one of them was a pediatrician and published in the medical journals.

In the 1920s there was a great flood of sunsuits, ultraviolet lamps, and cod liver oil. At least two companies made a plastic substitute for window glass, which would transmit the ultraviolet rays better than glass.

English and German investigators had also done research on vitamin D and so the cure for rickets spread throughout Europe, and the disease became rare both here and abroad.

At first, babies were given cod liver oil, but some of them could not tolerate so much fat and in the 1930s the drug companies began to make products of high vitamin D content. A few drops of these products supply the daily requirement of vitamin D.

Very little vitamin D is stored in the body and so it must be supplied daily. The FNB recommends 400 IU daily for infants and for children up to the age of 22. A unit is 0.025 mcg of the vitamin. The bones of children with an adequate supply of vitamin D not only develop normally, but they also grow longer, so that the average youth of today is taller than his ancestors of 50 years ago.

There is no recommendation of vitamin D for adults who have completed their growth, but there is a tendency to bone weakness among older people and so the vitamin should not be completely ignored at any age. It is contained in such natural foods as egg yolk and liver and in the body fat of mackerel and other fish. Also many foods available at the grocery have the vitamin added. And, of course, there is always sunshine.

VITAMIN E

While Fat Soluble A proved to be a mixture of vitamins A and D, another vitamin, which was found in lettuce, alfalfa, wheat germ, bean pods, polished rice, rolled oats and yellow corn, also was found to be soluble in fats and fat solvents. It was named vitamin E. McCollum in his *History of Nutrition* says that by May 1941 a total of 1248 papers had appeared in the scientific literature on the chemical nature and physiological action of this vitamin.

The chemists found it to be an oily substance of complicated structure with the simple formula, $C_{29}H_{53}O_2$ and called it *alphatocopherol*.

The absence of vitamin E has been found to cause muscular dystrophy in mice, mink, guinea pigs, monkeys, chicks, rabbits, and ducks, but in spite of the great variety of species affected, has not been found to have any effect on this disease in man. The role of vitamin E in human nutrition is still unsettled; most of the work to date has been done with experimental animals. Infants, however, definitely require it and 2 to 10 IU have been found sufficient. This amount is supplied by a liter of human milk. The requirement for older children and adults is not known but apparently varies with the amount of fat in the diet; it increases with the content of un-saturated fat. However, there appears to be little or no deficiency of vitamin E except in some infants.

VITAMIN K

In 1929 Henrik Dam, a student at the University of Copenhagen, was trying to determine whether hens can synthesize cholesterol. He fed several different diets and on one of them the hens developed hemorrhages under the skin and between the muscles. Dam thought they had scurvy and fed them lemon juice, but they did not recover. He also found that their blood was slow to clot. He tried the various remedies for deficiency diseases, but none of them helped.

Dam continued his investigation after graduation and found that the failure of the blood to clot could be remedied by adding one of several foods to the diet. This led him to conclude that the hemor-rhages and the failure of the blood to clot were caused by the lack of a dietary nutrient, which he named the *Koagulation* vitamin from the Danish way of spelling "coagulation." The name was soon shortened to *vitamin K*.

The discovery of vitamin K won Dam the Nobel Prize in physiology and medicine in 1943. He and others continued to investigate vitamin K, and within a few years its chemical nature and physiological properties were well known.

Like vitamins D and E it is a complicated substance, or rather one of several that have similar structures and the same physiological activity. Vitamin K_1, which is found in foods, has the formula $C_{31}H_{46}O_2$ and is not related chemically to either A, D, or E.

Vitamin K aids the production of the protein *prothrombin*, which in turn is required for the formation of *fibrin*, the protein of which a blood clot is composed.

Vitamin K occurs in green vegetables, tomatoes, cauliflower, egg yolk, soybeans, and all kinds of liver. It is also produced in the intestines by the action of bacteria. In adults on a normal diet there seems to be no danger of a vitamin K deficiency.

Doses of mineral oil, however, will prevent the absorption of vitamin K, just as it does that of A and D. The national Boards that suggest allowances have not thought it necessary to make recommendations for vitamin K, but there is one instance in which the physician is concerned with it. The newborn infant is generally deficient in the vitamin because its digestive tract does not contain any bacteria and its diet contains no vitamin K. Some doctors inject the vitamin either into the infant or into the mother before the birth.

CHAPTER 19

Water Soluble Vitamins

The original Water Soluble B turned out to be a more complex mixture than Fat Soluble A. Twelve distinct vitamins have been discovered that are soluble in water.

VITAMIN C

This vitamin prevents and also cures scurvy. I mentioned earlier that James Lind published a book on scurvy in 1753, in which he stated that earlier investigators had found that fresh fruits and vegetables prevent or cure scurvy and describes his own success with lemons and oranges. Later, the British, Spanish, and American ships used fresh foods to prevent the disease that had been known to kill half the crew on a long voyage.

The modern investigation of the cause and cure of scurvy began with experiments made by two investigators in Norway between 1907 and 1912. They tested corn, oats, barley, wheat, rye, and rice on guinea pigs and found that the animals developed scurvy and died after 20 to 40 days. But cabbage, cranberries, dandelion leaves, sorrel, or carrots added to the cereal diet, prevented the disease. These experiments proved that cereals do not cause scurvy, but that the fruits and vegetables contain something that the cereals lack. If the vegetables were dried, they no longer prevented the disease, and even the fresh ones lost some of their effectiveness if they were kept for a long time after harvest.

In 1914 Doctor Alfred Hess, a New York pediatrician who was the medical supervisor of an orphanage, noticed an increase in scurvy among the children. He investigated the cause and found that pasteurizing the milk destroyed its ability to prevent scurvy. As a remedy he added fruit juice to the diet and the scurvy soon disappeared from the orphanage. These results were given wide publicity, and fruit and tomato juice soon became a regular item in the diets of infants and children.

During the 1920s several research groups investigated the scurvy problem by feeding guinea pigs on a variety of diets. Many investigators were simply testing various foods for the presence of the antiscorbutic, some developed methods for determining the relative amount of it in different foods and some tried to extract it and determine its chemical nature, Sir Jack Drummond named it vitamin C.

The first to obtain the pure vitamin was Professor Charles Glenn King of the University of Pittsburgh, who isolated it from California lemon juice in 1931. In 1928 Albert Szent-Gyorgyi, a Hungarian chemist working in the biochemical laboratory at Cambridge University, isolated what he called a *hexuronic acid* from adrenal glands and also from oranges and cabbage. He determined its chemical properties and its formula, which is $C_6H_8O_6$. Dr. King announced in a paper published in 1932 that this acid is the same substance as the vitamin C he had extracted from lemon juice. Then, in a paper also in 1932, Szent-Gyorgyi, now at the University of Szegel in Hungary, also came to the conclusion that his acid was vitamin C. He and an associate continued the investigation and succeeded in getting 450 gm (over 1 lb) of vitamin C from Hungarian red peppers. The chemical nature of the substance could now be thoroughly investigated. The Hungarian chemist named the substance *ascorbic acid* in a report of January 13, 1933. Before the end of that year other chemists had determined its structural formula. It is one of the simpler vitamins, but even so its structure is complicated; its formula somewhat resembles that of glucose.

Ascorbic acid was synthesized the year that its formula was determined and is now available in large quantity without the need to extract it from tons of lemons or peppers. Scientists call it either ascorbic acid or vitamin C, whichever comes to mind first.

Fruits and vegetables, even different samples of the same variety differ in vitamin C content. For example, those that have had most sunlight contain more. Unlike vitamin D, however, sunlight on the animal, human or otherwise, does not produce any vitamin C.

Severe cases of scurvy in both children and adults have been cured by as little as 10 mg of ascorbic acid a day. Severe cases of scurvy are now rare, but an occasional case appears as a result of dietary ignorance, extreme poverty, or carelessness. If a mother has enough of the vitamin, her infant will be born with enough to last 4 to 6 months. Breast-fed infants seldom get scurvy because normal human milk contains about four times as much vitamin C as cow's milk and the latter has part or all of this vitamin destroyed by pasteurization.

Elderly people living alone are liable to scurvy. They have lost most of their zest for food and do not cook proper meals, but live on bread, sandwich meats, or other foods that require little preparation and contain little or no vitamin C. Unless they use fruit or fruit juices, scurvy is likely to develop. The first symptom is weariness and that aggravates a situation that is already bad.

Some people require more vitamin C than others, various kinds of infectious diseases destroy it, and it appears to have several functions in the body besides the prevention of scurvy. It is involved in the formation of collagen (tendons, skin), bones and teeth. It occurs in the adrenal glands, brain, pancreas, kidney, and liver and has been found to affect the action of the heart.

Two reports of effects of vitamin C have appeared recently. In November 1970, Professor Linus Pauling, of Stanford University and a Nobel Prize winner, published a book, *Vitamin C and the Common Cold* in which he states that doses from 250 mg to 5000 mg of ascorbic acid a day will prevent the common cold. Some doctors fear bad side effects from such large doses of acid. A large dose on an empty stomach will cause diarrhea and the formation of kidney stones has been claimed. The book has become a best seller as one might expect, and hundreds of people have followed its advice. Last winter, I took a 500 mg tablet at the first sign of a cold and two others at hourly intervals and got through the season without a cold. But a friend said that he took bigger doses than that and still caught cold. In fact too few supervised cases have been reported to establish the percentage of success, but it is not 100%.

Several studies of the effect of vitamin C and colds have been made both in this country and in Europe. Most of them by the use of 200 mg of the acid daily; only a few have been made with larger quantities. The results show that 200 mg reduces the number of colds by about 15%, and a daily intake of 1000 mg effects a reduction of over 60%. Some of the research scientists have reasons to believe that 4,000 to 10,000 mg is required for complete effectiveness. Vitamin C is a food, of course, and as usual the medical profession is slow to adopt any food therapy.

An even more recent report than Dr. Pauling's is that of Dr. Ralph Mumma of Pennsylvania State University, who found that vitamin C lowers the cholesterol content of the blood. What effect, if any, this property may have on atherosclerosis is yet to be determined.

Because of the many activities of vitamin C that have been reported, the amount a person must have may be subject to wide variation. Great Britain recommends 20 mg daily; South Africa 40 mg; Holland and Russia 50 mg; Japan 65 mg; and India 70 mg. Most of these countries vary the amount recommended with age and sex. The recommendations of the FNB are given in Table 19.1.

The vitamin occurs widely in fruits and vegetables. Some of the richer ones contain the number of milligrams indicated here in 100

TABLE 19.1
VITAMIN C INTAKE RECOMMENDATIONS OF THE
FOOD AND NUTRITION BOARD

Age	Amt. Daily, Mg
Infant (under 1 yr)	35
1–12	40
12–14	45
14–18	55
18+	60

gm of the food: hot peppers 300, parsley 172, orange juice 158, sweet peppers 125, broccoli 90, Brussels sprouts 87, collards 76, turnip greens 69, strawberries 59, lemons 53, mustard greens 48, cabbage 47, grapefruit 38, cantaloupe 33, lime juice 32, green onions 32, tangerines 27, spinach 28, asparagus 26, green peas 20, lettuce 18, lima beans 17, tomato juice 16, snap beans 12, mature onions 10.

Vegetables that have been in the market a long time after harvest lose a large part of their vitamin C, and cooking reduces it to about half that in the fresh food. If a vegetable is boiled in a lot of water and the water discarded the entire vitamin may be lost, for it is very soluble in water. Citrus fruits and other acid foods retain it better than those that are not acid.

VITAMIN B₁

I have already reported the discovery of a nutrient by Dr. Eijkman in 1906 and by Professor Hopkins in the same year, that cures or prevents beriberi. In the *History of Nutrition*, McCollum states that from its discovery in 1906 to the year 1941, 1489 investigators published 1617 papers on this nutrient, which became known as vitamin B_1 and *thiamine*.

By 1937 the vitamin had been isolated from foods, its chemical nature determined and it had been synthesized in the laboratory. It had also become commercially available. The simplest chemical formula for thiamine is $C_{12}H_{17}SN_4ClO$ and its structure makes a complicated picture.

The most dramatic work on vitamin B_1 was that done in the Orient that connected it with the disease beriberi. But it has also been found to be concerned with normal nutrition. It affects the metabolism of glucose, both in its oxidation to produce energy and in its conversion to fat. It also appears to affect the normal functioning of the digestive tract.

There are numerous signs of thiamine deficiency that appear long before the characteristic signs of beriberi. These include tiring easily, apathy, loss of appetite, moodiness, irritability, depression, constipation, numbness in the legs, and abnormal heart action. Continued deficiency causes beriberi, which results in brain damage and finally death.

Beriberi is still common in the Orient and it occasionally occurs elsewhere. In North America severe cases of beriberi occur in alcoholics; a survey made in the 1930s disclosed several cases of the disease in the United States.

The recommended allowances of the FNB increase with age from 0.2 mg for infants under two months old to 1.5 mg in the 18 to 35 period and then drops to 1.2 mg for adult males and 1.0 mg for adult females.

Thiamine occurs in foods of both animal and plant origin. Although the amount in any one food is small, the requirement is also small. Of the common foods, the following contain the number of milligrams indicated in each 100 gm: peanuts 1.14, Canadian bacon 0.92, lean pork 0.63, whole wheat 0.57, enriched bread 0.28, green peas 0.28, beef liver 0.26, lima beans 0.24, mackerel 0.15, dried beans 0.14, oysters 0.14, avocados 0.11, collards 0.11, asparagus 0.10, eggs 0.10 and potatoes 0.10.

VITAMIN B_2

The second vitamin that emerged from the water soluble B complex between 1919 and 1933 was called vitamin G in the United States and vitamin B_2 in England and Europe. Vitamin B_2 survived and vitamin G has long since been abandoned.

The vitamin was first prepared in pure form from whey in 1933 and was named *riboflavin*. Two research groups, working separately synthesized it in 1935 and it is now manufactured in large quantity.

Vitamin B_2 was at first known as the growth vitamin. Unlike vitamins B_1 and C it is not related to the cause and cure of any specific disease. It takes part in the activities of the cells of the various tissues and is essential to vigor, good health, and resistance to some infectious diseases. Symptoms of vitamin B_2 deficiency are not as specific as they are for thiamine and ascorbic acid. Among them are redness and soreness of the tongue and lips, cracks at the angles of the mouth, dermatitis, and poor vision.

Since vitamin B_2 is essential to the respiratory activity of the cells of the body, more than a bare minimum might be expected to improve the activity of these cells. No controlled experiments of this nature have been made with men or women, but there is some statistical evidence that good nutrition in general results in greater vigor, efficiency, and longevity.

Riboflavin is a yellow solid that is soluble in water; its formula is $C_{17}H_{20}N_4O_6$. It is not destroyed by the heat used in cooking, but it is very sensitive to light; exposure of a glass bottle of milk to bright sunlight has been found to destroy all the riboflavin in two hours.

The minimum requirement of riboflavin by the young varies with the number of Calories consumed, the amount of protein in the diet, and possibly other factors. The FNB recommends gradually increasing amounts from 0.4 mg a day for infants under 2 months to 1.7 mg for adults 22 to 75+.

Of the common foods, milk is probably the best source of riboflavin; a quart contains about 2 mg. The vitamin is present in most foods in small amount. In milligrams per 100 gm of food, beef liver contains 4.19, almonds 0.92, blue cheese 0.61, American cheese 0.46, eggs 0.30, bread 0.22, ham 0.22, broccoli 0.20, collards 0.20, asparagus 0.18, and many other foods contain from 0.1 mg to 0.2 mg.

NIACIN

The activity of a third member of the water soluble B complex is related to the disease pellagra. The presence of the disease in northern Spain was described in 1735, and it was also common in northern Italy, the Balkans, and Egypt in the 18th century, but it did not become important in the United States until there was an outbreak in the South between 1905 and 1910.

The first symptoms of pellagra are a sore mouth, then a rough, red skin followed by injury to the nerves and damage to the digestive system, spinal cord, and central nervous system.

With the outbreak in the United States, the Public Health Service began to investigate the cause of the disease. The first report was made by Dr. Carl Voegtlin, who experiments with diets for pellagra patients in a hospital in Spartanburg, S.C. He came to the conclusion that pellagra is a dietary deficiency disease because the patients recovered on some diets and not on others.

Dr. Voegtlin's results did not satisfy Dr. Joseph Goldberger, who was also in the U.S. Public Health Service, and so he undertook an investigation of the disease in state institutions in South Carolina, Georgia, and Mississippi. It took a year for Dr. Goldberger to convince himself that Dr. Voegtlin was right, but even then, he did not convince everybody else; one group of investigators made a survey and decided that the disease was infectious.

TABLE 19.2
NIACIN-INTAKE RECOMMENDATIONS OF THE FOOD
AND NUTRITION BOARD

	Age	Amt. Daily, Mg
Children	Infant–1	5–8
	1–10	8–15
Males	10–55	17–20
	55–75+	14
Females	10–18	15–16
	18–75+	13

One of the objections to Goldberger's work was that the patients in an experiment made in a prison did not develop a red skin. Twenty years later other investigators found that the redness occurs only when the patient is exposed to sunlight.

Dr. Goldberger and his associates continued their research and proved that certain foods cure the disease, but he died before the problem was fully solved. Others took up the investigation and their combined efforts disclosed that the absence of nicotinic acid in the diet is the cause of pellagra. This fact was definitely settled by 1935.

Nicotinic acid is a rather simple organic compound with the formula $C_6H_5NO_2$. It has this name because it was first made in the laboratory from nicotine long before it was known to be a vitamin. The name "nicotinic acid" has unpleasant implications for the name of a nutrient and caused strong opposition to including it in diets. Consequently, the biochemists devised the name *niacin* instead.

Niacin is a white crystalline solid, which is not destroyed at the temperatures used in cooking. Although nicotine is very poisonous, nicotinic acid is not at all toxic.

Scientists have decided that at least 9 mg of niacin a day is necessary to prevent pellagra. The recommended allowances of the FNB are varied somewhat with age and sex, but the general requirements are shown in Table 19.2.

Niacin occurs in many foods, for example, the following contain the indicated number of milligrams of the vitamin in 100 gm of the food: peanuts 17, chicken 12, canned tuna 10, turkey 8, canned salmon 7, lean pork 6, ham 4.5, bread 2.5, peas 2.3, lima beans 1.4, blue cheese 1.2, collards 1.2, and many other foods contain from 0.1 mg to 1 mg.

OTHER B VITAMINS

When investigators began to see that Water Soluble B is a mixture of several vitamins, some scheme for naming them became necessary. The British solved the problem by using subscripts, B_1, B_2, B_3 etc. and the mixture itself was called "the vitamin B complex," which turned out to be 11 separate vitamins. As each member was discovered and isolated in pure form, its chemical structure was soon unraveled and then the chemical names were used, as Drummond had suggested years before. Thiamine, riboflavin, and niacin have already been discussed. The other eight members of the "complex" are vitamin B_6, vitamin B_{12}, folic acid, pantothenic acid, choline, biotin, inositol, and para-aminobenzoic acid. Several of these eight vitamins have not had their importance in human nutrition established and we need not consider them further.

Vitamin B_6

Vitamin B_6 has been found to consist of several substances that are related chemically and perform the same function in nutrition. *Pyridoxine* is the main component of vitamin B_6. It is a solid, white, crystalline compound with the formula $C_8H_{11}NO_3$.

Pyridoxine occurs in lean meat, liver, whole grain cereals, and to a less extent in other foods. Milk contains 0.1 mg in a liter. The FNB recommends 0.5 mg to 1.2 mg for children and 1 to 2 mg for adults. The chief function of vitamin B_6 is its role in the metabolism of the carbohydrates, fats and proteins. Deficiencies of the vitamin are not common because the average mixed diet contains more than the body requires.

Vitamin B_{12}

Although chemists had reported the presence of cobalt in animal tissues as early as 1925, the agricultural chemists were the first to demonstrate its importance in animal nutrition. A serious disease known by various names, of which "coast disease" was one, attacked cattle and sheep in Australia, New Zealand, England, Scotland, Kenya, and Florida. The animals became emaciated, anemic, and died. Agricultural chemists began to search for the cause of the disease and in 1935 they found the answer; the grass of the pasture lands in the affected areas did not contain cobalt.

Pernicious anemia in humans had long been a problem until in 1926 Drs. George R. Minot and William P. Murphy of Boston hospitals discovered that liver in the diet will cure it. The discovery won them a Nobel prize in 1934 and, of course, started chemists on the track of the component in liver that cured this dreadful disease. In 1948 biochemists in England and the United States isolated vitamin B_{12} from liver and found it to be the curative factor.

With the discovery of vitamin B_{12}, the next problem was its chemical structure. This was solved much sooner than might have been expected, since it is an extremely complicated substance; the structure was announced in 1956 by a group at Oxford. Its simplest formula is $C_{63}H_{88}O_{14}PCo$, a total of 167 atoms of which one is cobalt. It was synthesized by the cooperation of nearly 100 chemists mainly from the United States and Switzerland; the final result was announced in 1972. Although vitamin B_{12} synthesis was a great achievement of the organic chemists, it has little significance for nutritionists at present, for the vitamin has been made for several years in large quantity by the fermentation of distillers wastes.

The cobalt in this vitamin seems to be all that is required by man or beast. The element occurs in nearly all animal and plant tissues especially leaves, and the requirement is so small that a mixed diet of natural foods will usually supply the requirement.

Vitamin B_{12} is the only one discovered to date that has an atom of a metal in its molecule. It is a solid that crystallizes in long, red needles. Its chemical name is *cobalamine*, but that name has not become popular and so it is vitamin B_{12} to practically everybody.

Vitamin B_{12} is an effective cure for pernicious anemia, but it also functions in the bone marrow, nerves, digestive tract, and elsewhere in the body. The FNB recommends an intake of 5 mcg daily for adults and 1 to 4 mcg for children.

The vitamin B_{12} content of foods in general has not been determined. However, liver has been reported to contain 40 to 60 mcg in 100 gm of the food, lean meat 1 to 3 mcg, and milk also contains some of it, but fruits and vegetables contain little or none.

Pantothenic Acid

Discovered in 1933, pantothenic acid was not isolated in the pure state until 1940. It is a viscous, yellow liquid, but it is marketed as the calcium salt, which is a white, crystalline solid.

This acid is required by all animal species that have been studied. Although, like many other vitamins, its absence does not result in any specific disease such as scurvy or pellagra, it is required in some of the complex chemical processes essential to normal health. The FNB recommends 5 to 10 mg in the daily diet. It occurs widely in meats, milk, eggs, and cereals. A mixed diet will likely contain 5 to 20 mg of pantothenic acid, so it is not a serious nutritional problem except in cases of special diets.

Folic Acid

In 1938 a research group discovered a vitamin deficiency in monkeys and so they called the nutrient that prevented it *vitamin M*. Several other groups began to investigate the subject, and in 1941 one of them isolated what proved to be vitamin M from spinach. Since they obtained the substance from leaves, they named it for the Latin word for leaves, *folia*. Consequently, vitamin M became folic acid, or *folacin*. Five years later two research groups of chemists in the laboratories of drug manufacturers determined the structure of folic acid and synthesized it.

One of the functions of folic acid in the body is its relation to certain types of anemia. The exact amount required is not definitely known, but it is less than 1 mg a day. It occurs in most foods, and the average American diet contains about 0.2 mg, therefore a deficiency is unlikely.

EXCESS VITAMINS

A question that always comes to the mind of a student of nutrition is: "What happens if one gets too much of a vitamin?" The research biologists have thought of that too and have spent considerable time and money to find out. The results of their many experiments and observations vary somewhat because some people tolerate more vitamins than others just as some tolerate more drugs than others. However, if vitamins are obtained from foods only, none of them will be consumed in harmful amount. But the vitamins are sold in pills, powders, and capsules, and therefore very large doses are available in any drug store. The richest preparations, are usually sold only on the prescription of a physician.

None of the water soluble vitamins has been found harmful, although 50 to 100 mg of niacin taken on an empty stomach may cause flushing and burning of the face and neck for a short time. Folic acid is restricted to 0.1 mg daily dosage for preparations sold to the general public because larger doses may cover up the symptoms of pernicious anemia.

The fat soluble vitamins are not as innocent as those soluble in water, but still the hazard is not very great. Arctic explorers have developed symptoms of too much vitamin A from eating the livers of seals and polar bears. The symptoms of too much vitamin A in children are vomiting and drowsiness; in adults the symptoms are headache, abdominal pains, vertigo, vomiting, and diarrhea.

The highest recommended daily allowance of vitamin A in normal diets is 5,000 IU. The results of experiments with large doses vary with the age and personal tolerance of the individual and the symptoms that are used to determine the excess. A child may begin to show symptoms with 50,000 IU daily. One report indicates that a harmful dose must be 20 to 30 times the recommended allowance, which would be at least 100,000 IU. Adults have taken 100,000 IU daily for 6 months with no toxicity symptoms, but 600,000 IU daily did produce symptoms.

Vitamin D is the most likely of the vitamins to produce ill effects although none has ever been reported when the vitamin was obtained from either food or sunlight or both.

The daily recommendation for vitamin D is 400 IU, and for infants this number should not be greatly exceeded, but older children and adults are much more tolerant. Children have had trouble on 40,000 IU daily and adults on 100,000. One observer reported that 1,800 IU retarded the growth of children, but others reported no evidence of harm in doses from 2,000 to 3,000 IU daily. However, overdosage varies with individuals and with the amount of calcium and phosphorus in the diet. The symptoms of overdosage in older children and adults are similar to those produced by vitamin A. If the overdosage is continued for some time, calcium deposits form in the soft tissues—primarily in the kidneys, but also in the heart, lungs, and blood vessels. Overdosage of vitamin A might occur from too enthusiastic prescription by a physician, but the results are easily remedied by cutting down the amount of the vitamin. A long-time overdosage of vitamin D is a much more difficult problem; recovery from calcification does not instantly follow reduction of the vitamin.

Toxicity of vitamin E is unlikely to be a problem. Daily doses as large as 800 IU per kilogram of body weight have been continued for 5 months without the detection of any harm. Vitamin K is likewise unlikely to be a problem, although it does interfere with the action of anticoagulant drugs and should be taken into account when such drugs are prescribed.

Thousands of people in the world suffer from a vitamin deficiency to one that is harmed by too much of any of them. A recent administrator of the FDA stated that enough of all the vitamins can be obtained from the common foods and that people waste their money on pills and capsules. He was quite correct in the first statement, but numerous surveys and observations have shown that few people do select a diet that supplies the required amount of all the vitamins. Many people have diets badly deficient in some of them. This was the reason for the food enrichment program which helps correct the lack of enough vitamins, but there are people who do not eat the enriched foods. People undoubtedly do waste their money, but very little of it on vitamin pills.

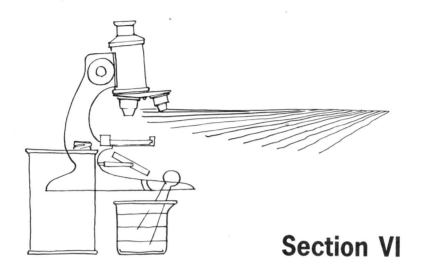

Section VI

Our Food Supply—
The Future

CHAPTER 20

What Now--What Next?

The facts of nutrition as stated in these pages are the results of long, tedious, and costly experiments and not the product of someone's imagination or casual observation. Man has always added anything to his menu that he could find, if it appealed to his taste or appeased his hunger. Thus, through the centuries, a food and beverage list has been accumulated by haphazard methods.

The safety of the common foods has been pretty well established by the long years that most of them have been eaten. However, the toxicologists are now beginning to look for possibly harmful substances in them. There is also a chance of contamination by pesticides, molds or other foreign matter, and so there is one precaution that should always be taken; wash any fruit or vegetable before you eat it and, except in a few cases such as bananas, wash it before you peel it.

PLANNING A DIET

There are so many essential features to a proper diet that the housewife or even the dietitian may feel discouraged—the task beyond her. Not at all. The first thing to consider is easy and needs to be done only once. Take stock of the persons to be fed. An elderly couple is a very different problem from the family with several young children, and a man who spends his days sitting at a desk needs less food than one who drives a truck or harvests watermelons.

(1) Calories may be no problem at all if there is plenty of money and no obesity. But if there is one or the other of these problems, consult Chap. 10 and select low-calorie foods or those that supply more Calories for the dollar, whichever eases the problem.

Some people seem to feel that only the food eaten at a meal counts, and they eat and drink more between meals than at meal time. If there is an obese member of the family, remove temptation; do not buy any candy, cookies, nuts, soft drinks, or beer.

(2) Although there is some protein in practically all foods, it is hard to get enough unless meat, milk, cheese, eggs, peas, beans, or lentils are eaten. But proteins are expensive and so it is a good idea to check each person's requirement against the allowance recommended in Chap. 13.

216

(3) Calcium is the most important mineral, and it may be deficient, especially if there are children in the family. Milk is essential in the diet of children, for it is exceedingly difficult to include enough calcium without it. Even with adults, calcium is a problem unless the diet includes milk or a very liberal amount of fruits and vegetables.

(4) Buy iodized salt. Seafood is the only other reliable source of iodine.

(5) It may be important to check on the first four vitamins for the general diet. The others are important only in special cases. Turn to Chap. 18 and 19 and check the vitamin content of the foods; the richest sources are recorded there. You may need to increase the milk, eggs, or green vegetables to get the recommended amount of vitamin A, more fruits and vegetables for C, and eggs or fortified milk for D.

NUTRITION IN THE UNITED STATES

Some idea of how important it is to plan the family menu is indicated by the results of surveys of nutrition in this country. A survey that was made in the 1930s found 200,000 cases of pellagra, and many cases of beriberi. In 1936, 75% of American diets were rated as "not good" and 33% as "poor."

The U.S. Public Health Service has recently issued a preliminary report on the results of examining the diet and health of 12,000 people in certain areas of Texas, Louisiana, Kentucky, and New York. They found 7 cases of starvation, 18 of rickets, and 5% of those examined had goiter. The survey included families with incomes up to $40,000 although 80% of those examined had incomes of less than $5,000.

Both goiter and rickets had been almost completely eliminated before the 1930s, the rickets largely by the addition of vitamin D to milk and the goiter by the general use of iodized salt. In those days the importance of iodine and vitamin D was widely publicized by nutritionists, dietitians, social services, teachers, government agencies, and popular writers. Then, during the war the government improved the nutrition by requiring the enrichment of flour and bread and the encouragement of home gardens. But with the economic splurge that has been with us since the war, everybody seems to have taken it for granted that with all the money people are now making, nutrition would take care of itself. In a Texas area surveyed, 40% of the grocers did not stock iodized salt. Apparently this neglect has become common; a salesman for a wholesale grocer in Florida tells me that many grocers pay no attention to whether or not their salt is iodized. Vitamin D milk and margarine are available, but their importance, especially to the young, is not generally realized.

Other surveys have been made in recent years. In 1965 obesity was the most common nutritional defect, but about the same time, nearly 25% of the infants between the age of 6 and 21 months were deficient in iron. In the late 1950s teenage girls had the poorest diets. They were low in vitamins A and C and in calcium and iron.

When the survey of the 1930s revealed the deplorable state of American nutrition, the Surgeon General of the United States called a conference of the prominent nutritionists of the day for a discussion of the best way to improve the people's diet. Vitamins had been known for 20 years at the time of the conference and as the knowledge of them increased, nutritionists, teachers, government agents, and others had urged the people to eat the foods that contain them—mainly fresh fruits, vegetables, and milk. Whole-wheat bread had also been strongly recommended.

Millers were criticized for not grinding more whole-wheat flour and the bakers for not baking more whole-wheat bread. Neither of them was at fault and so their defense was very simple. They did try to introduce whole-wheat products, but the people would not buy them. Furthermore, both the millers and the bakers had a problem. The whole-wheat flour did not keep well, for the eggs of the weevil, which were laid in the crease of the grain of wheat while it was still in the field, could not be removed and they hatched. One manufacturer of a muffin mix tried to sell a mix for whole-wheat muffins, but the packages sat on the grocer's shelves, and while the manufacturer waited for repeat orders, the flour on hand came alive with weevils. He gave over a ton of it to an employee who raised hogs on the side. Many of the packages that had been sold were returned because they too were coming to life, and the weevils were visiting neighboring items on the shelf. Naturally, he gave up the idea of making whole-wheat products.

The nutritionists at the Surgeon General's conference were well aware of the attempts to get the public to eat the natural foods that contain the most vitamins, and to use milk, fruits, and vegetables, and that it did have a little success. Cod liver oil and sunsuits for young children took pretty good care of vitamins A and D. The big problem revealed by the survey was the lack of the B complex. There were commercial campaigns for the consumption of spinach and raisins as sources of iron; but the raisins were expensive, and people did not like the spinach.

ENRICHMENT

After much discussion and argument during the years following the conference, the most logical solution to the problem prevailed; restore to white flour the nutrients lost in the milling process. The addition of the B vitamins and iron to flour had been suggested as early as 1936, but the government did not reach an official policy until May 27, 1941. The promptness with which the millers and bakers accepted the enrichment idea was partly a result of the decline in the use of flour, which was 300 lb per capita in 1909 and only 199 lb in 1940. Moreover, flour had been losing favor with dietitians who regarded it as a source of Calories and nothing else. They ignored the fact that flour has an average protein content of about 10%.

Enrichment increased the cost of the flour. In 1941 the cost to the miller was 12¢ a hundred-weight and is now about 1.5¢. This increase in the cost of the flour interfered with the acceptance of enrichment because the heavy consumers of bread were more concerned with the few extra cents than with nutritional requirements about which they knew little or nothing.

Within a year after the millers began to enrich the flour, 70% of the flour and bread was enriched. This is an amazing development when we consider that millers had to install special equipment to add the tiny amount of iron salts and vitamins and mix them thoroughly with the flour.

The noble efforts of the government and the miller to improve the nutrition of the population appeared to be doomed to failure, and some of the bakers were about to give up enrichment. The public, especially in the South, where the state of nutrition was the worst, refused to pay the extra cost of enriched flour and bread. Then came the war. In 1942 South Carolina led the way by passing a law that required enrichment. In January 1943 War Food Order No. 1 required the enrichment of all white flour and bread. The order was withdrawn in 1946, but by that time, 19 States had passed laws requiring enrichment. Beriberi and pellagra nearly disappeared, and since 1946 the enrichment program has been extended to other cereal products.

I have been asked frequently why the millers take the iron and vitamins out of the grain and then put them back again. The answer lies in the nature of the grain of wheat. The milling process has been described in Chap. 2, and reference to that will show that the flour consists mainly of the endosperm with very little of the aleurone layer and none of the bran and germ. The iron and vitamins are in these rejected parts of the wheat grain. The common flour represents only 70% of the wheat kernel.

The enrichment of the cereal foods is not done in a hit-or-miss manner by the individual miller. The government has set standards based on the analysis of several thousand samples of wheat and the opinions of several experts in the field of food and nutrition. These standards require 1 lb of flour to contain: thiamine 2–2.5 mg, riboflavin 1.2–1.5 mg, niacin 16–20 mg, iron 13–16.5 mg, calcium 500–625 mg, and vitamin D 250–1000 USP units. The last two items are optional, but if they are added, they must be declared on the label. Similar standards are set for other cereal products.

By 1930 the Walker-Gordon Laboratories, a specialized dairy in New Jersey, were increasing the vitamin D content of their certified milk by feeding irradiated yeast to the cows. In 1932, the Borden Company introduced irradiated milk in Detroit.

In 1933, the *Journal of the American Medical Association* in an editorial said:

> . . . the incidence of rickets is still too great and will continue to be until some cheap, generally available, agreeable source of vitamin D is provided. Vitamin D milk seems to offer promising possibilities of meeting these requirements.

It is hardly necessary to say that this statement by the influential medical journal gave the whole vitamin D milk project a terrific boost.

In 1934 the evaporated milk industry was adding 135 units of vitamin D to each pint of their product, and by 1945 the vitamin D content of evaporated milk had been increased to 400 units per pint, and that is now general throughout the industry. Fresh vitamin D milk is now marketed in all the states, and in most of them the standards require 400 units to the quart. In some states there is also available milk fortified with vitamins A and D, thiamine, riboflavin, niacin, iron, and iodine or some combination of them.

SHOPPING

Although food habits are probably the greatest obstacle to the improvement of the diet, cost also has its influence. The high cost of food is aggravated by advertising, salesmanship, and the housewife's surrender to convenience. When the farmer produced all his meat, milk, butter, eggs, cereals, vegetables, and fruits and his wife prepared them for the table, the cost of feeding the family was very little. The family itself did the processing. But as each task was handed over to someone outside the family, the cost increased. The miller ground the grain, the butcher dressed the meat, the baker made the bread and so on, until today, the housewife only needs to haul the food home from the market, heat it, and set it on the table.

Americans are also probably unique in insisting on a maximum variety of foods in all seasons; not only bananas that must come from the tropics and citrus fruit from California, Florida, or Texas, but also tomatoes from Mexico and other fresh vegetables from a southern climate. This means transportation over long distances, which is expensive.

The shopper has three and sometimes four choices of the same fruit or vegetable; it may be fresh, frozen, canned, or dried. The relative cost varies with the season, but at any time it will require considerable calculation. Besides the simple difference in price there is also the question of quality; in general, there is little difference in the nutritive value. Some people disdain canned food, but it is often better than the available fresh one; canned tomatoes and canned pineapple are both superior in flavor to the fresh product in most markets. Canned, frozen, and fresh peas differ in flavor, but which is the most desirable is a matter of taste.

Comparison of the cost of foods is complicated by the number of brands and package sizes to be found in most stores. It is difficult to say what food processor first issued a package of consumer size or what the product was, but by 1900 there were several such packages in the stores. Women baked their bread and so flour appeared in 25, 50, and 100 lb bags; there was no demand for smaller packages. Coffee, soda, baking powder, tea, and a few other items were in 1 lb, 1/2 lb, or 1/4 lb packages. Coffee was still available in bulk, and some stores carried Mocha, Java and several other kinds so the shopper could buy some of each and make her own blend.

Prepackaging was a great boon to the grocer, and so the idea grew rapidly and the cost of the food grew with it. Aside from convenience in handling, the packaging enabled the processor to present his brand name to the consumer. All these early packages were in simple units such as 1 lb, $\frac{1}{2}$ lb or 1 qt.

During the first half of the 20th century, packaging became more and more complex. Dry foods such as salt, sugar, soda, and coffee were packaged in cardboard containers lined with waxed paper if necessary, and those containers were always made to order because label information was printed directly on the package. This enabled the packer to use any size he chose and to change it whenever he ordered a new supply of packaging material.

Since the only legal limit on packaging was the requirement that the net amount of food must be declared on the label, the food distributor soon found reasons for odd size packages and for numerous sizes for the same product. One obvious reason for different sizes was a small package for a small family and a large package for a big family. Then came the idea that if two sizes are good more will be better; and it is better in one particular, that is, better for the distributor. The grocer must allot more shelf space to the product if he is to stock all the sizes, and the more there is on display, the more likely the shopper is to see it and buy it. Furthermore, odd sizes have the advantage of permitting an increase in price that may not be noticed by the casual shopper. If a 16-oz package is reduced to 14 oz and the price remains the same, the package is so nearly the same size that few shoppers would notice the difference, and the declared weight was often printed in small type and in an obscure place. Increasing prices by reducing the size of the package became very common with the rise in prices after World War I.

The odd size package, an advantage to the food processor, is most troublesome to the consumer. It is difficult to compare the cost of the same food in packages of different sizes. Suppose one package contains $6\frac{1}{4}$ oz and sells for 25¢, while another package of the same food contains $7\frac{1}{2}$ oz and sells for 35¢, which is the better buy? Some shoppers who are pressed for time or poor in arithmetic, solve such a problem by buying the larger package on the logical theory that the bigger the package the more economical it is. However, this is often not so. I recently noticed two jars of olives in which the olives were obviously the same. The jars looked alike except that one was slightly smaller than the other. The labels disclosed the fact that one contained 7 oz and the other 9 oz. The 7-oz jar was 49¢ and the 9-oz jar was 69¢. If the olives had been the same price the larger jar should have sold for 63¢. Also hand-packed products cost more but are no better. Recently, I noticed two jars of stuffed olives. One was packed by hand with the red peppers next to the glass and was priced at 69¢; the other had been filled by pouring the olives in and cost 47¢. The olives were the same and the jars the same size.

In 1966 Congress passed the Fair Packaging and Labeling Act, commonly called the Truth in Packaging Law. The purpose, as stated in the law is: "To regulate interstate and foreign commerce by preventing the use of unfair or deceptive methods of packaging or labeling of certain consumer commodities distributed in such commerce and for other purposes."

The law covers all commodities sold at retail except certain items that were already regulated by other laws, such as alcoholic beverages and tobacco. The FDA is charged with the enforcement insofar as it applies to foods, drugs, or cosmetics and the penalties are the same as those for misbranding under the Food, Drug, and Cosmetic Act.

The law does not contain any specification of package size or the number of different sizes that can be used for the same commodity; manufacturers and distributors were violently opposed to any such provision of the law. However, the law timidly recognizes the problem in the provision:

> Whenever the Secretary of Commerce determines that there is undue proliferation of weights, measures or quantities in which any consumer commodity, or reasonably comparable consumer commodities are being distributed in packages for sale at retail and such proliferation impairs the reasonable ability of consumers to make value comparisons . . . he shall request . . . [the distributors] to participate in the development of a voluntary standard . . .

Although this is no regulation at all, it may induce some distributors to reduce the number and complexity of their packages—Congress can and often does amend its laws.

In the five years since the law was passed it has not accomplished much, but the amount of food in the package does now appear on the front label, usually in larger type than formerly; one no longer has a long search for that information. Also a few packagers are dropping fractional ounces. The enforcement officers have recommended reduction in the number of sizes and a few companies are complying.

Price comparison is still far from easy. Consumer's Union gave 5 women, who were experienced shoppers, a list of 14 items and told them to disregard brands and buy the most economical package of each item in a large supermarket. They found 286 brands, types, and sizes. They spent 50 minutes on the project and the result was 32 correct choices and 38 wrong ones. Only 2 made the right choice from among 31 available breakfast cereals where the prices varied from 15 to 98¢ a pound. It took five women and a calculating machine 6 hours to calculate the most economic choice of each of these 14 items. Price comparisons are difficult but the variation in unit cost makes it worth trying if the cost of food is of importance to the shopper. Select the items most often bought and make one calculation at a time.

Aside from the difference in cost of the same foods there is a greater problem in the selection of foods used more or less interchangeably in the menu: olives and pickles; hot cereals, dry cereals and toast; rice and potatoes; meat, fish, poultry, cheese and eggs; ice cream, pies and canned fruit. In the selection of fresh fruit the shopper may have the choice of apples, bananas, grapefruit, oranges, pears, melons, grapes, and at times, several others.

Finally, there is the question of allergy. Some people cannot eat strawberries, mangoes, eggs, or some other food, and so the shopper must be prepared to recognize the foods some members of the family cannot eat and shop accordingly. No food is cheap if the family cannot or will not eat it.

CARE AND COOKING OF FOODS

After the shopper has made her purchases, she should get them home as soon as possible. Fresh foods lose their vitamin content, particularly vitamin C. Frozen foods deteriorate rapidly if they thaw. Once the food is at home, the fresh foods should be stored in a refrigerator with the exception of bananas, which lose their flavor at low temperatures.

Some cooks add soda to boiling vegetables to retain or increase the green color. This should never be done because it destroys both vitamin C and thiamine. Steaming vegetables causes less loss of vitamin C than boiling, and a pressure cooker destroys the least of the three methods of cooking. Vitamin C is easily destroyed by the action of the air; in one experiment, baked whole sweet potatoes retained 89% of this vitamin while those cut in half and then baked, retained only 31% of it. Of course, any of the water soluble vitamins is lost if vegetables are boiled in water and the water discarded.

FUTURE OF THE FOOD SUPPLY

In the previous pages I have emphasized the enormous quantity and variety of food available in this country. The question that concerns all of us is, how long will this abundance last. The population is increasing rapidly and farm land is fast becoming exhausted, or turned into housing developments, highways, and airports at the rate of several million acres a year. Machinery and fertilizer have increased food production from an average of 307 lb to the acre through the years 1947–1955 to 524 lb to the acre in 1964. Only 7% of our labor force is now in agriculture; we are no longer an agricultural country. In Russia 50% of the laborers are in agriculture and in the Orient, 90%. Our best land is now in use and any increase in farm land will require an increase in water supply or an increase in the use of fertilizer, or both. Our efforts to feed the people of other countries have already used up the huge surplus of grain we had only a few years ago, and both our population and that of the rest of the world is increasing.

Some people seem to think that we can go on increasing the food supply indefinitely. A few small increases are possible. For example, the common white flour is only 70% of the wheat grain; during the war years the government required it to be increased to 85% and that can be done again. The production of beef takes large areas of pasture land, and we can shift to more economical sources of protein, such as eggs, poultry, and fish raised in ponds. But even fish have to be fed. We cannot reduce our consumption of protein appreciably. About 12% of the calories of our diet now come from protein and the recommendation of the FNB is 10 to 12% from that source. Peas, beans, and lentils are more economical sources of protein than meat is, but they were not very popular substitutes during the war years.

Animals are poor converters of feed into food. Cattle usually convert only 4% of the energy of their feed into beef, although recent feeding experiments claim 10% conversion. Under special feeding conditions, cows convert 30% of their feed into milk. Poultry are much better energy converters than cattle. However, increasing the rate of conversion of feed to food cannot increase the food supply to any great extent except when the feed is something that cannot be used directly as food. Even that has its limits for land used to raise hay could also be used to raise grain or vegetables.

The food supply can be increased somewhat by the prevention of waste, especially by the elimination of insects, rats, mice, and other parasites on the human food supply.

The fact is that our food supply will need to be increased enormously within our own times and not at some vague future date. We are already familiar with scarcity and rationing in war time, and we now import 550,000 tons of meat annually.

In all the years from the advent of the human race to 1850 the population of the world reached 1 billion. The second billion appeared by 1930 and the third by 1960. In other words, the first billion took thousands of years, the second took 80 years, and the third arrived in 30 years; demographers predict that the fourth will be reached in less than 20 years. Even now, some informed nutritionists estimate that 10,000 people starve to death every day, and our own rich country contributes to the total.

Any big increase in the world food supply depends on water, land, and fertilizer. Very little unused arable land is available anywhere in the world unless water can be supplied on a huge scale to land that is now too dry to be of use for either farming or pasture. Further-more, experience with irrigation in Egypt indicates that it often creates more problems that it solves.

Fertilizer will soon become a problem. Of the 3 main plant nu-trients, nitrogen, phosphorus and potassium, the nitrogen problem was solved over 50 years ago by the invention of the Haber process for the fixation of atmospheric nitrogen.

For many years, Florida has been the chief source of phosphate fertilizer, and there are deposits in other states, in Africa, and else-where in the world. But all natural minerals are exhaustible; we now go far into Canada for iron ore, down to Venezuela, Surinam, and Jamaica for aluminum ore, to numerous countries for oil, and several places for nickel and gold. How long our phosphate deposits will last is hard to predict. The use of fertilizer in this country is less than a century old; before that the farmers simply moved to new land farther west as their eastern farms became less productive. The use of fertilizer has increased enormously in recent years, and the next century will use many times that of the last.

Before World War I our potassium supply all came from Ger-many, and many of us remember the consternation in this country when the war cut off all supplies from that source. Seaweed was harvested in the Pacific and burned for the potassium in the ashes. The sugar beet residue from the sugar factories was also burned for the same purpose, and contributed its mite. The government at once began a survey of the potassium content of the waters of the salt lakes in our western deserts. Searles Lake in California was found to contain about 2% potassium chloride in the brine beneath the crust of salt 90 ft thick that covered it. This lake became our main source of potassium for several years after the war. Then some brine wells in the Southwest came into production. These were our chief source until recently when rich deposits were found in Canada. The supply of potassium in North America is adequate at the mo-ment, but each ton of fertilizer contains from 100 to 200 lb of the element.

Education and prosperity tend to reduce the size of families, but neither of these factors can exert any important restraint on the growth of the population in the next half century. Even if the population does not increase at all, few centuries will pass before food must be provided by some means at present unknown, or people will starve.

Starvation seems to be the ultimate fate of the human race. How soon it will come cannot be predicted because more food can be produced as long as the phosphate and potassium hold out. Our present great prosperity only means that we are using up our natural resources faster. Agricultural production has increased in many countries, but so has the population, and although a general famine has been avoided, the production of food has always been one step behind the increase in population. The Food and Agricultural Organization of the United Nations estimates that only one-sixth of the present world population is well fed.

I end this chapter with a prediction: The next 100 years, perhaps the next 50, will see vast changes in our food supply in this country, including the disappearance of the less economical fruits and vegetables. Cucumbers, radishes, and watermelons will give way to carrots, beets, beans, and other crops that produce more food to the acre. Meat will become scarce and all foods will be expensive. And all these changes, and more, will have to be accompanied by some measures of population control.

Bibliography

ALBANESE, A. A. 1959. Protein and Amino Acid Nutrition. Academic Press, New York.

AGRICULTURAL RESEARCH SERVICE. 1972. Cheeses of the World. Dover Publications, New York.

ANDERSON, J. A. 1946. Enzymes and Their Role in Wheat Technology. John Wiley & Sons, New York.

ANON. 1965. Landmarks of a Half Century of Nutrition Research. Univ. California Press, Berkeley.

ARBUCKLE, W. S. 1972. Ice Cream, 2nd Edition. Avi Publishing Co., Westport, Conn.

ATWATER, W. O., and BENEDICT, F. G. 1905. A Respiration Calorimeter with Appliances for the Direct Determination of Oxygen. Publ. *42*, Carnegie Inst., Washington, D.C.

BAILEY, A. E. 1944. Industrial Oil and Fat Products. John Wiley & Sons, New York.

BAILEY, C. H. 1944. The Constituents of Wheat and Wheat Products. Van Nostrand Reinhold Co., New York.

BERGSTROM, G. 1961. Fish as Food, Vol. 1. Academic Press, New York.

BRINK, M. F., and KRITCHEVSKY, D. 1968. Dairy Lipids and Lipid Metabolism. Avi Publishing Co., Westport, Conn.

CORN INDUSTRIES RES. FOUND. 1958. Corn Syrup and Sugars, 2nd Edition. U.S. Govt. Printing Office, Washington, D.C.

DE LUCA, H. F., and SUTTIE, J. W. 1969. The Fat Soluble Vitamins. Univ. Wisconsin Press, Madison.

DYKE, S. F. 1965. The Chemistry of the Vitamins. John Wiley & Sons, New York.

EDSALL, J. T. 1951. Enzymes and Enzyme Systems. Harvard Univ. Press, Boston.

FDA. 1966. General Regulations for the Enforcement of the Federal Food, Drug and Cosmetic Act: Title 21, Part 1. U.S. Govt. Printing Office, Washington, D.C.

FOX, S. W., and FOSTER, J. F. 1957. Introduction to Protein Chemistry. John Wiley & Sons, New York.

FREED, M. 1966. Methods of Vitamin Assay, 3rd Edition. John Wiley & Sons, New York.

GARARD, I. D. 1969. Invitation to Chemistry. Doubleday & Co., New York.

GOLDBLITH, S. A., and JOSLYN, M. A. 1964. Milestones in Nutrition. Avi Publishing Co., Westport, Conn.

GREENSMITH, M. 1971. Practical Dehydration. Avi Publishing Co., Westport, Conn.

GUNDERSON, F. L. *et al.* 1963. Food Standards and Definitions in the United States. Academic Press, New York.

HALL, C. W., and HEDRICK, T. I. 1971. Drying of Milk and Milk Products, 2nd Edition. Avi Publishing Co., Westport, Conn.

HILDITCH, T. P. 1940. The Chemical Constitution of Natural Fats. John Wiley & Sons, New York.

JAMIESON, G. S. 1943. Vegetable Fats and Oils. Van Nostrand Reinhold Co., New York.

JENSEN, L. B. 1953. Man's Foods, Garrard Publishing Co., Champagne, Ill.

INGLETT, G. E. 1970. Corn: Culture, Processing, Products. Avi Publishing Co., Westport, Conn.

KLEINFELD, V. A., and DUNN, C. W. 1951. Federal Food, Drug and Cosmetic Act. Judicial and Administrative Record, 1949–1950. Commerce Clearing House, Chicago.

KOSIKOWSKI, F. V. 1970. Cheese and Fermented Milk Foods. Avi Publishing Co., Westport, Conn.

LAWRIE, R. A. 1970. Proteins as Human Food. Avi Publishing Co., Westport, Conn.

LEVITICUS. Chapter II.

LOCK, A. 1969. Practical Canning, 3rd Edition. Avi Publishing Co., Conn.

MANUFACTURING CHEMISTS ASSOC. 1971. Food Additives. U.S. Govt. Printing Office, Washington, D.C.

MATZ, S. A. 1965. Water in Foods. Avi Publishing Co., Westport, Conn.

MATZ, S. A. 1970. Cereal Technology. Avi Publishing Co., Westport, Conn.

MATZ, S. A. 1972. Bakery Technology and Engineering, 2nd Edition. Avi Publishing Co., Westport, Conn.

McCOLLUM, E. V. 1957. A History of Nutrition. Houghton Mifflin Co., Boston.

MEADE, G. P. 1963. Cane Sugar Handbook. John Wiley & Sons, New York.

MINIFIE, B. W. 1970. Chocolate, Cocoa and Confectionery. Avi Publishing Co., Westport, Conn.

MUTH, O. H., and OLDFIELD, J. E. 1970. Sulfur in Nutrition. Avi Publishing Co., Westport, Conn.

MUTH, O. H. *et al.* 1967. International Symposium: Selenium in Biomedicine. Avi Publishing Co., Westport, Conn.

NAT. ACAD. SCI.—NATL. RES. COUNCIL. 1966. Dietary Fat and Human Health. Publ. *1147*. Nat. Acad. Sci.—Natl. Res. Council, Washington, D.C.

NATL. ACAD. SCI.—NATL. RES. COUNCIL. 1968. Recommended Dietary Allowances. Rept. Food and Nutr. Board. Natl. Acad. Sci.—Natl. Res. Council, Washington, D.C.

NATL. ACAD. SCI.—NATL. RES. COUNCIL. 1971. Food Colors. Natl. Acad. Sci.—Natl. Res. Council, Washington, D.C.

NEAL, H. E. 1968. The Protectors. Julian Messner, New York.

PARRY, J. W. 1969. Spices, Vols. 1 and 2. Avi Publishing Co., Westport, Conn.

PAULING, L. 1970. Vitamin C and the Common Cold. W. H. Freeman and Co., San Francisco.

POTTER, N. N. 1973. Food Science, 2nd Edition. Avi Publishing Co., Westport, Conn.

RIEPMA, S. F. 1970. The Story of Margarine. Public Affairs Press, Washington, D.C.

SCHULTZ, H. W. 1960. Food Enzymes. Avi Publishing Co., Westport, Conn.

SCHULTZ, H. W., and ANGLEMIER, A. F. 1964. Proteins and Their Reactions. Avi Publishing Co., Westport, Conn.

SHERMAN, H. C. 1914. Food Products, 1st Edition. The Macmillan Co., New York.

SHERMAN, H. C. 1952. Chemistry of Food and Nutrition. The Macmillan Co., New York.

SHERMAN, H. C., and SMITH, S. L. 1931. The Vitamins. Chemical Catalog Co., New York.

SHRODER, J. H. 1939. Food Control. Its Public Health Aspects. John Wiley & Sons, New York.

SIVETZ, M., and FOOTE, H. E. 1963. Coffee Processing Technology, Vols. 1 and 2. Avi Publishing Co., Westport, Conn.

STADELMAN, W. J., and COTTERILL, O. J. 1973. Egg Science and Technology. Avi Publishing Co., Westport, Conn.

SULLIVAN, M. 1927. Our Times, Vol. II: America Finding Herself. Charles Scribner's Sons, New York.

UNDERWOOD, E. J. 1962. Trace Elements in Human and Animal Nutrition. Academic Press, New York.

USDA. 1962. Magnesium in Nutrition. Home Economics Res. Rept. *19*, Agr. Res. Serv., U.S. Govt. Printing Office, Washington, D.C.

USDA. 1967. Food and Your Weight. Home and Garden Bull. *74*, U.S. Govt. Printing Office, Washington, D.C.

U.S. DEPT. COMMERCE. 1935. Hearings Before a Subcommittee on Commerce, U.S. Senate, 74th Congress. U.S. Dept. of Commerce, Office Tech. Serv. P.B. Rept., Washington, D.C.

U.S. DEPT. HEALTH, EDUCATION, AND WELFARE. 1967. Federal Food, Drug and Cosmetic Act. U.S. Govt. Printing Office, Washington, D.C.

U.S. PUBLIC HEALTH SERV. PUBL. 1966. Obesity and Health. U.S. Govt. Printing Office, Washington, D.C.

TRESSLER, D. K. *et al.* 1968. The Freezing Preservation of Food, Vols. 1, 2, 3, and 4. Avi Publishing Co., Westport, Conn.

VON LOESCKE, H. W. 1949. Outlines of Food Technology. Van Nostrand Reinhold Co., New York.

WAGNER, A. F., and FOLKERS, K. 1964. Vitamins Coenzymes. John Wiley & Sons, New York.

WEBB, B. H., and WHITTIER, E. O. 1970. By-products from Milk. Avi Publishing Co., Westport, Conn.

WEISS, T. J. 1970. Food Oils and Their Uses. Avi Publishing Co., Westport, Conn.

WHITE, J. 1954. Yeast Technology. John Wiley & Sons, New York.

WILEY, H. W. 1929. History of a Crime against the Food Law. Published privately, Washington, D.C.

WILLIAMS, E. W. 1970. Frozen Foods: Biography of an Industry. Avi
   Publishing Co., Westport, Conn.
WILLIAMS, R. J. 1950. The Biochemistry of B Vitamins. ACS Monograph
   110. Van Nostrand Reinhold Co., New York.
WOODROOF, J. G. 1970. Coconuts: Production, Processing, Products.
   Avi Publishing Co., Westport, Conn.

General References

The following list of publications will prove useful to those who wish to pursue the subject of food and nutrition beyond the scope of this book. Most of the magazines mentioned in Chap. 6 are now out of print, but the larger libraries will have the files for the early years of the century. The library of any college of agriculture has an abundance of literature on food production, and a source of information frequently overlooked is the many publications of the U. S. Government. A letter to the Superintendent of Documents, U.S. Govt. Printing Office, Washington, D.C., will bring a list of publications on nutrition, legal control of food, or almost any other subject. Many of these publications are free, and none are very expensive.

EMERSON, GLADYS A. 1965. Nutritional Status U.S.A.: Landmarks of a Half Century of Research. Univ. California Press, Berkeley.

HARRIS, R. S., and VON LOESECKE, H. 1960. Nutritional Evaluation of Food Processing. Avi Publishing Co., Westport, Conn.
> This book was written by a long list of specialists, and covers the effects of various factors on the nutritional value of natural food as well as the effects of the various food processes from the harvest to the kitchen.

JENSEN, L. B. 1953. Man's Foods. Garrard Publishing Co., Champagne, Ill.
> This is a brief survey of food from the Paleolithic epochs and indicates the effect of nutrition on human development. It contains over 20 pages of references.

LI CH'IAO-P'ING. 1948. The Chemical Arts of Old China. Journal of Chemical Education, American Chemical Soc., Easton, Pa.
> One chapter each is devoted to the following topics: salt, vegetable oils and fats, sugars, soybeans, and alcoholic beverages and vinegar.

McCOLLUM, E. V. 1957. A History of Nutrition. Houghton Mifflin Co., Boston.
> This excellent book contains some information about ancient foods, but primarily covers research in nutrition from the middle of the 18th century to 1940.

MEYER, LILLIAN H. 1960. Food Chemistry. Van Nostrand Reinhold Co., New York.
> Contains recent information not easily available elsewhere.

SHERMAN, H. C. 1948. Food Products. The Macmillan Co., New York.
The early chapters describe the various nutrients and their functions, the latter ones treat the common foods and their influence on nutrition. There is also some discussion of food management, economics and use. Many references.

VON LOESECKE, H. W. 1949. Outlines of Food Technology. Van Nostrand Reinhold Co., New York.
This is a general survey of the technology of the common food processes and the references at the end of each chapter make it a good starting point for a thorough study of each process.

WATT, BERNICE K., and MERRILL, ANNABEL L. 1963. Constitution of Foods. Agricultural Handbook No. 8. U.S. Dept. Agr., Washington, D.C.
An authoritative compilation of a long list of foods.

NATL. ACAD. SCI.—NATL. RES. COUNCIL. 1966. Dietary Fat and Human Health. Publ. *1147*. Natl. Acad Sci.—Natl. Res. Council, Washington, D.C.
A report of the Food and Nutrition Board on the effects of the components of the natural fats on human health.

NATL. ACAD. SCI.—NATL. RES. COUNCIL. 1968. Recommended Dietary Allowances, 7th Edition. Natl. Acad. Sci.—Nat. Res. Council, Washington, D.C.
A report of the Food and Nutrition Board which contains a brief discussion of each nutrient and a long list of references.

USDA. 1959. Food. The Yearbook of Agriculture. U.S. Govt. Printing Office, Washington, D.C.
This is an excellent and inexpensive item for any home library. It contains a brief history of nutrition, a discussion of each nutrient, nutrition and health, quality of food, food preparation and costs.

USDA. 1964. Nutritive Value of Foods. Agr. Res. Serv., U.S. Govt. Printing Office, Washington, D.C.
Similar to the Watt and Merrill publication, but lists fewer foods, and the quantities are given in kitchen measurements: cup, tablespoon, 1-in. cube, etc. It lists 500 foods.

U.S. PUBLIC HEALTH SERV. PUBL. 1966. Obesity and Health. Publ. *1485*. U.S. Govt. Printing Office, Washington, D.C.
A thorough discussion of the subject including methods of prevention and control.

Appendix: A Useful Table

	Age[2] years	Weight Kg	Weight Lb	Height Cm	Height In.	Kcal	Protein Gm	Fat-soluble Vitamins Vitamin A Activity IU	Vitamin D IU	Vitamin E Activity IU
Infants	0–1/6	4	9	55	22	kg × 120	kg × 2.2[5]	1,500	400	5
	1/6–1/2	7	15	63	25	kg × 110	kg × 2.0[5]	1,500	400	5
	1/2–1	9	20	72	28	kg × 100	kg × 1.8[5]	1,500	400	5
Children	1–2	12	26	81	32	1,100	25	2,000	400	10
	2–3	14	31	91	36	1,250	25	2,000	400	10
	3–4	16	35	100	39	1,400	30	2,500	400	10
	4–6	19	42	110	43	1,600	30	2,500	400	10
	6–8	23	51	121	48	2,000	35	3,500	400	15
	8–10	28	62	131	52	2,200	40	3,500	400	15
Males	10–12	35	77	140	55	2,500	45	4,500	400	20
	12–14	43	95	151	59	2,700	50	5,000	400	20
	14–18	59	130	170	67	3,000	60	5,000	400	25
	18–22	67	147	175	69	2,800	60	5,000	400	30
	22–35	70	154	175	69	2,800	65	5,000	—	30
	35–55	70	154	173	68	2,600	65	5,000	—	30
	55–75+	70	154	171	67	2,400	65	5,000	—	30
Females	10–12	35	77	142	56	2,250	50	4,500	400	20
	12–14	44	97	154	61	2,300	50	5,000	400	20
	14–16	52	114	157	62	2,400	55	5,000	400	25
	16–18	54	119	160	63	2,300	55	5,000	400	25
	18–22	58	128	163	64	2,000	55	5,000	400	25
	22–35	58	128	163	64	2,000	55	5,000	—	25
	35–55	58	128	160	63	1,850	55	5,000	—	25
	55–75+	58	128	157	62	1,700	55	5,000	—	25
Pregnancy						+200	65	6,000	400	30
Lactation						+1,000	75	8,000	400	30

Source: Natl. Acad. Sci.—Natl. Res. Council (1968).

[1] The allowance levels are intended to cover individual variations among most normal persons as they live in the United States under usual environmental stresses. The recommended allowances can be attained with a variety of common foods, providing other nutrients for which human requirements have been less well defined. See text for more-detailed discussion of allowances and of nutrients not tabulated.

[2] Entries on lines for age range 22–35 years represent the reference man and woman at age 22. All other entries represent allowances for the midpoint of the specified age range.

Water-soluble Vitamins							Minerals				
Ascorbic Acid Mg	Folacin[3] Mg	Niacin Mg equiv[4]	Riboflavin Mg	Thiamine Mg	Vitamin B_6 Mg	Vitamin B_{12} μg	Calcium Gm	Phosphorus Gm	Iodine μg	Iron Mg	Magnesium Mg
35	0.05	5	0.4	0.2	0.2	1.0	0.4	0.2	25	6	40
35	0.05	7	0.5	0.4	0.3	1.5	0.5	0.4	40	10	60
35	0.1	8	0.6	0.5	0.4	2.0	0.6	0.5	45	15	70
40	0.1	8	0.6	0.6	0.5	2.0	0.7	0.7	55	15	100
40	0.2	8	0.7	0.6	0.6	2.5	0.8	0.8	60	15	150
40	0.2	9	0.8	0.7	0.7	3	0.8	0.8	70	10	200
40	0.2	11	0.9	0.8	0.9	4	0.8	0.8	80	10	200
40	0.2	13	1.1	1.0	1.0	4	0.9	0.9	100	10	250
40	0.3	15	1.2	1.1	1.2	5	1.0	1.0	110	10	250
40	0.4	17	1.3	1.3	1.4	5	1.2	1.2	125	10	300
45	0.4	18	1.4	1.4	1.6	5	1.4	1.4	135	18	350
55	0.4	20	1.5	1.5	1.8	5	1.4	1.4	150	18	400
60	0.4	18	1.6	1.4	2.0	5	0.8	0.8	140	10	400
60	0.4	18	1.7	1.4	2.0	5	0.8	0.8	140	10	350
60	0.4	17	1.7	1.3	2.0	5	0.8	0.8	125	10	350
60	0.4	14	1.7	1.2	2.0	6	0.8	0.8	110	10	350
40	0.4	15	1.3	1.1	1.4	5	1.2	1.2	110	18	300
45	0.4	15	1.4	1.2	1.6	5	1.3	1.3	115	18	350
50	0.4	16	1.4	1.2	1.8	5	1.3	1.3	120	18	350
50	0.4	15	1.5	1.2	2.0	5	1.3	1.3	115	18	350
55	0.4	13	1.5	1.0	2.0	5	0.8	0.8	100	18	350
55	0.4	13	1.5	1.0	2.0	5	0.8	0.8	100	18	300
55	0.4	13	1.5	1.0	2.0	5	0.8	0.8	90	18	300
55	0.4	13	1.5	1.0	2.0	6	0.8	0.8	80	10	300
60	0.8	15	1.8	+0.1	2.5	8	+0.4	+0.4	125	18	450
60	0.5	20	2.0	+0.5	2.5	6	+0.5	+0.5	150	18	450

[3] The folacin allowances refer to dietary sources as determined by *Lactobacillus casei* assay. Pure forms of folacin may be effective in doses less than $1/4$ of the RDA.

[4] Niacin equivalents include dietary sources of the vitamin itself plus 1 mg equivalent for each 60 mg of dietary tryptophan.

[5] Assumes protein equivalent to human milk. For proteins not 100% utilized factors should be increased proportionately.

Index

Coffee, 64–65
  dried, 31, 65
Cold storage, 68
Collagen, 175
Collier's Weekly, 71, 75
Combustion, theory, 111
Consumers Union, 223
Copper, 175–176
  sulfate, 80
Corn, 7, 14, 18–20
  meal, 18
Cream, 42
Creamery, 43
Cyclamates, 103

Dehydration, 31–33
Dextrin, 20–21, 150
Dextrose. *See* Glucose
Diet, early American, 9, 13
  planning, 216–217
  of primitive man, 2
  special, 128–129
Digestion, 148–150
Diseases, deficiency, 188
Distillation, destructive, 139
Domestication, plants and animals,
    3, 6
Drying foods, 27–29

Eggs, dried, 34
Eijkman, C., 186–188
Elastin, 175
Elements, chemical, 111, 164–165
Energy, 119–124
Enzymes, 147–148, 175

Fat, 135–139, 158–159, 181
  beef, 139
  butter, 139
  chicken, 139
  consumed, 158
  diet, 159–162
  in food, 160
  pork, 139
  unsaturated, 161–163
Fat Soluble A, 190, 194–195
FDA. *See* Food and Drug Ad-
    ministration
Fertilizer, 226–227
Fish Commission, 83
Fisher, E, 134–135, 142, 155
Flour, 15–18
  enriched, 26, 219–220
  whole wheat, 17, 218
Fluorine, 176–177
FNB. *See* Board, Food and Nutrition

Food, 145
  ancient, 3–4
  army, 28, 33
  browning, 27
  canning, 11–12, 34–38
  color, 95–96
  commercialization, 68
  cooking, 224
  dehydrated, 34
  dehydrators, 31–33
  dried, 31
  drying, 11, 27–30
  energy value, 131–132
  enrichment, 169, 219–220
  fresh, 31
  frozen, 31, 38–41
  future supply, 224–227
  habits, 13
  pattern in 1900, 68–69
  preservation, 11–12, 27–41, 68–70
  problems, 8
  processing, 14
  reconditioning, 99
  refrigeration, 38–39, 68
  salt content, 179
  standards, 80–81, 97–98
  storage, 8
  taboos, 5
  technologists, 30–33
  tolerances, 98–99
  wars, 28, 30–33, 36, 185
Food and Drug Administration, 89, 94,
    105
Foodstuffs, 145
Formaldehyde, 69–70, 80
Frauds, 70
Fraudulent, 89
Freezing, 38–41, 50–51
Fructose, 134, 150

Gelatin, 152–153, 154–155
Glucose, 20–21, 134, 145, 150, 159
Gluten, 17
Glyceride, 53, 138–139, 150
Glycerol, 136, 138–139
Glycine, 141–143
Goiter, 172–174, 217
Grain, 14–15
Grapes, 27
GRAS, 103–105

Heat, 121
Hemoglobin, 168, 175
Homo sapiens, 2–3
Hopkins, F. G., 187–188
Hunger, 2, 108–109
Hydrogenation, 53
Hydrolysis, 20, 150